Plan Your Escape

Secrets of Traveling the World
for Less Than the Cost
of Living at Home

By

Wayne Dunlap

AuthorHouse™
1663 Liberty Drive
Bloomington, IN 47403
www.authorhouse.com
Phone: 1-800-839-8640

Contact Wayne Dunlap at:
Plan Your Escape Now
PO Box 642, Del Mar, CA 92014 USA
e-mail: wdunlap@UnhookNow.com

First published by AuthorHouse 10/13/2011

ISBN: 978-1-4567-9568-9 (e)
ISBN: 978-1-4567-9569-6 (sc)

Please visit our website and
sign up for our **FREE travel tips at
www.PlanYourEscapeNow.com**. Reprinting
rights, premium sales, and trade
promotions are available for
organizations.

Library of Congress Control Number: 2011918352

Printed in the United States of America
This book is printed on acid-free paper.

Design and composition by MCD
Cover design by Alden Webber
Back cover photo by Tom Lafleur

Other than finding bargains and information available to everyone, when this book was published the author has not benefited financially or from special arrangements from any of the resources listed in this book.

This publication contains the opinions and ideas of its author. It is intended to provide information on the subjects addressed in the publication. It is sold with the understanding that the author and publisher are not engaged in rendering travel or any other kind of personal services in the book. Travel policies are subject to change, so the reader should confirm this information or consult a competent professional before adopting any of the suggestions in this book or drawing inferences from it. Please do as much research as possible and any decision you make is yours and your responsibility.

The author has used his best efforts in preparing this book. The author and publisher make no representation or warranties with respect to the accuracy of completeness of the contents of this book and specifically disclaim all responsibility for any liability, loss, risk, or inconvenience, personal or otherwise, which is incurred as a consequence, directly or indirectly, of the use and application of any of the contents of this book.

Because of the dynamic nature of the Internet, any web addresses or links contained in this book may have changed since publication and may no longer be valid. The views expressed in this work are solely those of the author and do not necessarily reflect the views of the publisher, and the publisher hereby disclaims any responsibility for them.

I dedicate this book and the love and gratitude from which it was written to my wife, Pat. It is to her I owe much of my happiness and without her continued support this book would not exist.

Acknowledgments

First I would like to thank all those travelers we have met and who enhanced our travel experience and knowledge. A special thanks goes out to travelers over the centuries that have blazed a path for the rest of us.

My wife, Pat, and son, Alden, have been instrumental in inspiring, contributing, and supporting the creation of this book. Alden did a great job designing the book cover. I offer thanks to Diane Uke and Tom and Kathy Lafleur who let us stay with them between trips while our home was rented and to Bill & Pat Allen who provided valuable editing comments.

I would like to express my gratitude to Sarah Gamber, David & Anna Smith, Bob & Susan Kovitz, Susie & Steve Ladow, Pat & Bill Allen, Joe & Dolores Mos, Aki & Kay Sasaji, Cheri Sogsti & Greg Retkowski, Andy Achterkirchen, Noelia Da Mata, Kristy-Lee May, and Bruce Sherman who have provided their travel insights that appear in Appendix A. This book is better because of them.

Finally, I acknowledge Ariela Wilcox, a literary agent in Del Mar, California, who believed in this book from the first time we met in line at the post office and has expertly coached me through the process of getting it published and into your hands.

Table of Contents

Appendix

Preview

Do you dream about traveling the world or living somewhere for a few weeks to a month or more but don't know how you could afford it or even think it is possible? Now you can do it! We reveal proven secrets the travel industry would prefer you did not know and how to give your life more meaning through travel.

Plan Your Escape, Secrets of Traveling the World for Less Than the Cost of Living at Home is a comprehensive step-by-step "how-to-do-it" guide essential for turning your travel dreams into reality making travel an adventure, not a problem. We show you how traveling the world or living somewhere for 1-2 weeks or 2-6 months can be safer, easier, and more affordable than you think. This book gives you the practical resources and advice missing in travel guidebooks.

We reveal hundreds of cost-saving tips and bargain-finding strategies so powerful we were able to travel the world for months, which we could never have afforded otherwise. With these tips, worth 100's of times the cost of this book, you can stretch your typical vacation costs to cover a month or more of travel. In many places in the world we learned how to do it for less than a $100 a day for the both of us and we show you how you can too!

My wife, Pat, who joined me on our worldwide travel adventures calls this the how-to-do Eat, Pray, Love book. She says: *"Having had it all, but choosing to run away with my husband and best friend, has been the most rewarding lifestyle change one can make and has brought us closer together."*

My wife and I sold our business, rented our home, and traveled the world for 2 years visiting 51 countries and are members of the exclusive Travelers' Century Club. In total we have visited 100 countries and island groups on 6 continents as well as 43 states in the U.S. We have done home exchanges and taken 26 cruises on 12 different cruise lines on ships ranging from 10 to 3,000 passengers as well as over 70 trips together taking cars, trains, buses, organized tours, and independent travel all over the world. Traveling is our passion!

We met scores of people along our worldwide journeys who asked hundreds of questions. We realized many people dream of taking a travel adventure but felt it would be too expensive with too many unknowns or didn't know the best way to pack or where to begin to make it actually happen. This detailed book combines real-life answers with countless hours of research from travel experts. We address the concerns you may have as well as the ones you may yet be aware of. We wish we had this book when we started.

We show you how to start out slow, choose the right trip for you, and work up to longer trips or stays. We present ideas about how to get a reluctant partner interested in travel and how to bring you closer together even on a 24/7 basis. **Plan Your Escape** is the travel-planning guide Americans need. You too can unhook from your current routines and live your travel dreams.

In addition to having hundreds of practical ideas with easy to follow step-by-step planning and organizational guidelines, **Plan Your Escape** addresses many other concerns Americans have about traveling and living away somewhere. It starts with a focus on fears and uncertainties. It goes on to refute the myth that extended travel and stays are just for the rich. Included to assist Americans in achieving their travel dreams are comprehensive packing check-off lists for women and men, a five-month planning and preparation guideline for getting started, practical travel advice from other experienced travelers, and ways to save time and money from extensive up-to-date hidden secrets from the best Internet travel websites and smartphone apps. Also included is the most current information on how to: pack less and have more, save money, stay safe and healthy, choose your designation, plan your trip, avoid tourist scams, pay your bills, stay in touch, set up a travel blog, take travel photos like a pro, and deal with your home and possessions.

We went to see the world and were pleasantly surprised how the experience improved our life. **Plan Your Escape** also provides insight for the wonderful life changing aspect a travel or living-away adventure can have on you and will greatly improve your enjoyment of your life and give it more meaning. It is no longer the exclusive privilege of the young to leave behind responsibilities at home and work to seek adventure.

Numerous research studies have shown that the natural high that comes from dopamine flooding your brain when you buy something new is temporary. The high from stuff goes away and you have to continue buying more to get the high again. These studies also show your pleasurable memories of travel experiences remain with you the rest of your life.

Now is the time to learn how to take and how you can afford a travel or living-away adventure that will improve your life forever!

Plan Your Escape Now!

Introduction

We had it all! We studied and worked long and hard for decades and achieved the American dream - beautiful home and furnishings, successful business, good friends, lovely parties and dining out, luxury cars, wonderful vacations, and a comfortable routine. But we spent our lives working to pay for all of it with much of our weekends maintaining all the stuff. One day we had enough. We wanted to fill our car with gas, drive anywhere until it stopped, and start a new life.

Why? Is the American dream enough? There had to be more to life. We learned much more about ourselves traveling around the world for two years visiting 51 countries (and are members of the exclusive Travelers' Century Club, having visited 100 countries and island groups on 6 continents as well as 43 states in the U.S.). Believe us, there is so much more to life than we thought.

Come take a dream journey with us. Close your eyes. Remember it's just a dream. Image you are traveling the world cruising the islands of the Caribbean, having a margarita under a palapa on a warm sandy Mexican beach, staying a couple of weeks in the Alsace wine villages in France, visiting beautiful exotic island beaches in Thailand, wandering the Champs Elysees and the Eiffel Tower in Paris, enjoying sexy tango dancers in the streets of Buenos Aires, climbing the steps of the Great Wall in China, admiring the grand spectacle of the Great Pyramids of Giza, hiking in a rain forest in Costa Rica, witnessing the glory of Argentina's Iguazu Falls or America's Grand Canyon, adventuring the ancient rock-carved city of Petra or the magical ruins of Machu Picchu, living a month in a villa in Tuscany, and more.

How about simple delights like falling asleep on a white sandy beach under a palm tree while listening to the waves gently wash ashore, pulling into an exotic port of call on a cruise ship, watching the sun set over the ocean while having a wonderful dinner, swimming with dolphins in warm ocean waters, learning to cook real Italian food (or just eating it!), having a picnic on a sunny day tasting fine wines overlooking elegant vineyards, or waking up to days full of promise and excitement? How about not having to go home after a wonderful vacation?

Keep your eyes closed… your dream continues. Imagine places you have always wanted to see. In your dreams, the world is at your feet and month after month you travel to places you have only dreamed about, spending time to get to know the place and people not as a tourist but as a traveler experiencing and learning much more how to enjoy your life. The world is a wonderful place! Now, stop reading… actually close your eyes and take a dream travel journey – you know the one you have wished for.

Finished dreaming? Welcome back to the reality of your job, errands, meetings, traffic, long days, bills, family, house, shopping, cooking, cleaning, laundry, mortgage/rent, pets, maintenance of your yard and stuff, repairs, projects, the ringing phone, demanding people, negative news, obligations, commitments, expectations, worries, routines, and everything else keeping us from living our dreams.

One day is much like the next wishing for the weekends that end too soon because we need to take care of so many things. We change jobs or routines, take short vacations, move the furniture around, buy new things, stay busy with errands, and try to relax watching too much TV. In spite of everything we do it never seems quite enough. Think about it… if our coveted 'lifestyle' routines were so fulfilling and desirable, wouldn't there be shelves of books about "The Joys of Living a Routine"?

Something is missing… what about our dreams? What if your dreams can actually be your reality where everyday is an experience you choose and you wake up excited about the day? Can you really live your dream?

You can! My wife and I did it. We unhooked from what was expected of us and traveled the world for 2 years visiting 51 counties. In total, 100 countries and island groups in our lifetime. The experience has permanently improved our lives… much more than we ever could have imaged!

Plan Your Escape Now!

Chapter 1

Don't Wait Until 'Someday'

In this chapter...

Why We Procrastinate – Inertia and Fear

Overcoming Fear of Travel

Turning Dreams and Goals into a Plan of Action

We have all said it... "Someday I will _____". You can fill the blank. Because you are reading this book, you probably have also said "Someday I would like to travel to and see _____". Many of us dream about traveling the world or experiencing living somewhere for a while. All too many people get to a point in their lives when achieving travel dreams is impractical, resulting in regrets. What holds us back from realizing our dreams while we are healthy and still able to do so? Something we take for granted that can change at any time.

Why We Procrastinate – Inertia and Fear

"Twenty years from now you will be more disappointed by the things you didn't do than by the ones you did do. So throw off the bowlines, sail away from the safe harbor. Catch the trade winds in your sails. Explore. Dream. Discover."

~ Mark Twain

"Without new experiences, something inside of us sleeps. The sleeper must awaken."

~ Frank Herbert

Procrastination can come from several things such as disinterest, inertia, and fear. You have already expressed an interest in travel by reading this book leaving inertia and fear.

Inertia

Inertia keeps us in familiar routines. We have spent a large portion of our lives doing what others tell us to do – school, college, job, marriage, children, house, and work to pay for all of it. It becomes more difficult to start something new than to keep doing what we are familiar with. Beliefs are easier to hang onto than to reevaluate.

> *"Whenever you find yourself on the side of the majority, it is time to pause and reflect."*
>
> ~ Mark Twain

Many of us believe a travel adventure would be wonderful but we worry that major changes are not going to be easy. This causes us to be intimidated and uncomfortable. So we make excuses and put our dreams off to another day. We continue doing the same things in our comfort zone. Tomorrow quickly becomes next month, next year, never, or even worse; past the point in your life when you have health and physical problems so you must live with regrets.

You are born, live, and then die. These are the cards we have been dealt – no way out. Our human mortality is not something we like to think about, but we should. Instead of ignoring or fearing our mortality we should view it as a wake up call. Yes, our time alive on this earth will run out and before that we will become unable to do many of the things we want to do. If we had infinite time we could take all the time we want to live this wonderful experience but the reality is we don't have unlimited time. So, we should make use of every day before physical and other limitations start to exclude possibilities.

Fear

Fear is not a sign of weakness. It affects all of us. If we let it, fear can paralyze us into inaction. There are so many possible fears…

- Isn't the world a scary place?
- Do we have the abilities to do this?
- How can we afford a travel adventure?

- Won't we miss our friends and family? Don't they need us?
- What about our home and possessions?
- How do you plan for a longer trip or stay? How do I make time to do so?
- What will we do if we get sick?
- What if I make a mistake?
- Are we worthy of such an adventure?
- What if your family and friends start disliking you for doing something different with your life?
- Can anything be better than our current lives? ... and the list goes on and on.

Most of these 'fears' are actually uncertainties – fear of the unknown. In this book, we provide realistic answers to these unknowns and many more travel challenges. When it comes to travel, countless millions of people have done it before you, making it straightforward to follow them. Also, there are millions of people dedicated to the travel industry everywhere in the world to help you.

"I've had many troubles in my life, most of which never happened."
~ Mark Twain

All too often we let rationalization of fears overwhelm us causing us to take the safe path. It is usually the case that most of what we perceive as fears never happens. It's the concerns and beliefs we project onto every situation that create our fears. The important thing is to avoid mistaking our thoughts for reality. Playing it safe can kill your dreams by telling yourself they were never worth pursuing and you were only kidding yourself because you were never good enough to make them real.

"It is often safer to be in chains than to be free."
~ Franz Kafka

We do not recommend foolish or risky behavior. Sometimes playing it safe is important but when we let ourselves be held back because of uncertainties or not wanting to be different from others is when we opt for playing it safe over living our dreams. This causes us to feel unfulfilled where dreams and happiness remain out of reach.

We have been conditioned to think we should avoid anything that causes any fear. In many cases, this is too strict of a rule. Fear is a natural emotion that comes up in many situations and should be respected to save us from bad experiences. Sometimes venturing into the unknown can be good because it lets us know we are exploring the potential of our time on this earth and makes us feel more alive.

"Nothing will ever be attempted, if all possible objections must first be overcome."

~ Samuel Johnson

Fortunately, you are much more capable than you think and your dream of travel is achievable. With the practical ideas presented in this book and a little determination, you can overcome possible hurdles (real and perceived). Once the decision is made and you achieve your dreams of travel, you will discover most of your 'fears' were just not as insurmountable as you believed.

Overcoming Fear of Travel

"Whether you believe you can or you can't, you're right."

~ Henry Ford

We need to learn the difference between the fear that keeps us alive and the fear that keeps us from living. The first can save you from potential dangerous things like dark alleyways and sleazy characters. The fear that keeps us from living is of the unknown. It limits our potential for wonderful things

There are several varieties of fears we have about traveling to new places. First, the numerous issues involved with the practicalities of travel keep many from considering travel adventures. This book offers practical solutions to many concerns you may have as well as the ones you may yet be aware of that may keep you from traveling the world.

Isn't the World a Scary Place?

"Nothing in life is to be feared. It is only to be understood."

~ Marie Curie

When negative things happen, it is natural for us to worry and plan around it. It is unfortunate this natural human tendency also keeps us from doing some of the most rewarding things in life. Sometimes it causes us to go out of our way to avoid possible danger we read about in biased and sensationalized media stories.

Real or exaggerated, we cannot change our media's reporting of stories. What we can change is our reaction to the fear. We can accept fear is a natural human emotion, understand it, and move on without letting the daily news imprison us.

Hollywood movies and TV shows are exported all over the world. Guns, shootings, explosions, car chases, and scandals influence people around the world about our daily life. We had a wonderful guide in Japan who showed us some interesting things in her city for a day. When we took her to lunch, we learned her favorite American TV shows were "Real Housewives" and "OC". She believed most Americans lived this way and was surprised when we explained to her it was just 'Hollywood'. Our media gives us the same impression of people living in other parts of the world.

Photos of the worst part of any disaster or disturbance are shown and stories are often exaggerated to seem shocking in order to 'sell' the story. We can overcome knee-jerk reactions with perspective, not reaction. It is better to understand the circumstances by reading several sources about an event or place with a bad reputation and decide for yourself. Keep in mind that many events are isolated within a small area. The whole country is rarely affected. In time things return to normal. We view many 'disasters' as opportunities to achieve great travel bargains – see the section "Follow the Disaster" in Chapter 7 ("Finding Great Travel Bargains").

People seem to need the stimulation derived from fear so the news media dishes it out to us daily making the world appear to be an awful place. Think about it... in a world of nearly 7 billion people, is the real 'news' only about crashes, killings, wars, disasters, scandals, and hate? - of course not. We have found the best way to overcome the fear initiated by our negative media is to turn off the 'news'.

We have learned the world is a much less scary place than we were led to believe. We have traveled to 100 countries and island groups as recognized by the exclusive Travelers' Century Club including several months in Islamic countries. All over the world people have been friendly and kind to us. Their values are not much different from ours. They want to live their lives well, support their families, and be good human beings.

We have met hundreds of world travelers and not a single one has told us the world is a scary place. Quite the contrary, they tell us how lovely people around the world are and what a beautiful wonderful world we live on. And we agree!

> *"We live in a wonderful world that is full of beauty, charm and adventure. There is no end to the adventures we can have if only we seek them with our eyes open."*
>
> — Jawaharial Nehru

Turning Dreams and Goals into a Plan of Action

> *"Go confidently in the direction of your dreams. Live the life you have imagined."*
>
> ~ Henry David Thoreau

We are all busy so how do we have time to prepare and plan a travel adventure? Start by cutting back on the distractions. Be honest with yourself and evaluate your daily schedule. How much time do you spend watching TV and movies, reading escape novels, shopping, chatting on the phone, reading and sending e-mail and text messages, surfing the Internet, or playing video games? For most of us it is hours each day that could easily be devoted to making plans to achieve our dreams and goals. Tim Ferriss, author of the best selling book The 4-Hour Workweek, reminds us to ask: "Am I inventing things to avoid the important?"

> *"Things may come to those who wait, but only the things left by those who hustle."*
>
> ~ Abraham Lincoln

To accomplish new goals and dreams, you have to get off autopilot and change goals to plans. If you do not plan for a travel adventure you will never get there. Start by focusing on the wonderful experiences you will have instead of fears. Write down what you want to do and where you want to visit. Then tell yourself you deserve to live your life to the fullest and you can do it.

"Dreams are messages sent by talent."
~ Barbara Sher, author, *It's Only too Late if You Don't Start Now*

Go to Chapter 6 ("How Planning Can Enhance Your Experience") to help you formulate a travel plan best for you. Then go to Chapter 17 ("Getting Started on Your Travel Adventure – A Step-by-Step Guide") and follow the step-by-step guidelines. By taking action to change your goals into a plan you are on your way.

Take the first step today and you will be on the road enjoying your dream travel adventure before you know it.

To get you excited, in the next chapter we describe how travel can improve the rest of your life.

Chapter 2

Travel Can Improve Your Life

In this chapter...

Renew Your Playful Spirit and Love of Life

Improve Your Health and Creativity

Have an Adventure

Letting Go – A Reevaluation of What is Important

A New Perspective of What is Important to Enrich Your Life

A New Start

In this chapter we illustrate many ways travel has improved our lives. These ideas have been confirmed over and over by the travelers we have met along the way. Getting away from your regular routines for an extended period of time is almost like having an out of body experience. You have a chance to evaluate and reassess what is working for you and what is not.

Like any habit, it takes more than just a few weeks to reevaluate the familiar routines of your existing life. In a shorter timeframe you will miss your old habits and lifestyle instead of having a chance to reassess them. It is when you are gone for a longer time past the homesick and culture shock period that you will begin to let go and reevaluate your life. The payoff can be vast improvements for a more fulfilling and enjoyable life.

One of our most famous American writers said it well:

"If one advances confidently in the direction of his dreams, and endeavors to live the life which he has imagined, he will meet with a success unexpected in common hours. He will put some things behind, will pass an invisible boundary; new, universal, and more liberal laws will begin to establish themselves around and within him."

~ Henry David Thoreau, Walden

Renew Your Playful Spirit and Love of Life

"We don't stop playing because we grow old; we grow old because we stop playing"

~ George Bernard Shaw

Travel or living somewhere else for an extended time is much different than the experience we have from our shorter vacations. In a week or two we are just coming down from the stress and worries of our 'normal' life. If you were like us, too often we crammed too many things into our vacations and had to come home to relax allowing no real time away from our routines.

Escaping from the humdrum of every day life, travel can renew your playful spirit. Away from the daily routines of jobs, maintenance of home and possessions, and regular habits, you have a chance to make simple daily decisions of "what would be fun to do today?"

Do you want to take a walk or drive among beautiful sights, explore famous wonders, experience and learn something new, eat exotic foods or learn how to cook them, meet interesting people from all over the world, spend more time with your travel partner, improve a skill like photography, read a book, or just relax and watch the world go by? Imagine having fun day after day, doing what you want to do instead of what you have to do, and rediscovering your love of life! Travel can bring this to reality.

Improve Your Health and Creativity

"Health is a state of complete physical, mental and social well-being, and not merely the absence of disease or infirmity."

~ World Health Organization, 1948

Traveling can relieve a lifetime of pressures, anxieties, and stress. Because you are in new situations, you literally leave the past behind. Your physical and mental health improves.

You begin seeing things in a new light invigorated about life. Because a traveler must deal with new challenges and learn new ways of doing things, your confidence of problem solving improves along with your self-confidence, creativity, imagination, and ability to think outside of the box. When returning home, you become more willing to try new things and take on new possibilities to make your life more fulfilling and enjoyable.

Have an Adventure

Adventure can stimulate your life. Our lives become rather predictable and routine after years commuting back and forth to our jobs; running errands on the weekends to the grocery store, dry cleaners, and hardware store; taking care of the kids and home; and watching television at night to unwind. At times there is little excitement to look forward to.

Because of worldwide travel, our life is more exciting now and full of adventure and promise of more for the future. Some of our best memories are of our journeys through Europe on trains, touring New Zealand by car, and visiting the Greek Islands by ferries. We look forward to more exciting activities like when we zip-lined over the jungle canopy in Costa Rica, rode an elephant across a river in Thailand, snorkeled in the Red Sea in Egypt, were in the middle of the no-holds-barred Palio horse race in Siena Italy, took a jet boat ride and climbed a glacier in New Zealand, or just tasted fabulous wine overlooking a vineyard on a summer day in the famous French Cote d-Or wine villages.

Travel affords you the opportunity for so many unique exciting adventures that you can choose the ones you will most enjoy.

Letting Go – A Reevaluation of What is Important

"When one door closes another door opens; but we so often look so long and so regretfully upon the closed door, that we do not see the ones which open for us."

~ Alexander Graham Bell

"Some of us think holding on makes us strong, but sometimes it is letting go."
                                          ~ Herman Hesse

Traveling can bring your life into perspective and help you determine what is important for you. For thousands of years, farmers have separated the valuable grain from the worthless chaff by throwing their harvest up and letting the wind blow away the chaff. Traveling is like the wind. A traveling experience allows you the opportunity to get away from what you believe is vital to evaluate and better understand what is worth holding on to and what you should let go. You can discover characteristics about yourself you never knew existed and as you travel you leave behind habits and prejudices as you reevaluate your life.

"When I let go of what I am, I become what I might be."
                                          ~ Lao Tzu

An extended trip or living away also gives you a chance to reevaluate your existing priorities with new perspectives breaking habits and forming new ones that will make your life more enriched and enjoyable. You start asking yourself questions. After living out of a 40-pound suitcase for months, does more stuff really make you happy? Are a house and many possessions with all the costs, time to maintain, and lack of mobility the best way to live or does it keep you from living? Were we put on this earth to work and stress to pay for more stuff or could we enjoy life differently? After being away from certain demanding relationships, do the cons outweigh the pros and are you better off without them? The best path to health and happiness is often not a path of adding to or gaining something, but of removal or letting go.

"None are more hopelessly enslaved than those who falsely believe they are free."
                                          ~ Johann Wolfgang von Goethe

So many of us are too consumed with making money and gaining possessions to appreciate the value of experience and relationships. Western society encourages us to believe we should climb to new heights and acquire more money, processions, power, and important friends. Advertisers and the media dictate what we are supposed to want. We gauge our 'success' by what others have, creating desires for even more. This quest for 'success' gives us less choice on how we spend our time and whom we spend it with.

Unfortunately, too many of us buy into all this trying to fit in. All too much of it is 'having it show' and we don't feel better off because others around us have similar things. Also, going faster makes us feel we are always behind. This definition of 'success' often leaves too little time to develop fulfilling experiences of life and supportive relationships. Realizing your dreams can make you be and feel better off than someone else who let others define what is success.

"In the end these things matter the most. How well did you love? How fully did you live? How deeply did you learn to let go?"
~ Buddha

Great lessons can be learned by letting go of the past and the accumulation of possessions, inflexible viewpoints, negative emotions, demanding and unsupportive friends and relatives, and other baggage that is holding you back. Letting go of what is not working in your life makes room for the wonderful things that do. If you don't define life then life defines you.

Spending some time away from your current routine and busy schedules allows you to jump off the treadmill and throw your life up in the wind. What is still valuable becomes even more precious. What can be reassessed for a more fulfilling and deeply satisfying life becomes more apparent.

A New Perspective of What is Important to Enrich Your Life

"The world is a book, and those who do not travel, read only a page."
~ St. Augustine

"One's destination is never a place, but a new way of seeing things."
~ Henry Miller

Travel will give you a new perspective of the world and your life. One of the things you will realize is the world is a big place and you live in just a small part of it with limited experiences. With 197 countries and almost 7 billion people in this world, traveling will expose you to amazing new experiences and ideas. There is a whole world of experiences you don't know about but can learn if you listen and observe. Other people in the world who have grown up with different beliefs and experiences can enlighten you assisting you in making improvements to live a more gratifying life.

Once we see beyond rationalization of our existing life, our perspective expands from "sure makes us appreciate what we have at home" to "what can I learn to improve my life?" Travel will help you do this.

People Around the World Are Friendly, Kind, Generous, and Happy

"Travel is fatal to prejudice, bigotry, and narrow-mindedness."
~ Mark Twain

"To travel is to discover that everyone is wrong about other countries."
~ Aldous Huxley

"Perhaps travel cannot prevent bigotry, but by demonstrating that all peoples cry, laugh, eat, worry, and die, it can introduce the idea that if we try and understand each other, we may even become friends."
~ Maya Angelou

Meeting people from other cultures will teach you that your beliefs of the world acquired from years of mass media are not the way it really is. We agree with the hundreds of travelers we have met, who have spent significant time away from home, who tell us the world is a wonderful place and the people are friendly, kind, and generous. The people you meet have desires and needs like us. They are interested in supporting their families and living a good life.

An incredible perspective that you will gain is even in seeing poverty in your travels there are happy people everywhere in the world. The lack of money and possessions do not keep them from being happy and enjoying their life. We met more unhappy people when we return to America. We can learn much from the people we met around the world.

We Need Less Possessions to Be Happy

"Money never made a man happy yet nor will it. There is nothing in its nature to produce happiness. The more a man has, the more he wants. Instead of filling a vacuum, it makes one."
~ Benjamin Franklin

How much of what you own really improves the quality of your life? Are you buying new things because of necessity or out of compulsion, from a desire to impress, or because others have it? Have we become convinced buying things is the only way to have a good 'lifestyle'?

"Most of our troubles are due to our passionate desire for and attachment to things that we misapprehend as enduring entities."
~ Dalai Lama

From traveling for months stopping to live in places with only 40-pound suitcases, we realized how independent we are of our possessions. It became clear to us we need much less stuff to be happy. In fact, life can be better without it liberating us to enjoy life instead of being slaves to a 'lifestyle'. The pursuit of the latest style leads to conformity. Impressing others with possessions has become less important and letting go of possessions gave us more time that would have been required for maintenance and making more money to pay for it.

The time you save can be used to peruse what really makes you happy. More time for family and friends, satisfying volunteer time to enrich your life, hobbies you always wanted to pursue, enjoyment of the outdoors, improving or changing your career, and much more. How does a fun get-together with family or friends compare to working an extra day to pay for more stuff? How does spending time helping others compare to having matching saucepans or a new purse? How does winning a photography contest or having your friends complement you on a new dish you learned to cook compare to having a new gadget? Does a walk along the beach every week compare to taking care of the yard? How does having your mate and family love you compare to showing off a larger home, newer car or furniture, or the latest electronic gadget?

"You may have occasion to possess or use material things, but the secret of life lies in never missing them."
~ Gandhi

It is often a question of more time to live a more satisfying enjoyable life or more possessions. The best tradeoff for you becomes clearer when you travel away from home for a longer period and have a chance to gain new perspectives of what is important to enrich your life.

A New Start

> *"Once you have traveled, the voyage never ends, but is played out over and over again in the quietest chambers. The mind can never break off from the journey."*
> ~ Pat Conroy

> *"Travel is more than the seeing of sights; it is a change that goes on, deep and permanent, in the ideas of living."*
> ~ Miriam Beard

Reevaluate Your Limits

Confidence gained from travel experience can help you better face fears allowing you to escape your routines and alter old habits. You will be surprised at the amazing talents you have. Knowing you can overcome many challenges from travel gives you self-assurance you can use to examine new ideas in your job, relationships with friends and family, and other life challenges. Travel expands your limits for what is possible on any given day or circumstance. You open yourself up to an entire new world of possibility.

Create a Closer Relationship with Your Travel Partner

When I asked my wife what was some of the improvements our travels had achieved for her, she quickly said it brought us closer together. Except for raising our wonderful son, nothing has made our lives together happier and more interesting than seeing this amazing world together. Sharing the experience has revived and strengthened our relationship giving us memories for a lifetime that we talk about for hours.

Learn to Live in the Now

> *"As you walk and eat and travel, be where you are. Otherwise you will miss most of your life."*
> ~ Buddha

Living in the now has become a Zen cliché. This is how it affected us. Without mental distractions or major worries about yesterday and tomorrow we were able to be totally involved with what we were are doing right now. Our stress went down and we became more peaceful. We obtained a heightened sense of awareness and increased sensitivity to others as well as ourselves. Living in the moment makes us more positive and happy.

Learn to More Fully Appreciate Home and Good Friends

"There is nothing like returning to a place that has remained unchanged to find the ways in which you yourself have."
                                                             ~ Nelson Mandela

One of the many reasons we travel is to investigate other options in the world including places to spend the rest of our lives. Were we just lucky to be in the best place in the world? Millions of Americans have decided to live full time in other countries. They believe they have a better life and were glad they traveled and investigated their options.

We have visited many of the popular places North Americans want to visit around the world. Although they are lovely, we have reconfirmed that our home, friends, and family in San Diego, California, are great for us. Sometimes you have to travel the world to discover your home for the first time. We also have great fun at parties now with loads to talk about because people are naturally curious of what is out there in the world.

Simplicity Improves Our Life

"Simplicity is the ultimate sophistication."
                                                             ~ Leonardo da Vinci

"The ability to simplify means to eliminate the unnecessary, so that the necessary may speak."
                                                             ~ Hans Hofmann

Travel imposes a life of simplicity, reducing your possessions to the few items that fit in your suitcase and making it difficult to acquire new things. At home, these lessons of simplicity can help you live in a more purposeful and satisfying way. Scientific studies have shown that new experiences (and the memories they produce) are more likely to produce long-term happiness than new possessions. Taking a friend to dinner, for example, brings more lasting happiness than spending on a new item of clothing. Friendships affect your life in ways more possessions cannot.

> *"A man is rich in proportion to the number of things he can afford to let alone."*
>
>   - Henry David Thoreau

Travel has given us a chance to evaluate our dependency on possessions and has shown us the value of the simple joys of life. We find pleasure in being open to new experiences and opportunities as they present themselves, learning new skills, laughing over dinner with our friends, spending more time with our wonderful son, and playing together wherever we are. These activities make us feel more fully alive.

Read on and learn about even more benefits you can derive from travel and stays away.

 ***Chapter 3***

Additional Benefits of Travel or Living Away Somewhere

In this chapter...

A Transition To Your Next Phase of Life

Chance to Slow Down and Discover New Experiences

Live Your Dream

A Better Mid-Life Crisis

Chance to Volunteer and Contribute

Learn Better Ways to Live Your Life and Give It More Meaning

"The traveler sees what he sees. The tourist sees what he has come to see."
~ G.K. Chesterton

Our travel experience has enriched our lives in more ways than we can count. We have undergone meaningful life changing improvements, which have allowed us to live a more joyful and happy life. Here are some of the ways travel can make your life even better than you thought possible.

A Transition To Your Next Phase of Life

"Two roads diverged in a wood and I – I took the one less traveled by."
~ Robert Frost

A trip or living away can be a great way to separate life stages. It can give you a chance to reevaluate your life and determine how you want to live your next phase of life as well as provide closure on the previous one.

Some of these prominent life transitions are:

• Entering retirement
• Prior to experiencing health and physical limitations
• Divorce or failed romance
• Becoming an empty nester
• Mid-life crisis or turning 50
• Experiencing the loss of a spouse, parent, or other loved one
• Between jobs, schools, relationships, or serious illness
• Leaving your job and becoming self-employed or before starting a business
• Job burnout or a sabbatical from career
• Boredom and loneliness or a craving for excitement
• Experiencing serious depression or stress
• Wishing to further develop a passion such as learning to cook, a new language, or a sport
• Desiring to give back and contribute
• Hunger for spiritual enlightenment
• Need for change, challenge, or a new start from old baggage
• Receiving an inherence

In addition to the above life transitions, taking an extended trip or stay (also called sabbatical or gap year) at any time in life can be very beneficial in establishing a fulfilling life-work balance. In Appendix D ("Recommended Reading") two books are listed providing insight in how to as well as the benefits of taking a long break from your job and career. If you are considering it but do not think it is wise or even possible, you should read these books before dismissing the possibility.

Chance to Slow Down and Discover New Experiences

All too often, our life at home is based on getting as much done in a day as possible. We rush to work, hurry through meals, and we even multi-task when we are with family and friends. Because of the many tasks we take on, this might be necessary or done to make us believe we are busy and productive. It likely does little to make us happier or create a more fulfilling life.

There are many packaged tours targeted to our short vacation timeframe and notion of travel and leisure. They are a good way to see many of the great attractions in the world and a good way to get you started in travel. Unfortunately, many package tours can be as rushed and rigidly confined just as our work life is. Later in this book we suggest ways to incorporate guided tours with independent travel to gain the best advantages of both.

One of the big advantages of extended travel is it allows you a chance to slow down and let things happen. Freed from strict schedules, you begin to do things and meet people most tourists overlook in their hurry to see the attractions. You have the choice each day to do a lot or just relax and have your biggest decision of the day be where to have your next tantalizing meal.

Wayne catching up on his reading floating in the Dead Sea in Israel.

Extended travel gives you the chance to discover off-the-beaten path opportunities. In Rotorua in New Zealand, the owner of our hostel told us about two small rivers, one hot water and other cold water. The place they joined created a natural warm spa surrounded by trees only the locals knew about. With some bread and cheese, we had a wonderful afternoon soaking in the natural warm water after exploring the amazing Wai-O-Tapu Thermal Wonderland in the morning.

In Jerusalem, we met a couple who invited us to their home for a traditional dinner to celebrate Shavuot, a major Jewish holiday. This occurred after we had a long talk with the Muslim family who owned the hotel we stayed in. These two insightful experiences gave us a much better understanding of issues in the Middle East. It is these kinds of experiences that can happen when you slow down during an travel adventure.

Live Your Dream

Exploring the world and experiencing new things is a dream shared by many of us. Traveling allows you to live your dream.

A Better Mid-Life Crisis

'Having a mid-life crisis' is now a cliche. This reassessment of life typically occurs between the age of 40 and 60. It is a period of self-doubt, sometimes dramatic, when we sense the passing of youth and pending old age. It can be triggered by a number of things such as extramarital affairs, physical changes such as menopause, death of parents, job burnout or unemployment, empty nest, or just feeling unhappy with your life and lifestyle.

The result may be a desire to make significant changes in basic aspects of your life such as in career, marriage, romantic relationships, big-ticket expenditures, or physical appearance. The stereotype mid-life crisis can be expressed by major changes and expensive conspicuous consumption spurred by insecurities such as a new career, body work, abuse of alcohol, divorce, younger mates, 'younger' designer clothes, and new toys like sports cars, boats, jewelry, and gadgets.

Researchers have found that midlife is often a time for reflection and reassessment. This is not always accompanied by the psychological upheaval popularly associated with a mid-life crisis. Some of the renewed desires are a need for adventure and change, decisions about what to do with the rest of their life, anger at your spouse for feeling tied down, and a desire for new, passionate, and intimate relationship.

Traveling the world is defined by excitement, challenge, and adventure. It is also a chance to reconnect passionately with your mate and reassess your life for improvements for the future. What could be a better antidote to the trials and tribulations of a mid-life crisis?

Chance to Volunteer and Contribute

Some of the most rewarding pleasures that give our lives greater value come from helping others. Taking advantage of the opportunity to do something worthwhile and give back by making a difference in people's lives can enrich your life and give it more meaning. Many people have taken an extended travel excursion volunteering somewhere in the world where they are needed.

Learn Better Ways to Live Your Life and Give It More Meaning

"A mind that is stretched by a new experience can never go back to its old dimensions."
~ Oliver Wendell Holmes

"Do not follow where the path may lead. Go instead where there is no path and leave a trail"
~ Ralph Waldo Emerson

Life is an endless learning journey and when you travel you learn new things everyday. The following are examples of ways traveling have improved our lives and give it more meaning.

By taking more time to explore new places, you are exposed to new cultures and ways of doing things giving you new and refreshing perspectives. We learned much more being there physically then reading about it. Travel has opened us up for self-discovery from other points of view and values. We learned many better ways to live our lives and have made changes to enjoy life even more.

We are better equipped to deal with problems and move on. We get disturbed about minor inconveniences much less often. We have learned to go with the flow and have more patience.

The more we travel in our big wonderful world the smaller our own self-importance has become. We are no longer the big fish in our small pond.

There are many people and beliefs out there that challenge any arrogance we had. We realized we were not as important and knowledgeable as we thought we were. We now enjoy many more new experiences and activities we discovered from listening to others. Some of these have made permanent improvements to make our lives even better in the future.

The famous member of the Beatles, John Lennon said, "Life is what happens while you're busy making other plans." We now better appreciate that many opportunities to enjoy life are not always planned. We are more flexible and open to enjoying new experiences and saying 'yes' when invited to join others or try new things.

Our travel experience gives us a chance to make new friends and create lasting relationships. People who love to play the card game bridge love to go to tournaments. People who crave long bike rides can't wait to cycle with their friends. Why? They are with people who share a kindred spirit. There is a kindred spirit shared by travelers and friendships are easy to establish. We have stayed in the homes of people we met and stay in touch with others all around the world.

There are many other things we have learned. We have a much better sense of geography, history, and current events allowing us to view world news in a much better light. We have learned the value of laughter and try to practice it regularly.

"And the end of all our exploring
Will be to arrive where we started
And know the place for the first time."

~ T.S. Eliot

Very importantly, travel has helped us appreciate the good things we have in our life. The petty annoyances we were sometimes allowed to dominate our attitudes and moods have become less important. When at home, we enjoy our family and good friends more, do more fun things we enjoy, and worry less about what others are doing or thinking.

We also have gained a greater appreciation of how lucky we are living in America. Beyond the usual expressions of missing home from the typical homesick tourist returning from seeing the sites, a long-term travel experience clearly illustrates the freedoms and opportunities we may have taken for granted. We are not trapped in repressive economic systems, class structures, and societal norms. We are free to choose and make our life what we want it to be.

Finally, we are happy and have fabulous experiences and memories to cherish and share with friends as we grow older. We have tapped into the spice of life!

You have to be rich to afford an extended travel adventure – right? Wrong! In the next chapter we share ways how you can stretch your dollar further while traveling.

Chapter 4

Traveling the World Can Cost Less Than Living at Home

In this chapter...

Travel on Less Than $100 a Day for a Couple

Eliminate a Large Amount of Expenses from Your Normal Life

Other Priceless Returns on Your Travel Investment

"You must be rich!" is often the response we receive when we are asked about our traveling and we respond we were out for two years. Even for a month, an extended trip around the world or living away somewhere is just for the rich - right? How can backpacking college grads that are broke do it? Right now people with much less money than you have are having the time of their lives on worldwide travel adventures touring and living for months and months. How do they do it?

Traveling can be less expensive than you think. In many places in the world we learned how to do it for less than a $100 a day for the both of us and we show how you too can do it in Chapter 7 ("Finding Great Travel Bargains"). Also, you do not need to continue incurring many of the expenses you normally do living at home.

Travel on Less Than $100 a Day for a Couple

We all know the costs of our typical vacations can be expensive. Who hasn't justified a travel indulgence by thinking, "we are on vacation"? So how can we afford to go for a month or more? With knowledge, research, planning, and flexibility, your travel adventure can be more affordable than you think.

For example, flying across the world and back incurs one of your largest expenses and it is the same whether you stay for 2 weeks or 2 months. The expensive resort hotels and fancy restaurants that were justified because you had only a few weeks of vacation each year are not necessary. In fact, local hotels and restaurants can be more enjoyable than the expensive ones.

You don't have to do the expensive shows, side trips, and attractions to fill your day. Many of these 'authentic' shows are nearly forgotten dances put on just for the tourists. Watching the sunset, taking walks through amazing new places, visiting less touristy sites, meeting new interesting people, or relaxing and reading a good book can lead to as good or better experiences.

When we visited one of Europe's most beautiful palaces, the palace of Versailles outside of Paris, we took a picnic lunch with us. While we enjoyed our wonderful French baguette and cheeses overlooking the beautiful gardens, the caretaker's cute daughter came and sat down next to us with her little Scottish terrier dog and shared our lunch. She was about 7 years old and spoke no English. We spoke no French but the three of us 'chatted' for about an hour. We remember our French picnic and the caretaker's daughter as much as our visit through the palace.

Great travel bargains can be found if you know where to look. Prices are less expensive in many places of the world and travel savings can be had everywhere when you use the cost-saving ideas presented in Chapter 7 ("Finding Great Travel Bargains"). Also, interesting photos are better than souvenirs.

We set a daily budget of less than $100 for the both of us when we are traveling. This doesn't include extra expenses such as flights, cruises, car rentals, and optional but can't be missed expensive excursions. In many places in world, we can find clean suitable lodging accommodations near the important attractions for $40-60/night for a private double room (dorm rooms for single travelers can be had for $10-30/night). Good meals for the day for both of us can be done for another $30-50 leaving some left over for a good beer or glass of wine, entrance fee to an attraction, and transportation around town or a bus transfer to the next destination.

Spending less than $100/day for the both of us is achievable and we have done it for weeks on end. For some travel options (i.e. cruises, organized tours, resorts) and some destinations such as larger cities and the more developed parts of the world (i.e. Western Europe, Japan, Australia, New Zealand) this budget is difficult to maintain and we need to raise it. Also, there are wonderful excursions (e.g. boat trip to Iguazu Falls, Argentina, or day excursion to Milford Sound, New Zealand) that should not be missed.

If you are accustomed to staying and eating in more expensive places, a higher daily budget can be set. The travel advice and Internet websites and apps presented in this book offer savings on a wide range of travel options. Also, there numerous tips on how to save on other travel needs.

In Chapter 7 ("Finding Great Travel Bargains") we detail many ways you can significantly reduce your travel expenses. These are the 'secrets' the travel industry would prefer you did not know.

Eliminate a Large Amount of Expenses from Your Normal Life

During short vacations, we continue to incur the expenses of our normal life. For extended travel or stays, many expenditures you currently have become unnecessary. Among many other expenses you don't need are: a house/apartment, car, most of your clothes, and related expenses (i.e. home and auto insurance and maintenance, gasoline, groceries, utilities, cable TV and other entertainment, Internet services, dry cleaning, and cleaning and maintenance services). Magazine and newspaper subscriptions can often be suspended. Gym/club memberships can be reduced or suspended while you are away.

We spend more than we think. In America we have become more productive in doing most everything allowing us a higher standard of living. Instead of exchanging higher productivity for more time, we have exchanged it for more stuff. Many Americans cannot put their car in their garage because it is full of stuff. The owners of Walmart have become the richest people in America because of this. Their slogan is "Save Money. Live Better." Of course, by living better they mean more stuff. Walmart's slogan should be "At Walmart, you can have more stuff for the same money."

Our society convinces us that a good 'lifestyle' is to spend big for status and the required accessories - bigger homes in nicer neighborhoods, second homes or timeshares, newer cars, more and larger TV's, recreational vehicles (i.e. RV's, boats, motorcycles, jet skis), the latest electronic gadgets, home entertainment systems, computers, printers, pricy vacations, trips, home renovations, new furniture, kitchen wares, other new items for the home, current clothing fashions, jewelry, watches, gym/golf/club memberships, parties, and other stuff.

In addition, other smaller things add up - eating out, shopping excursions, newer phones, gifts, movies, shows, and subscriptions for items we don't read or use. Possessions are easier to buy now than ever before. Because of the Internet we do not need to leave our home. Check out your monthly credit cards statements.

We need to earn more money to pay for all this and our taxes (even percentage wise) go up. When we started adding up all our taxes it was approaching half our income. Surprised? We were. Think about it – federal income tax, state income tax, local income tax, sales tax, Social Security, Medicare, disability, property tax, capital gains tax, corporate business tax, unemployment tax, gasoline tax, auto license and registration fees, excise taxes (i.e. liquor, tobacco, airfare), utility bill taxes, gift tax, inheritance tax, estate tax, severance tax, yield tax, transfer tax, renters tax, hotel and rental car tax, building permit fees, licenses, and tolls and use tax for bridges and parks.

I had a saying when I ran for the U.S. Congress, "If it moves, we tax it." Remember, even if you do not have one or more of these taxes levied directly on you, you pay it indirectly through higher prices for goods and services. If you add it all up, probably 25-50% of your income goes to taxes.

If you add up all these expenses, the cost of living to sustain the 'American way' is expensive. Most of these expenses can go away when you take an extended trip or stay.

Even your home expenses (i.e. rent, mortgage, property tax, utilities, cable, insurance, repairs, maintenance, security service, upgrades, HOA fees, supplies) can be covered. We rented our home out for the time we were away. The rent covers our home expenses with a little extra positive cash flow. More about renting your home, even for a week or two, is presented in the next chapter. Another option is to house trade reducing your lodging expenses while spending time to get to know another place in the world.

When you find bargains while traveling and eliminate expenses from home, you truly can travel the world for less than it costs to live at home. We do.

Other Priceless Returns on Your Travel Investment

What about the added benefits of travel or extended stays? How do you put a price on getting closer and reconnecting with your spouse, memories of a lifetime, or reclaiming your health, reducing your stress, and avoiding depression? How much are these things worth: taking control of your life and becoming excited, recharged, and viewing your life full of possibility?

What would an economist say about the value of new abilities gained from overcoming travel challenges such as improved skills in decision making capability, problem solving, planning, and communication; ability to adapt to new situations; and renewed courage to take on new things? How would a psychologist value increased self-confidence, love, joy, fulfillment, personal development, independence, passion for new experiences, peace of mind, and being happy?

Our society has convinced us that material investment and extravagant consumption is more important than personal investment. Instead of trading time to pay for more possessions, many people are discovering a new definition of wealth from those who are rich in time to live, do the things they want to do, and enjoy life fully.

When you consider all the potential benefits of a travel adventure, we get close to priceless!

Chapter 5

What to Do with Your House and Possessions

In this chapter...

Renting Your House

Home Exchange and House Sitting

You have made a major investment of money and time in your home and possessions. What do you do with them while you are gone on a trip or extended stay?

Renting Your House

Your house expenses (i.e. rent, mortgage, property tax, utilities and cable, insurance, security service, repairs, maintenance) can be covered. You can rent your home for a few weeks or much longer. Many people prefer renting a furnished home with kitchens, etc. when they go on vacation. This could be for two weeks or so during summer or winter if you are near a winter resort. Short-term rentals during special seasons of the year usually receive a higher than average monthly rent. One of our neighbors has rented their home to a European family every summer for years. Years ago, we rented our home for 6 weeks and took our son for his first tour of Europe. Other families must relocate for a few months for the parent's work requirements.

The Bedouins in Wadi Rum, Jordan, moved their tents within hours - you may need a little more planning

Longer-term rentals can be done with people relocating within your town or moving to your area but who are not ready to buy a home. We rented our house for the 2 years we were on our round-the-world travel adventure. The rent covered our expenses with a little extra positive cash flow. If you plan to have an extended trip, then you should consider renting your house arranging short stays with friends and family if you return for short periods of time.

Renting your house has some tax advantages, especially longer term. You should talk to your tax accountant. Also, if you rent your home for just a year or two, you will still be eligible for the Federal capital gains tax exemption if you lived in your home for at least two of the past five years. Don't go over three years because you will lose the tax exemption and your gain will be taxed as a capital gain. It is also wise to check first with your mortgage lender and insurance company to make sure there are no restrictions or additional insurance coverage required (e.g. rider to cover the contents and furnishings).

What to Do with Your Possessions

Rent your home furnished, if possible, so you do not need to deal with the furniture and other items in the house. When you return from your travel adventure, possessions will probably be less important to you. Unclutter your house and life now by lending out or selling off as much stuff as you can that the tenants will not be using.

Have a garage sale or use **Craigslist (www.craigslist.org)** or **eBay (www. ebay.com)**. Sort through your clothes, books, etc. and give to charity a majority of the items you cannot sell. Giving books to your local library is a good way to see them get good use. Get rid of anything you have not used for a year or so. For storage of any items you decide to keep and do not want the new tenants to have, you can put a lock on one of the closets. Renting an external storage unit or storing some things in friends' homes can also be done.

For people who do not own a house, you can reduce the amount of possessions that may need to be stored or lent out by using the same methods.

How to Rent Your Home

You can rent your house on your own or with a real estate agent. If you choose to do it on your own, we found placing ads with photos on *Craigslist (www.craigslist.org)* to be very effective in finding tenants. Getting professionally done photos is worth the investment. Start off your description with the major 6-8 most desirable features with brief bulleted statements. Make clear when it is available and state the monthly rental price. You may want to develop your own website to help people, especially those from out of town, get excited about renting your home. Your Internet provider often offers easy-to-use web building and hosting capability.

We also let our friends and family know about it. Sometimes neighbors know of people who would like to relocate to your area. For shorter-term rentals you may want to try listing in *HomeAway (www.homeaway.com)*, *Villas International (www.villasintl.com)*, and *VRBO (www.vrbo.com)*. Your area may have other effective ways to advertise such as newspaper and local magazine ads.

To make your house rent as quickly as possible, you should repair everything, replace old knobs and fixtures (i.e. lighting, faucets), and clean it inside out and from top to bottom including the windows, carpets, floors, sinks, and all the drawers and closets. Cleaning up the garden and a fresh coat of warm neutral-color paint is very helpful in making your house more appealing.

Eliminate the clutter, remove outdated furniture and anything dirty or stained, and simplify decorations removing personal collections and photos. Yes, that photo of grandma has to go and maybe some of the furniture. Open shades to all windows to let in as much light as possible. Lighten dark areas with lamp lighting. Clear off all the walls, shelves, drawers, and closets of personal items leaving just those things that enhance the decor or what a new tenant will need.

Your tenants may not keep things up as well as you so try to make everything as low maintenance as possible. Install a drip system for the garden and arrange for any maintenance to be done. We wrote a document explaining how to use everything in the house along with maintenance suggestions and contacts of maintenance/repair companies, local restaurants, movie theatres, grocery stores, and other nearby attractions. This document is great for a new tenant and makes for an extra selling feature.

We ask for a monthly rental fee slightly lower than the market rate. This allows us to rent our property consistently. Only one month of lost rent can be a lot of months of a few extra hundred of dollars. This also lets us find good tenants more quickly and be able to choose a better one. You do not want to have tenant problems. When we rent our home, we take the first month's rent up front so the tenant is always paying one month ahead.

Take a security deposit equal to a month's rent (more if the tenant has pets or other special circumstances). The security deposit is returned at the end of the rental period if no damage occurred. Any damage other than normal wear and tear is deducted from the security deposit. You should take detailed photos or video of every room, article of furniture, and all items left at your house.

Take time to find a good tenant. The best may not necessarily be the first one interested. Have each prospective tenant complete an application and do reference and credit checks.

Some simple screening guidelines are:

1) Income should be least three times rent verifiable with pay stubs

2) Call two prior landlords to see if they had problems

3) Using a social security number, do a background and credit check at **E-Renter.com (www.e-renter.com)** for about $30.

Your state landlord association can also help with this. Be careful when turning potential tenants away. For example, refusing tenants for non-financial reasons, like families with children, race, sexual orientation, etc. could violate fair housing laws.

Get a standard lease agreement signed. Real estate documents can be found at business and bookstores, online at **Ez Landlord Forms (www.**

ezlandlordforms.com), or from your real estate agent. We use the standard California lease agreement. A lease agreement also is good for bringing up and working out issues (e.g. plant watering) before you begin your relationship.

Make sure you are clear about your needs in the terms of the lease agreement. Make it is clear to the new tenant when you plan to return. If your plans are more open ended, you may want to consider a 12-month lease that converts to month-month after the end of the first year.

Once You Rent Your Home

When rented, ask your tenants to direct deposit the monthly rent into your checking account or send the rent payments to a trusted friend or family member to deposit for you. When you set up your bills to be paid automatically you cannot wait to arrive home to deposit rent checks – see Chapter 9 ("Paying Your Bills While You Are Away"). Have the renter change the utilities to their name and billing. Apply for a PO Box mailing address and mail forwarding. Plan for someone to do repairs while you are away. We left our tenants with a complete list of handymen and other maintenance/repair contacts to call if something urgent arises. Arrange to have your pets stay with friends and family. You can arrange for your cars to be used by the tenants or stored in a safe place like a friend's garage or driveway.

It can take time to find a good tenant and get your house ready to show. Start the process five months or more before you plan to leave. If you do find a good tenant before you plan to leave, it may be beneficial to stay with friends or in inexpensive short term lodging in your town for a while or start your travel adventure early.

Also, if you are taking a series of longer trips with a break to come home for major events like the Christmas holiday, send out an e-mail message a couple of months before to friends and family asking to stay with them. You may want to expand your list of contacts making house and pet sitting service available in exchange for a place to stay. Many people believe it is a good idea to have the pets and yard taken care of and someone reliable staying in their house while they are gone.

Home Exchange and House Sitting

Another option is to exchange your home reducing your lodging expenses while spending time to get to know another place in the world. Free or low cost long-term lodging can be obtained though home exchange. We have done a home exchange (also known as house swap) and it worked out well. You live in each other's home and work out other arrangements like use of cars and home, maintenance, and pet care. To find more information about home exchanges, you can go to:

- *Intervac (www.intervac.com)*
- *HomeExchange (www.homeexchange.com)*
- *HomeLink International (www.homelink.org)*

Another option is to have a house sitter come stay at your home while you are away. Friends and family are good sources for this. You also use these websites to help you find a house sitter:

- *HouseCarers (www.housecarers.com)*
- *MindMyHouse (www.mindmyhouse.com)*
- *The Caretaker Gazette (www.caretaker.org)*

You can improve your changes of being accepted as a house sitter by contacting homeowners and posting an add on the websites listed above, providing references, networking with friends, and possibly offering a security deposit.

How do you determine where to go and plan for a travel adventure? Read on...

Chapter 6

How Planning Can Enhance Your Experience

In this chapter...

Deciding Where to Go

Doing Your Homework is Fun

Organized Tours vs. Independent Travel On Your Own

Flexibility

Making a Commitment

"If you have built castles in the air, your work need not be lost;
that is where they should be. Now put the foundations under them."
~ Henry David Thoreau, Walden

Traveling or living away somewhere does take some planning. How do you decide where to go in this great big world? How do to get there and get around when you are there? Where do you stay? How do you find the best places to eat and things to do? This chapter will help you get started in in your planning process.

Planning is good. Picking out destinations you want to visit, putting together a good itinerary during the best times to go, deciding how you want to do it, and finding good bargains can greatly enhance your experience. You will probably want to make a least a few flight bookings and possibly an organized tour. Arrangements can be hard to make in busier seasons. Good preparation is especially important for those beginning to travel. Combining the advice in this book with a positive, confident, and willing-to-learn attitude will overcome your lack of knowledge.

Over planning is not necessary. Your plan should not become a rulebook where you overlook great unplanned happenings and encounters as they come up. Some of our best experiences have been spontaneous and having overly detailed itineraries makes that difficult.

Give yourself plenty of time before leaving to plan your trip. Chapter 17 ("Getting Started on Your Travel Adventure – A Step-by-Step

Guide") gives a five-month step-by-step planning and preparation guideline. You will have time to enjoy the process and it will make the anticipation of the trip more exciting.

Deciding Where to Go

All destinations are potentially wonderful in their own way. There is hardly a corner of the world that doesn't have some hidden treasure. You may already have some ideas of great places in the world you would like to visit and attractions you would like to see. In the case you do not have one special place or have too many places you want to travel to, here are some ways for you to decide on your next travel designation.

There are so many wonderful places in the world!

Explore Your Dreams

A funny story thing happened in Italy during one of our first trips to Europe. We were taking the train from Paris to Venice. Watching the map was my job on this trip and my wife,

Pat, was not aware of the cities we passed through. The train was slowing down for a stop and the conductor yelled out "All passengers for Pisa please prepare to depart."

Pat asked me, "Pisa? Is this the Leaning Tower of Pisa, Pisa?" I answered in the affirmative and she said, "We have to get off the train!" As a child growing up in New York her family had tomato sauce cans with a picture of the Leaning Tower of Pisa on them. When she told her family she was going there someday they would make fun of her thinking it was just a dream. With her feet barely touching the ground, Pat visited her 'Leaning Tower of Pisa' that day. What is your 'Leaning Tower of Pisa'?

Venice, Italy! – the city of my dreams.

The first thing you should explore is your dreams. If you did not do the dream exercise in the Introduction chapter, let's do it now. Close your eyes and start imaging the places in the world you would like to visit and explore. Stop reading now, actually close your eyes, and dream about traveling the world… What did you dream about? It is probably a good place to start.

Talk to Your Friends and Other Travelers

One of the best sources of information on good places to travel to is from other travelers. The opinion of people you trust can give you the pros and cons of trips they have taken.

What is Your Traveling Personality?

Another way of deciding is to think about your traveling personality. Are you a first time traveler, intellectual, romantic, or adventurous? First time travelers are probably a little nervous and concerned about things you do not know. A good place to start is touring Europe with classics such as London and Paris. Europe is developed with excellent travel accommodations and famous attractions with an abundance of culture, history, and leisure opportunities.

The history buff and intellectual that can't get enough of museums, architecture, and archeological sites will enjoy Europe, Egypt, Jerusalem, China, and Japan. The romantic who loves sunsets, beautiful beaches, and romantic fantasies will love Santorini, Venice, Paris, Caribbean islands, Bali, Fiji, and Tahiti. The adventurous type can get their thrills in New Zealand, the Amazon, and Costa Rica. For those who have travel experience, go to India, Africa, Thailand, or Papua New Guinea. Of course, a great choice is seeing more of North America… that has it all.

These listings just scratch the surface of the numerous places in the world to visit and enjoy. We maintain a personal list of future travel trips that keeps getting longer as we meet other travelers from around the world who tell us about their adventures and home countries.

Usually our travel adventures include a little of all the travel personalities. We explore a region of the world including several countries so we can include famous historic attractions, beautiful surroundings, relaxing and romantic beaches, and adventurous activities.

A Curiosity About Your Ancestry

Tracing your ancestry can provide for an exciting experience. An interesting story is about how we came to discover and visit our ancestral origins. We did not know the background of our name 'Dunlap'. One day we received a solicitation in the mail for Scottish-related items to purchase with our last name on the front of the brochure. This is the first time we learned our name is Scottish. Later that week we were invited to a fun evening at the Magic Castle in Los Angeles where you are entertained all night by various magicians. One magician interrupted his show and told us that today was his birthday and he was Scottish.

The following week we attended an event for Make-A-Wish where about 5,000 people came together in the largest fund raising event in San Diego. A drawing was held for two round-trip tickets to American Airlines' newest hub. Guess who won the tickets - us! Guess where they were for – Glasgow, Scotland - about 30 miles from the village of Dunlap! The world can be a strange fascinating place at times. So off we went to discover our heritage.

It was fun because the village of Dunlap has a population of only 200 (with 2 pubs!). Hundreds of years ago, the Dunlap's were dairy farmers who invented hard cheese. Because of this, cheese could be stored and shipped making the Dunlaps rich. They gave money to the then king of Scotland for a war and received a clanship. We were invited to visit the Dunlap manor and spent an evening with a retired university professor who's hobby it was to collect Dunlap artifacts. We did continue on to visit other parts of northern Europe. This discovery of our ancestry has been one of the highlights of our travels.

What is Your Budget?

Finding great travel bargains can extend your travel days and experiences much further. We often choose our designation region because of special deals that may come in specific areas. To assist you, we have compiled loads of great ideas on helping you find travel bargains. Carefully read and start using the ideas presented in Chapter 7 ("Finding Great Travel Bargains"), especially the sections "Big Savings Traveling During Off Season" and "Follow the Disaster", so you can include sensible estimates of costs and best times to go when deciding on your travel destinations.

In order to make your travel budget go even further, travel to developing nations, where people make less money. These regions include Eastern Europe, Central America, South America, Southeast Asia, the Middle East, and India.

Ease of Travel

When planning our next travel adventure, we take in account easy vs. hard travel. Good traveler infrastructure and no language barriers characterize easy travel places while harder travel places are more challenging with less infrastructure and a language barrier. If our last trip was a hard one we consider doing an easier one next to keep our enthusiasm for travel high. People who are starting their world travel should consider beginning with easier travel destinations.

Easier travel destinations include USA, Canada, UK, Ireland, Scandinavia, Australia, New Zealand, South Africa, and Singapore. Although English is spoken widely in the world, examples of designations with a little more language barrier are France, Italy, Spain, Germany, and Japan. Examples of harder travel designations are India, Cambodia, Bolivia, Syria, Uganda, China, and Morocco.

Travel Advisories and Warnings

For an updated list of countries the U.S. government has issued travel warnings you can go to the **U.S. Department of State's website (www.travel. state.gov)**. Do keep in mind that a disturbance in one area or city causing the travel advisory may not be widespread across the whole country. You can also find specific information about each country. For the latest rules pertaining to flights, you can go to the **TSA's website (www.tsa.gov).**

Planning Assistance Websites and Smartphone Apps

There are several good travel websites and apps that can help you decide where to go based on your travel preferences. Several interesting ones are:

- **Gecko Go (www.geckogo.com)**
- **Trip Base (www.tripbase.com)**
- **iExplore (www.iexplore.com)** for more active and adventurous trips

With the above ideas in mind, start brainstorming with your travel partner. Don't be overly judgmental and just let the ideas flow. Some of the off-the-wall ideas may spark the perfect trip. Once you have decided on a travel destination, get a map of the world and see where it is located and what other places around that area may also be fun to explore. Now you have a kernel of a plan.

A trip planning smartphone app called **mTrip** is available for the Android and iPhone for 28 cities. You input your travel dates, lodging, and what you want to see and do and mTrip will calculate a daily itinerary with reviews and directions.

Doing Your Homework is Fun

Researching and planning the details of your trip or living away can take some time. It can also be fun. Reading about places you dream about is exciting and adds to the anticipation of your travel adventure. Learning your options from the experience of others can lead you to wonderful new places and possibilities.

Visit Your Bookstore's Travel Section

Reading about our chosen destinations gets us excited and the anticipation of the trip is one of the wonderful things about traveling. One of the first things to do after deciding on a destination or region of the world to visit is to go to your local bookstore's travel section. Some of the larger bookstores have large sections for travel guidebooks with multiple offerings for most places you can image.

If you do not have a favorite travel guidebook series you use, a good way to pick the right travel guidebook for you is to review the different guidebooks for a destination you have already visited. See how they rate places you visited and how their suggestions and descriptions fit your impression of the place. When you find one that agrees with your experience, style of travel, and other tastes, you have found your travel guide series for other places.

Pick up and review each travel guidebook for your destinations. Look at the publication date to see if it is current. See how they are organized and what kinds of places they recommend for activities, lodging, and eating. Check the prices listed in the guidebook to see if they are within your travel budget. Different travel guidebooks may be more appropriate for different destinations. Always consider new travel guidebooks because your preferences may change.

If there is one thing we splurge on it is travel guidebooks. A $28.99 price for a travel guidebook may seem expensive at first glance but if it is the right guidebook for you, it will save you that in your first day and greatly enhance your travel experience. Because we tend to group several destinations together in a region of the world and sometimes pick up several different guidebooks for each destination, our travel guidebook budget (if you can call it that) can easily exceed $100 for an extended travel adventure.

Travel guidebooks are great for:

- Getting the feel of a place
- Understanding historical significance and cultural nuances
- Finding where the major attractions are located
- Deciding what is best for you
- Discovering interesting day trips
- Learning how to get around with maps included
- Obtaining advice on local customs
- Acquiring tips on accommodations and places to eat

Do keep in mind the limitations of relying exclusively on the advice of travel guidebooks. They send everyone to the same places. Discovering your own adventures is also important to enjoying travel experiences.

To reduce the weight of your luggage, leave travel guidebooks behind or trade them for other books when you move on. You may not need to take the whole book with you on the trip. Tearing out or photocopying the sections you need will lighten your load.

If you are planning to visit only a city or two in a region, you can save money on your guidebooks. **Lonely Planet (www.lonelyplanet.com)** allows you to download only the chapters you need from their guidebooks for $4.95/chapter. Chapters can then be printed or viewed on PDF-compatible devices. If you purchase the entire guidebook as digital chapters, you will save up to 80% on the price of the printed version. Introductory sections of guidebook, including the index, are included for free.

Please do not take this as a definitive recommendation because your needs may be different than ours. For budget travel full of experiences exploring areas on our own, we have gravitated to the "Lonely Planet" series of travel guidebooks. We also like and use other travel guidebooks. Frommer's offer all-purpose guidebooks covering all ranges of travel budgets. They are easy to read and offer rankings of attractions

Order Tour Brochures

Go online and order brochures from the major tour operators. They will provide sightseeing itineraries and other suggestions such as hotels and restaurant recommendations. You can use them to help plan your independent tour or maybe decide one of the tours is best for you.

Some tour operators are listed later in this chapter. You can find many more by doing an Internet search using the words "tours" and the name of the place you are planning to visit (e.g. "tours France").

Do Research on the Internet

While reading and marking the best things in your travel guidebooks, you should not use them as your only source of information. The information provided is limited and some of it can be outdated. Because so many people use travel guidebooks sending people to the same places, you may miss many great experiences. Go online and research the vast amount of information pertaining to your destinations. The following are just a few of the many travel websites that can assist you in your planning.

We have found *Wikitravel (www.wikitravel.org)* is a very good website to learn about our city or country destinations. Just type in your destination (i.e. city, country) in the search box. Another good informational website is done by the *CIA (www.cia.gov/library/publications/the-world-factbook/index.html).*

Online travel forums can be an excellent source to find answers to your travel questions. You can obtain a vast amount of information on any topic by doing an Internet search with your question (e.g. "how to get from London to Paris"). Information from several online forums and informational websites will be displayed.

Lonely Planet (www.lonelyplanet.com) is world-renowned and their "Thorn Tree" travel forum is a good source for your hard-to-find-answers questions. *Frommer's Travel Talk (www.frommers.com/travel_talk)* is another source for general travel advice. *Trip Advisor (www.tripadvisor.com)* offers a large number of user reviews and also has good selection of things-to-do suggestions. *Yelp (www.Yelp.com)* provides user reviews useful in selecting restaurants, stores, banks, and other places. Yelp is also available as an app for the Android, BlackBerry, iPhone, iPad, and Windows Phone 7. At *CruiseCritic (www.cruisecritic.com)* you can learn more about cruising. *Johnny Jet (www.johnnyjet.com)* is a comprehensive travel information resource website.

Other interesting information and planning travel websites people recommend are:

- *Gadling (www.gadling.com)*
- *World Hum (www.worldhum.com)* owned by the Travel Channel
- *Rick Steves (www.ricksteves.com)* for Europe
- *VirtualTourist (www.virtualtourist.com)*
- *Trip Wolf (www.tripwolf.com)*
- *UNESCO World Heritage Sites (http://whc.unesco.com)*
- *Travel and Leisure (www.travelandleisure.com)* for upscale travel

For researching events you can use:

- *Frommer's Whatsonwhen (www.whatsonwhen.com)*
- *World Reviewer (www.worldreviewer.com)* for lists of activities around the world
- *Festivals Media (www.festival.com)*

Younger and student travelers can locate good information suited to them from these travel websites:

- *STA Travel (www.statravel.com)*
- *International Students Travel Conference (www.stc.org)*
- *IIEPassport (www.iiepassport.org)* for international options for study

More mature (nice for senior) travelers may discover interesting travel opportunities using these travel websites:

- *AARP Destinations (www.aarp.org/travel)*
- *Elderhostel Road Scholar (www.roadscholar.org)* for traveling and learning overseas.

Best Time to Go

The sections "Big Savings Traveling During Off Season" and "Follow the Disaster" in Chapter 7 ("Finding Great Travel Bargains") offer guidelines for your decision of when it might be the best time to go.

Our stopover in Fiji – can't wait to go back.

Consider Stopovers

Often there are opportunities to stop in places where you have flight connections and stay for some time. Because you need to or could stop there anyway, the extra flight cost is often minimum. We have done this many times such as

Melbourne, Australia, on the way to New Zealand and a wonderful week in Fiji on the way back home. We also stopped in Iceland on the way back from Europe and had a wonderful experience. Each time we spent some time in a new place and completely enjoyed ourselves.

Overland Travel

By only flying from city to city you miss out on some of the best parts of the travel experience. The world that exists between major cities can be as interesting as the big cities. If you are flying from place to place, you should consider overland travel with 'open jaw' flight reservations not leaving for your next destination from the same city you came into. We often do this. For example, after touring Israel, we flew to Turkey, took gulet boats through southern Turkey, ferries through the Greek Islands to Athens, from where we flew home. After our sweep through Asia, we flew to Christchurch in southern New Zealand, rented a car, and drove across both the South Island and North Island of New Zealand flying out of Auckland in the north.

You should consider including overland travel between flights to enhance your travel adventure.

A Note of Warning About Proof of Onward Travel

Countries use proof of onward travel to insure visitors do not overstay their tourist travel limitations. If you have flights scheduled for your entire trip, you only need to keep your itinerary and flight tickets handy to show border control officers. For most travelers the limits, commonly 90 days, are usually not a problem. Although if you travel with flexible schedules without onward travel booked you may have troubles crossing borders or exiting countries, even being detained. Having proof of onward travel may be a cause of concern that needs to be addressed.

Some countries requiring proof of onward travel for non-residents are Peru, New Zealand, United Kingdom, United Sates, Philippines, Indonesia, Brazil, and some others. Others that may also be a concern are Japan, Thailand, Singapore, Indonesia, Chile, and Ecuador. This list may change over time so it is best to check the requirements. For current information on visa requirements and limits of the countries you plan to visit, go to the **U.S. Department of State's website (www.travel.state.gov).**

A good way to deal with this if you do not have onward flights scheduled in advance is to ask your travel agent or the agent who booked your flight for advice.

Organized Tours vs. Independent Travel On Your Own

The choice of using an organized guided tour or exploring the world independently provides an interesting tradeoff for travelers. We have used several good companies that provide excellent organized tours and have enjoyed our travel experience with them. We have also explored many regions of the world totally on our own keeping our costs down.

Organized tours will make your travel experience easier with less hassles and provide you with knowledgeable guides that make your visits to the attractions much more interesting. Because they use large group buys to negotiate their travel accommodations, many organized tours can provide you a reasonably good value. Some organized tours offer more free time to allow you some flexibility to do your own exploration. Tours are a good way to travel for the beginning, less adventurous travelers, and those traveling solo so they can make friends. They also are worthy to consider for all travelers for many harder or more adventurous travel destinations such as India, Egypt, China, Costa Rica, etc.

Some of the drawbacks of tours can be with tight itineraries you have little time to explore on your own, you must wait for the group, and you must leave places where you might want to spend more time. Organized tours take you to places where most tourists go and sometimes you will be overwhelmed by vendors attempting to sell you things making the experience less enjoyable.

When we visited Bali for the first time traveling on our own, we experienced the beauty and wonder of Bali craving to return one day. When one of our cruises stopped at Bali for the day, the vendors overwhelmed us and a taxi driver took us to a place where we did not ask to go. If this second experience had been our only one of Bali, we would have a totally different opinion of Bali.

Check out travelers' reviews on the Internet of the company and tour you are considering. Some questions to ask before booking an organized tour are:

- What is included in the price and what is extra (i.e. tips, taxes, fees, meals, entrance fees, optional excursions)?

- How many meals are included?
- Where does the tour start and end? Are airfare and transfers included?
- How large is the group?
- What is the typical makeup of the group (i.e. age, level of activity, English speaking)?
- What is the expected level of difficulty and activity (i.e. walking, stair climbing, adventure)
- How do you travel and what type of accommodations do you stay in?
- Does it include free time to explore and shop on your own?
- Are the sites you want to see on the tour?
- Are there optional excursions and what do they cost?
- What are the qualifications of the trip leaders?'
- How much travel time is there on buses, etc.?
- How much time each day is devoted to planned souvenir shopping? (Note: some tours offer lower prices because they take you to many 'factory tours' where the company or guide gets a commission on everything that is purchased. Some people love to shop and you can spend hours every day waiting around in shops.)
- Can you leave the trip at the end to travel independently and return home on a later date?
- Ask about any special considerations (i.e. diet, medical conditions, disabilities) you have?

There are numerous organized tour companies. Many specialize in certain areas of the world. You can find those by doing an Internet search for the word 'tour' and the place you place to visit. *Johnny Jet (www. johnnyjet.com)* has a listing of tour operators for many places in the world. To start your research we have listed below a few popular companies that feature tours to many places.

General:

- *smarTours (www.smartours.com)*

- *Gate 1 (www.gate1.com)*
- *Overseas Adventure Travel (www.oattravel.com)* featuring smaller groups
- *Trek America (www.trekamerica.com)* for U.S. tours

Adventure:

- *Wildland Adventures (www.wildland.com)*
- *Gap Adventures (www.gapadventures.com)*
- *Tauch (www.tauch.com)*

Spa Vacations:

- *Spa Finder (www.spafinder.com)*

Educational Travel (i.e. cooking, language, cultural, art, photography, writing, golf, tennis):

- *Shawguides (www.shawguides.com)*

Volunteer opportunities worldwide ranging from assisting people, teaching, improving parks, building homes, participating in an archeological dig, or working with animals:

- *International Volunteer Programs Association (www.volunteerinternational.org)*
- *Global Volunteers (www.globalvolunters.org)*
- *Volunteers For Peace (www.vfp.org)*
- *Idealist (www.idealist.org)*

Traveling Independently

Traveling on your own requires more research and time spent finding good accommodations and things to do. Many experienced travelers prefer this option and learn how to overcome the added challenges without too much difficulty. You can travel less costly on your own, meet new people, and you are free to go where you want to and stay as long as you wish. You can stay and dine in small quaint places that cannot accommodate large groups. Once you are confident of your travel skills, the advantages of having flexible schedules and itineraries with reduced costs can greatly enrich your travel experience.

Getting Started

A good way to start out is to learn how to travel by taking organized tours. At the end of the tour you may want to try some travel on your own before returning home. Check with the tour company to delay your return flight. We did this when we visited Costa Rica. We enjoyed a wonderful expertly guided tour of the national parks and then delayed our flight home to stay 5 additional days independently enjoying Costa Rica's wonderful beaches.

As your confidence increases but you are not quite ready for being completely on your own, you may want to consider some of the new types of tours that provide more flexible escorted tours. These include more free time. There are also customized tours where only flights and hotels (and maybe a few extras like car rentals and a local host) are provided.

We plan most of our travel adventures now to be on our own with high consideration of a flexible (more free time) organized guided tour for a portion of our trip. Once your travel experience grows, you may want to try this. We did this in the Middle East. We started on our own in Cairo and the Red Sea. Then we did an organized tour of the Nile River Egyptian wonders and the rose city of Petra in Jordan benefiting from an expert guide and visiting many attractions without having to plan it all. After that we went on our own again through Israel, Turkey, and some Greek Islands – a wonderful trip combining the advantages of an organized tour with mostly independent travel.

Flexibility

"The traveler was active, he went strenuously in search of people, of adventure, of experience. The tourist is passive; he expects interesting things to happen to him."
~ Daniel Boorstin

During our lives, we have learned to play by the rules of home that reward us for following firm routines and procedures. There is a time for the more experienced traveler when less is more when it comes to planning your travel adventures. When traveling independently, you are in charge of your own schedule. You can find great things you did not know about by adopting a new attitude that prepares you to be open to things that come your way. Possibilities grow from asking questions rather than knowing all the answers.

We ask questions and advice from fellow travelers, locals we meet, and managers of hotels and restaurants about options, ideas, hot spots, etc. For reference, we take photos of maps and schedules on train station walls and bus stops. The benefits of the information age are a precious resource for the modern-day traveler. Knowing your options, not your future, gives you opportunities to be flexible.

Be open-minded instead of seeking evidence for conclusions you have already made. Try to overcome predetermined beliefs by not setting limits. Give yourself challenges to try new things. At first I was not overly excited about trying a room with the bathroom down the hall or touring an area without hotel reservations. My wife got me to try both and I learned it is not anywhere near as problematic as I thought it would be. We now love to try new activities, foods, and things we never did before.

Be open to new ways of traveling, the side trip you did not plan, a local festival you did not know about, or spending more or less time in a place you are visiting.

Relax

See the sites and then spend some time off the tourist area. Relax at a sidewalk cafe and have a coffee, beer, or glass of wine. Then just sit and watch the world go by. It is a national pastime in many countries.

Allow Things to Happen

In Viet Nam, we started to have some fun with two boys on a bicycle by taking a photo of them and showing it to them on our camera's screen. Although we could not speak each other's language, in a short time I was riding their bike and laughing with them. We went on to do something fun that night but we remember the two laughing boys on the bike as a highlight.

Be Open to Things that Come Up

In Supetar on Brac Island in Croatia, staying in a guesthouse in a private neighborhood above the city gave us a unique experience. In addition to playing on the beautiful white stone beaches during the day and enjoying harbor-side restaurants at night, we were able to sit with the local men who gathered every afternoon for a serious contest of bocce ball. We were able to learn about everyday local life as well as take advantage of the attractions.

A Traveler Seizes Opportunities

When a group of fun-loving people invites you out to dinner or their home, be flexible to change your plans and go for it. Some of our most memorable travel experiences have been enjoying the company of other travelers and locals. We had Thanksgiving dinner with a bunch of joyful Australians in New Zealand. In Uruguay, we met two travelers who, after an upbeat conversation at breakfast, invited us to share their car for a day exploring the wonderful beaches around Punta del Este. In Jerusalem, we were invited into a couple's home for a traditional family Shavuot dinner after meeting them in the market. Be fun and positive and be ready to say 'yes' to these experiences.

Have a Flexible Itinerary

When you become more confident as a traveler, making no lodging reservations and not deciding in advance on how long you will stay, will allow yourself to enjoy your travels much more. Sometimes you will love a place and want to stay longer. We fell in love with Dubrovnik, Croatia, living like the locals getting fresh fruit at the morning market. We enjoyed the town and beaches during the day and there was an international film festival with screenings at night. What a great time! Because we were being more flexible on that trip, we extended our stay from a few days to a week.

Sometimes you would like to slow down, rest, and enjoy a place. We fell in love with many other places, like the Greek Islands of Santorini and Crete, and stayed many more days than we had planned. Sometimes a place is just not for us so we leave early allowing more time for other places.

Having more flexibility in your itinerary also allows you to make changes when presented with a good opportunity. On our train trip through Europe, we met a traveler who raved about Munich. We changed our plans and went to Munich. We had a marvelous time and wished we could thank that guy we met on the train.

Finding Lodging on a Flexible Schedule

When we are being flexible in our itinerary, we decide a couple days before we leave one destination that it is time to explore our next destination. Then we start looking for lodging for the next place. We use the travel websites and strategies listed in Chapter 7 ("Finding Great Travel Bargains"). We also talk to fellow travelers and our hotel management.

They will often have suggestions for your next destination and may even call to reserve it for you. Booking at least a day or two before provides more options because sometimes the better places get booked with last minute arrivals. Finding suitable last-minute lodging while on a flexible schedule may not be best during peak travel seasons. It is easier when you travel during non-peak seasons.

It is possible to find suitable lodging the day you arrive at a destination although it can be more stressful. Local tourist bureaus and city information centers are often good sources and we have had good luck using them finding lodging the same day we arrive. Sometimes people will meet you when you arrive at your destination offering lodging. When we took ferries through the Greek Islands, people would meet us at the dock offering rooms. We have used these options with reasonable success. It is important to ask a lot of questions.

Some exceptions would be if you know your specific dates you will be at a destination. In this case, booking much earlier affords you more options. This is also valid if you are traveling during high season, when a special event is planned, or in areas where lodging is less plentiful. When we travel independently, we like to have our lodging reserved for a few days at the first destination of our trip because we know we are going to be there and our flight may come in late making finding a place stressful. You can usually extend your stay or find other lodging if you decide to stay longer.

Making a Commitment

"A journey of a thousand miles must begin with a single step."
~ Lao Tzu

There are so many ways we rationalize our familiar routines and procrastinate making changes. A good way to begin your travel adventure is to imagine you are doing it and the fun and joys you will have. Then decide when you are going and block out that timeframe on your calendar.

"The world is full of people who would love you to behave in whatever ways are most convenient for them."
~ Dr. Wayne W. Dyer, author,

Pulling Your Own Strings

"No matter who says what, you should accept it with a smile and do your own work."

- Mother Teresa

To reinforce your commitment, tell friends, family, and organizations you are involved with you are going and when. Some will be supportive. Prepare yourself to hear their concerns for not doing it. Keep in mind they may be coming from their own fears or even jealousy. They could be reacting to missing you or just not being able to understand what you are doing or why. They may also take your growing freedom as subtle criticism or a threat to their own way of life and dismiss you as irresponsible and selfish. It's OK. Actually, you are taking responsibility for your freedom and happiness. Don't let them hold you back on living your life.

"Conventional people are roused to fury by departure from convention, largely because they regard such departure as a criticism of themselves."

-Bertrand Russell

Have a plan for those who depend on you before you announce your plans. When they are assured their needs will be addressed, they will become more supportive of your plans.

To anchor the start of your planning, book the initial flight, tour, or where you plan to stay. You are on your way. Expect to have worries and doubt and maybe wake up at night. It's normal. We have done this more than once and even now, after years of traveling, worries still come up from somewhere inside us.

To help you with the details of realizing your travel adventures, we have provided a step-by-step guide in Chapter 17 ("Getting Started on Your Travel Adventure – A Step-by-Step Guide"). Be assured you are more capable than you think you are. Many have done it before you and it is not as hard as you might think.

In the next chapter we detail how you can find those great travel bargains the travel industry would prefer you did not know about.

 *Chapter 7*

Finding Great Travel Bargains

In this chapter...

This chapter will give you practical ways to stretch your typical vacation expenses to cover a month or more of a wonderful travel or living away adventure by presenting powerful cost saving tips and bargain-finding strategies worth 100's of times the cost of this book. These cost saving tips are so good and comprehensive we were able to travel the world for 2 years visiting 51 countries, which we could never have afforded otherwise.

These cost-saving tips and bargain-finding strategies are suitable for trips or stays of 1-2 weeks or 2-6 months. We have detailed the proven secrets we discovered as well as those from many travel experts from our research on how to dramatically reduce your travel costs. Many of these 'secrets' the travel industry would prefer you did not know.

The suggestions in this chapter include budget accommodations as well as more pricy lodging options. Budget travel does not have to be an inconvenience. In fact, having a thick wallet has a tendency to insulate you from the cultures, people, and unique learning experiences. It should be noted you could set a higher budget if you are accustomed to staying and eating in more expensive places. The travel websites and apps presented in this book offer savings on a wide range of options.

There is not a single best place to research prices and book your trip. You need to do some research and shop around to achieve the best deal for you. The suggested travel websites and smartphone apps presented in this chapter are some of the most popular and useful ones when this book was written. Innovations in the travel industry are happening fast. Always be on the lookout for new travel websites and apps that may offer you even better bargains and service for your travel needs.

It is wise to have printed confirmations of all reservations. Although reservation systems around the world have improved, occasionally there occurs a mistake. Having proof helps solve any issue, especially if there is a language issue.

Big Savings Traveling During Off Season

One of the best secrets to enjoy your travel adventure and save money is to go off season where you can achieve 20-50% savings off peak-season pricing. A more descriptive explanation of the best off-season times would be the 'shoulder' seasons at the beginning and end of the peak tourist season when the weather is usually good without the crowds. This varies in different parts of the world.

Often spring and fall have nice weather, less crowds, and better bargains. Except in northern or southern countries, summers can be hot, expensive, and packed with tourists, especially in July and August in the northern hemisphere, when schools are out and many people take their vacations. Many Europeans take a month off in August and restaurants and other places can be closed.

There are tradeoffs when planning for off-season bargains. For example, if you don't mind cold weather, some of the best deals can be had during winter when the weather is usually cold and dark. In places that are tropical or nearer the equator, winter is a good season to visit.

Summers are a wonderful time to visit many areas in the far north or south of our earth (i.e. Canada, Baltic countries, southern Chile and Argentina). Also keep in mind in the southern hemisphere the seasons are opposite of the northern hemisphere. In New Zealand they are skiing when Europeans are sweating in record-breaking temperatures. New Zealand's peak summer and more expensive season is mid-December through early February when their schools are out. We had beautiful weather in New Zealand in November and in Chile and Argentina in January and February. Keep this in mind when you are planning your trips.

The best time to go and off-peak seasons vary in different places in the world. You can easily learn the best times by consulting your travel guidebooks or searching on the Internet with a phrase such as "best time to go to Paris".

With a little careful planning you can enjoy good weather and save money. You can move around the world avoiding the expensive peak season taking advantage of the best or near best time to go in each area. Make a chart of the places you wish to visit with the best time to go and you may see a pattern that will work well for you.

Follow the Disaster

We have had some wonderful trips costing us almost half the normal cost by using our 'follow the disaster' travel-planning model. This idea takes some careful explanation.

When a country experiences an unexpected tragedy, people will cancel their planned trip. For months, sometimes years, tourism will be significantly reduced to that country. What many people see as potential risk, we recognize as a potential travel bargain. Let's examine this concept a bit deeper. The terrible 9/11 incident in New York saddened and concerned all of us. As bad as it was, a couple of months later were you concerned to walk around your hometown? Would you have been concerned to visit San Francisco? If you answered 'probably not' then you are a candidate to consider the 'follow the disaster' travel-planning model.

After the tsunami that hit Thailand in and around Phuket, Thailand became a travel bargain. Of course, Phuket in the south needed time to recover. We planned our Thailand trip to start in Bangkok over 500 miles away from Phuket and worked our way north to Chiang Mai and Chiang

Rai. What a wonderful trip! Hundreds of miles away there was no evidence of any problems and we took advantage of much reduced tourist crowds and amazing prices including our flight to Thailand.

We have benefited from many more examples of this. When China

Going for a ride on an elephant in Thailand.

experienced the SARS outbreak, people were rightfully concerned about traveling there. Fortunately for us they stayed concerned long after the outbreak was over. For about half of what you would normally expect to pay, we took a terrific trip to China visiting the Great Wall, Forbidden City, and Tiananmen Square in Beijing; the terracotta soldiers in Xian; the beautiful canal city of Suzhou, and the modern city of Shanghai.

Even political and terrorist incidents can provide travel bargains. For a fraction of the normal prices we went to virtually unaffected places such as Bali after the bombing of the disco, Fiji after their coup, and more recently found amazing bargains during peak seasons in the Greek Islands after the demonstrations in Athens. For over a year the whole world was on sale after 9/11. It was like being a kid in a candy store for 'follow the disaster' enthusiasts.

This concept also applies to economic recessions. Our 2-year travel adventure that inspired the writing of this book was much more affordable because we did it during the global economic downturn starting in 2009. We were able to negotiate much lower hotel prices even in peak times for hotels that were only 40% occupied when a couple years previously required a year in advance to get a reservation. Flights, tours, cruises, car rentals, and meals were all significantly more affordable.

A Word of Caution

A word of caution is more than appropriate when considering the 'follow the disaster' travel-planning model. First, 'follow' is the key word. Be sure conditions are safe where you are planning to visit. Usually you will have time to do so because people are overly concerned for a period of time after any disaster. Do your research, be aware of travel warnings, and talk to travel experts knowledgeable of the country you are planning to visit.

Last Minute Travel

Last minute travel is defined as much as 2-3 months before departure with even better deals appearing the last few weeks. Although it is not always easy, being flexible will give you more options for the best last minute travel deals. Cruises, hotels, and sometimes airlines are the best bets for last minute deals. They want to book their offering so they will offer discounts if they are not full. Keep in mind most of the last minute travel deals will be nonrefundable and they do book out if you wait too long trying get an even better deal.

A good way to learn of last minute deals is to click on last minute deal offerings on the travel websites mentioned in this chapter. You can also sign up for their e-mail newsletters. Some other good travel websites that will alert you by e-mail of special travel deals and last-minute deals are:

- *LastMinuteTravel (www.lastminutetravel.com)*
- *LastMinute (www.lastminute.com)*

- *TravelZoo (www.travelzoo.com)*
- *Budget Travel (www.budgettravel.com)*
- *CheapCaribbean (www.cheapcaribbean.com)*

There are many others where you can sign up for the e-mail updates and newsletters.

First Learn to Recognize a Good Price

Any budget-searching traveler should be ready to book a great fare as quickly as it appears. Since pricing for travel changes constantly, you first must be able to recognize a good price for your flights, hotels, cruises, tours, and car rentals. Keep in mind many hotels, cruises, and tours quote prices per person and don't always show all the taxes and fees.

Popular General Travel Websites and Smartphone Apps

Finding travel bargains can take some time but the payoff is worth it. Start by using the following popular travel websites and other travel websites and apps mentioned in this book as well as the ones you have found to be useful:

- *Kayak (www.kayak.com)* - also available as apps for the Android, BlackBerry, iPhone, IPad, and Windows Phone 7
- *Yapta (www.yapta.com)*
- *Expedia (www.expedia.com)* - also available as iPhone app
- *Travelocity (www.travelocity.com)* - also available as Android and iPhone apps (more on the way)
- *Orbitz (www.orbitz.com)* - also available as iPhone and Window Phone 7 apps
- *SideStep (www.sidestep.com)*

Enter in a variety of dates and start a journal writing down the lowest prices for different dates and places. Do this for all your travel needs (i.e. flights, tours, hotels, cruises, car rentals, excursions).

Kayak (www.kayak.com) is getting good reviews as one of the best travel websites and smartphone app (available for Android, BlackBerry, iPhone, iPad, and Windows Phone 7) for finding the bargains on flights, hotels, cruises, and car rentals. With no booking fees, Kayak combines searches across many sources including more than 400 airline websites, online travel agencies, and other travel sites, including some international ones, in its search for the best fares and fees. Kayak's Buzz gives you ranges of airfares to your destination based on departure time. They also have interesting tools which allow you to see the best fares for similar routes searched by other Kayak users as well as fare alerts.

New travel websites are appearing regularly. Read the travel section of the newspaper and research popular travel information websites to keep abreast of the latest developments. Certain travel websites concentrate in different regions of the world and you can obtain even better information and bargains for that region. You can usually find recommendations of good regional travel websites in your travel guidebooks.

Online Bounce Back Offers

Making use of online bounce backs offers is a powerful way to achieve some amazing travel bargains. If you use the Internet and have given your e-mail address to any online company, you have probably received bounce back responses. These are e-mail responses to you offering products. The online travel industry also uses bounce back responses. The marketing reasoning goes like this. If you did not book the deal when you were on their website, you are probably not coming back and are looking elsewhere. So, they feel since they have lost you why not try a better price.

Bounce back offers do not happen all the time. We have refined our online searches to the point where about 25% of them result in bounce back offers - sometimes with very good deals.

This is how it works. Do your searches for various timeframes as described in the previous section and be sure to fill out and submit their online form including your e-mail address. Do not book it at this time. Move to another website or log off and wait. Sometimes as soon as an hour you may find the deal you were looking for. Sometimes waiting a day or so will yield you the results you are looking for. If we have time, we wait for 3 days sometimes receiving offers along the way.

Online Auctions

Great bargains can be found using online auction travel websites. Many people say **Priceline (www.priceline.com)** can deliver cheaper fares for hotels and flights and **Hotwire (www.hotwire.com)** is good for finding discount hotel rates and car rentals. Priceline is available as an app on the Android, iPhone, and iPad. What should be remembered is there are tradeoffs for these bargains. For hotels, you do not know exactly where you are staying although you can choose general neighborhoods and ratings of hotel. You cannot expect the best rooms for heavily discounted prices. For flights you lose control over things like airline carrier, time of day of travel, and length of layovers although they claim to not be unreasonable. The details are available after your reservation is paid for. Your purchases are often nonrefundable.

Before attempting an online travel auction website or app, do your basic research as described above waiting for the bounce back offers to come back to you. Keep good notes in your journal. When making your bid, some experts advise taking about 20-30% off the lowest price you have found. You may want to try even more. Carefully review your bid and read the rules before making your bid. You could be stuck if you make a mistake or a reservation that doesn't fit with your plans.

To see get an idea of what prices are being accepted and declined on Priceline for particular dates for airfares, hotels, and car rentals, you can go to **BiddingForTravel (www.biddingfortravel.com)** and **BetterBidding (www. betterbidding.com)**.

Online bounce backs also work for the online auction sites and apps like Priceline and Hotwire. Often when doing a Priceline bid you will receive their response to raise your price. Maybe try waiting and see what happens.

How to Save on Flights Costs

Because the cost of flights, especially international, tends to be one of the large expense items of traveling, it is important to find the best prices as possible. If you plan to book your own flights, good deals can be found by being flexible. The lowest price may not be the best deal for you if it means saving $50 but having a long layover, early morning departure, or multiple stopovers. Here are 19 valuable tips to use to save on the cost of flights:

1) ***Keep your departure and return dates flexible if you can.*** One week may be much less expensive than another. Sometimes a day or two difference will yield great savings. Calendar-based fare tools on travel sites such as Travelocity and Expedia will show you the less expensive dates to fly to your destination. Use the 'flexible' option, if available, when choosing dates. Sometimes flying on a Tuesday or Wednesday and sometimes Saturday will yield the best fares where Monday, Friday, and Sunday are often the most expensive. For international flights, the cheapest days to fly are Monday through Thursday.

2) ***Search fares on several websites.*** Fares can vary widely.

3) ***Avoid holidays.*** Check to be sure your destination city is not celebrating a holiday or special festival. Remember in other parts of the world they celebrate different holidays at different times of the year. Move your arrival date or destination city to avoid the busier time.

4) ***Book your flight as early as you can.*** This sometimes gives you access to the cheapest seat inventory.

5) ***Use discount airline carriers (e.g. Southwest in the U.S. and easyJet and Ryanair in Europe).*** Be careful to understand any add-on fees.

6) ***Flying 'red-eye' at night or very early in the morning can often yield good bargains.***

7) ***If you are traveling just one-way, also check the round-trip fares.*** Sometimes they are less expensive than one way only.

8) ***Having more stops with different routing, longer layovers, and longer total flight time often yield savings.***

9) ***Tour one region of the world more extensively rather than making many longer air flights.***

10) ***Check for departures and arrivals from other airports in the area.*** Driving or taking public transportation at either end of your trip may save you hundreds of dollars. Also, airline hub cities (usually the country's capital or largest city) will have cheaper flights than going directly to smaller cities. You can use local ground transportation (i.e. train, bus, ferry, car rental) to go the rest of the way and possibly save on the airfare.

11) ***Timing of the week and even the day can help in finding better deals.***
Many people find better deals on flights early in the morning and
late at night when airlines frequently release new prices. Some
travel experts say Tuesday afternoon is best when the sales are often
in place. Prices are highest on average on weekends.

12) ***Ask for senior, student, or other discounts.***

13) ***Join frequent-flyer programs and use credit cards that award extra
miles for purchases.*** The miles add up and can be used for free
flights. You can research and compare programs at ***CreditCards
(www.creditcards.com).***

14) ***Use a fare-tracking travel website such as Yapta (www.yapta.com) to
help find low airfares – more details presented below.***

15) ***Once you find a good deal, first check directly with the airline's
website.*** Sometimes they offer special promotions to places nearby
that may be an even better deal.

16) ***Use your frequent flyer miles for tickets for expensive flights.*** If you
plan to use frequent flyer mileage, you need to do so in plenty
of time in advance and be willing to be flexible in your dates.
Often six months or more prior is necessary. Although one trip
we were lucky and got almost all our flights using frequent flyer
mileage in less than a month before leaving (don't count on
it). ***MileBlaster*** is a smartphone app, available for the Android,
Nokia, iPhone, and iPad, that will help you keep track of all
your frequent flier programs.

17) ***When traveling or booking last minute, be sure to get an e-ticket
issued.*** Paper tickets need to be mailed and can be lost or stolen.

18) ***Use Seatguru (www.seatguru.com) to help you choose a good seat.***
Remember to have some cash for airport taxes and departure fees.

19) ***If you need to cancel a flight, do it before the plane takes off.*** This
will give you a better chance of getting a refund or credit. Call the
airline's customer service number, even when waiting in line at the
airport. You may receive quicker service. If you cancel or miss your
flight reservation along the way, always re-confirm your return flight
because the airline may consider it canceled.

For our international flights we have had good experience finding discounts using **AirTreks (www.airtreks.com).** They have staff experienced with worldwide travel, RTW (round the world) tickets, and sourcing complex international airfares. They will assist you in planning and customizing your itinerary, suggesting interesting stopovers, providing price estimates, and offering customer support after you have made your reservations. Their website has a trip planner tool that provides you fare estimates. It is wise to do your homework first to learn what is a good price and where you want to go.

Flycheapo (www.flycheapo.com) maintains a database of low-cost airlines and where they fly in Europe.

Make Use of Fare Alerts

Because airlines regularly change their fares, setting up fare alerts to catch the best sales can save hundreds of dollars. You can set alerts on several of travel websites mentioned above. Many people say **Yapta (www. yapta.com)**, an acronym for "Your Amazing Personal Travel Assistant", is one of the best to use to track airfares for a specific flight (also hotels) before and after purchase. Yapta continues to track fares after you have purchased your ticket. If a significant change in the fare is made, Yapta will notify you. You may be able to obtain refunds or credit if you have booked directly with the airline or hotel.

Carefully Read the Offer for Extra Fees

Airline pricing is becoming very competitive. As airline companies unbundle their services to offer lower prices for just the flight, many now charge for services that were previously included. This is good for the bargain-seeking traveler because it lets others pay for costly overweight baggage and other services you do not need.

Some fees must be paid such as departure and other taxes, change fees, and to redeem frequent flier miles. If you are aware of them, other fees can be minimized such as checked baggage and over-sided or over-weight baggage. Following the guidelines in Chapter 13 ("How to Pack Lighter and Still Be Prepared") will help you avoid excessive baggage fees. You should consider renting large baggage items such as surfboards, golf clubs, and skis at your destination. Other fees can be avoided by booking your flight and printing your boarding pass online, bringing your own snacks in your carry-on bag, and avoiding inflight movies, drinks, and other extra expenses.

It pays to read the fine print to better understand any hidden fees. Finding a low airfare is important but keep in mind a super low promotional fare may not be the best fare when all the taxes and fees are added on and many are non-refundable or have a fee for changes.

When you arrive at your destinations, use mass transit, if possible, instead of taxis.

Spending Less for Lodging

When you are traveling, lodging can be your largest expense. Resort and upscale hotels can be pricy and will diminish your travel budget quickly. At the 'better' hotels, mandatory taxes, resort fees, service fees, parking fees, Internet access fees, processing charges, energy fees, and other add-ons (i.e. minibar, porter, fitness center, early check-in, in-room safe) can add up to 20% extra to your bill. So it is important to consider ways to reduce costs on lodging.

You should keep in mind if you plan to be out and about enjoying the place you are visiting, you are not going to be spending a lot of your time in your room. You can spend more for lodging if you prefer, although all you really need is a clean comfortable bed, hot shower, and a reasonably quiet room located in a good area convenient to the places you want to explore.

Depending on the type of lodging, here are some questions to ask:

- Is the price 'per person' or total?
- Depending on your preference, is the room non-smoking, has twin or double beds, and does it have air conditioning?
- What, if any, are the additional fees (see list in the first paragraph above)? Note: when you book on the Internet, these charges may not be clear so it is often wise to call the hotel.
- Do they honor discounts (i.e. AAA, ARRP, corporate)?
- How many total rooms do they have?
- Are they near a noisy area such as a bar or busy street?
- What facilities (i.e. pool, laundry) do they have?
- Do you need to share a bathroom?

- What type of breakfast is served and is it included?
- Do they have Internet access or TV?
- Are there any common areas besides the dining room?
- If you have a car, is there parking?
- What is the cancellation policy?
- Is the rate negotiable?

Budget Lodging

Small mid-range family-run hotels, B&B's, guesthouses, pensions, and hostels can be less stylish than the more expensive places. We think they can be charming, full of character, located closer to the main attractions, travel budget stretching, and provide more opportunities to meet people. They are often run by interesting people who love to help you and located in historic locations a short walk to the action, restaurants, and attractions. You do need to do your homework so you do not get into a bad place. Getting advice is easy if you make use of **TripAdvisor (www.tripadvisor.com)** - more on that later.

Staying at budget lodging does not have to be a sacrifice. In fact, we have found when traveling we have more fun and better experiences in less expensive lodging than when we stayed in luxury hotels where it is harder to meet other people. Often budget lodging, especially hostels, have meeting areas more conducive to gathering with other travelers. We meet and talk to other fellow travelers and learn more about the place we are visiting as well as other places in the world. On many occasions we have shared a travel experience for a day or night after meeting and getting to know fellow travelers from all around the world. These experiences greatly enhance our enjoyment of traveling.

At first budget accommodations may take a bit of getting used to if you have been accustomed to higher end hotels and resorts. Although they are clean and functional, many times you will be staying in an older place without a fancy lobby in rooms with furniture that may not match and no maid service after the first night (do you really need new sheets every day?). Sometimes great bargains can be had even in the best part of town if you can give up features like an elevator or share a bathroom with other guests, although most will have ensuite bathrooms in your room with a shower and toilet. This may feel a little uncomfortable at first but it is not hard to get use to, especially when you consider you can stretch your travel budget to cover months of travel instead of weeks.

You can locate many nice budget accommodations, in addition to higher priced hotels, by using the travel websites and apps mentioned previously in this chapter in section "First Learn to Recognize a Good Price". Other popular hotel reservation websites are:

- *Hotels.com (www.hotels.com)*
- *Venere (www.venere.com)*
- *HotelsCombined (www.hotelscombined.com)* that searches over 30 hotel reservation sites
- *LateRooms (www.laterooms.com)* for last minute hotel bargains

When searching, use the pricing feature to sort for the range of pricing you want. Around the world, $30-100 usually can give you a private double room and will sometimes include some sort of breakfast in the morning. A higher price range will show the fancier accommodation options.

Reserving a nice place to stay in an area that is close to the things you want to do does enhance your experience so we spend some time to select the hotels, guesthouses, hostels, and home exchanges where we stay. First, we do our homework (see Chapter 6 - "How Planning Can Enhance Your Experience) and learn what areas in the city we are visiting we most want to stay in or near. Then we bring up the website's map of lodging for that city and start reviewing places with the highest ratings to stay in that area.

We normally opt for a double (or twin) private room with air conditioning in warm climates and an ensuite bathroom, although we have become comfortable with sharing a bathroom down the hall if we find a nice place in a good location with a good price. We like free or low fee Internet availability typically more available for no charge at less pricy places. Wi-Fi or Internet connection in the room is nice because we bring our computer laptop along. We look for free parking if we have a car and we request a quiet non-smoking room with a double bed, if available.

Staying in budget lodging does not mean you cannot use the facilities of a local resort. Many resorts have a day-use fee intended for cruise passengers or tour groups allowing you to use their facilities for the day.

This way you can have the experience of a more expensive resort and sleep for a fraction of the price.

Ideas for Negotiating Hotel Rates

The smaller lodging places sometimes can have options for bargaining for even better prices, especially in the off season. We contact several options in our next destination and get a range of pricing. Then we make an offer to our favorite place at the lowest price we received. We remind them we are booking direct and they will save booking agency charges. We also inform them we are on a budget traveling around the world and are willing to accept a less expensive room. You can sometimes get better deals if you stay longer (3 or more nights) and offer to pay in cash. Sometimes they will have a less renovated room, maybe up some stairs, they may make available to you or they may just agree to give you a standard room for the lower price knowing you are about to book with their competition. If they do agree, be thankful.

When inquiring about pricing, be sure to mention any discount group (i.e. AAA, AARP, corporate) you are involved with. If you show up without a reservation and they appear not to be busy, ask for the off-season or other discounted rate. They would rather fill their rooms than to see you leave. If all else fails, ask for a room upgrade for the same price. We have received many better rooms this way.

Before booking a reservation, we carefully read many recent user reviews as well as the description of services offered for free or for a fee to be sure of what we are getting. Be sure to inform your hotel of your arrival time so they do not give your room away. If you are staying just a night or two, don't unpack your suitcase. Just take out the items you will need for your short visit.

Before accepting any room, is wise to check it out first. If it is not to your liking, they may have a better room available or you may want to move on if you feel you can locate more suitable lodging.

Hostels Offer a Good Budget Alternative

Often with even better pricing, hostels offer a good alternative. Today hostels have a higher standard of comfort than a generation ago offering dorm, single, double, and family rooms. Some are located in prime areas. Although the average age of hostel regulars do tend to be in their twenties, people of all ages use hostels (like us!).

Although simple, many hostels are quite good and have community rooms, sometimes nicely furnished, to sit and meet fellow travelers. Many also include breakfast in the morning and have kitchens where you can prepare some of your own meals. Most owners/managers go out of their way to answer questions and make suggestions of the best places to visit and eat. Often, for an extra charge, they provide additional services such as excursions to local attractions and other fun things to do. They will even tell you of off-the-beaten-path places only locals know about.

After experiencing budget accommodations we do not consider them an inconvenience now. In fact, we often prefer staying at a nice hostel. One time when we were searching on the Internet for lodging for our next destination, we found an upper scale hotel on sale. I mentioned to my wife I was just about to book it but heard nothing back from her. I said it again and received the same nonresponse. When I asked her what she was thinking she told me, "I like staying at hostels so we can meet more people." The young people make us feel younger and we meet fellow travelers of all ages and share stories of travel around the world. Sometimes we pop some microwave popcorn to share and we are instant celebrities.

Two popular websites to locate and book hostels and budget hotels around the world are **Hostelworld (www.hostelworld.com)** and **Hostelbookers (www.hostelbookers.com)**. These websites do not charge a fee. They make their money by collecting about 10% of the booking up front from you when you make a reservation using your credit card and then you pay the remaining balance to the hostel when you arrive. Many places require payment in cash. Another very popular hostel website is **Hostelling International (www.hihostel.com)**.

This websites have listings for thousands of hostels as well as other budget accommodations worldwide and you can view photos, read descriptions, locate them on a local map, and read reviews from previous customers. Based on the user reviews, the hostels are given a rating to help you quickly sort out the better ones.

Hostelworld offers local tours and other travel services. Although they list many of the same hostels, we often check both Hostelworld and Hostelbookers because occasionally they will have some different listings, availability, or pricing. Other good websites are available for reserving hostels and budget accommodations that specialize in certain regions of the world.

Other Lodging Bargain Alternatives

There are many other ways to save on lodging. Consult your travel guidebooks and ask your fellow travelers for recommendations for lodging and good websites and apps to find accommodations. Some of the best lodging bargains we have stayed in came from suggestions from other travelers we met and owners/managers of the place where we were staying.

Staying at quaint inns and B&B's can be very enjoyable and some can be less costly. You may locate them at **BedandBreakfast.com (www. bedandbreakfast.com)**.

In many places in the world, for additional income people add an apartment or guesthouse adjacent to their home or offer their second or vacation home for rent. We have stayed in many of them and they can be very enjoyable. Using **AirBnB (www.airbnb.com)** you can locate owner-rented private studio apartments, second homes, and rooms in 181 countries often for less than the cost of a hotel. AirBnB is available as a smartphone app on the iPhone.

You may want to look into a relatively new trend of no cost or low cost rooms from people opening up their homes to travelers. **Crashpadder (www. crashpadder.com)** will help you locate these rooms in private homes.

For Longer Stays and Living Somewhere for a While

For longer stays, you can obtain savings by renting furnished homes, villas, and apartments, by the week or even monthly. This is especially economical if you have a larger group. You can learn more about home rentals at **HomeAway (www. homeaway.com)**, **Villas International (www. villaintl.com)**, and **VRBO (wwwvrbo.com)**.

Free or low cost long-term lodging can

Consider staying longer in beautiful places like Strasbourg in the Alsace wine region of France.

also be obtained though home exchange. We have done home exchanges (also known as house swap) and it worked out well for us. You stay in each other's home and work out other arrangements such as use of cars, pet care, etc. Be sure to spend time via e-mail or voice to get to know the person or family with whom you are exchanging. Also be sure you are familiar with the area the home is located, ask for references if they have them, and leave detailed instructions for the use of your home. To find more information about home exchanges, you can go to:

- *Intervac (www.intervac.com)*
- *HomeExchange (www.homeexchange.com)*
- *HomeLink International (www.homelink.org)*
- *Craigslist (www.craigslist.org)*

House sitting is also an option to obtain lodging in exchange for caring for the house, pets, plants, etc. Learn more by going to: *Housecarers (www. housecarers.com)* and *The Caretaker Gazette (www.caretaker.org)*.

For the more adventurous you might want to try homestays or couch surfing where you sleep in a spare bedroom or on people's couches, often at no cost. It is a great way to meet locals and find out what is going on in the area. A couple of websites specializing in this type of lodging are *Servas International (www.servas.org)* and *CouchSurfing (www.couchsurfing.com)*. Check out the profiles and users reviews before making your decision.

Check User Reviews to Assist Your Selection

We do not reserve any accommodation without referring to one of our favorite travel websites. *TripAdvisor (www.tripadvisor.com)* has a huge archive of user reviews and ratings of over a half million lodging properties and attractions. You can also get quotations on hotels rooms from several popular hotel-booking websites and apps. TripAdvisor is also available as an app for the Android, iPhone, iPad, and Windows Phone 7.

When searching for a place to stay, we put up two web browser windows. In one we are searching various travel websites for lodging and the other has TripAdvisor where we can get user reviews of the place. You should not be turned off of a place if it has a few poor reviews. Some people are just plain hard to please. You should also keep in mind the price you are paying. A good review for a budget hotel is like a great review for a more expensive hotel. Pay more attention to recent reviews (you can sort for them) because the service can change for the better or worse over time.

Using TripAdvisor is also helpful for us in planning what we will do. They offer a list of the top attractions. Many user reviews contain detailed information about where to eat and what activities are enjoyable. It is good karma to add your user reviews if you use TripAdvisor.

Save Money on Meals and Enjoy Local Experiences

We try to eat healthy to maintain our vitality, avoid disease, and control our weight (see Chapter 11 - "Staying Healthy"). At the same time we believe experiencing local cuisines is literally the 'spice of life' that greatly enhances our excitement for travel.

When we first started traveling, we only had two weeks of vacation so we splurged on many of the fancy restaurants in the area we were visiting. Now that we are out for months at a time, in addition to wanting to minimize our expenses, we have found the local family-run restaurants often offer an even better dining experience. The food can be very good and the atmosphere more unique to the area you are visiting.

For breakfast, we try to have some fruit, non-sugary cereal or oatmeal, coffee or tea, and maybe a local pastry and fruit we have purchased the day before. Often the hostel or hotel where we stay will have something offered for breakfast. While we are exploring areas of the place we are visiting we use our noses to locate potential places for lunch or dinner when we get hungry. We look for places that have many people, especially locals. This is usually a good indication of a good economical place. Walk a few blocks away from tourist areas (unless you can't resist the view) and you may find some less expensive but equally as good options.

Often we opt for dining recommendations

Having a traditional breakfast at our Ryokan in Nara, Japan.

from locals, fellow travelers, or people operating our hostel or hotel. We have had mixed results from using recommendations from travel guidebooks. After getting the recommendation, some of them let their quality and service go down because they have so many customers.

We have found many ways to reduce our meal costs and still have good dining experiences. When we choose a more expensive place we try to go for lunch because it is usually less expensive. Also, like they are accustomed to do in many parts of the world, we often make lunch our bigger meal and just have appetizers for dinner. Early bird and the daily fixed-priced specials are usually a good deal. Remember tipping is not expected in many countries. Grabbing a local dish from a clean street vendor and sitting somewhere nice to people watch can provide a cheap and interesting experience.

There are times when we just purchase some items at the store and prepare a meal in our hostel if kitchen facilities are available. There are usually interesting people around to spend the evening with.

Save Money While Seeing the World on Cruises

Cruising can be an enjoyable way to see the world and meet new interesting people. We have been on 26 cruises on 12 different cruise lines. Some were on large ships with 3,000 people and some have been on small boats with as few as 10 people. We have done the large-ship European, Indonesian, Japanese, Baltic Sea, Hawaiian, New England, and Panama Canal cruises as well as many Caribbean and Mexican cruises. We have also taken cruises to more remote places on smaller boats such as a gulet boat in the Turkish Turquoise Coast, felucca boat down the Nile River, Windjammer barefoot boats in the Caribbean, as well as other ships around the islands of Fiji, Tahiti, Greece, and the Great Barrier Reef.

What surprises many people is that cruising can be an economical way to travel. Especially during particular less popular weeks, many cruises can be a bargain when you consider they are all inclusive including lodging, transportation, great food (and more food), entertainment, shows, movies, lectures, shopping, activities, dancing, swimming, work out and other recreational facilities, and a relaxing enjoyable travel experience. Cruises can take you to many interesting places, you can do as little or as much as you like, and there is no need to move luggage around, wait in airports, or worry about finding accommodations and transportation. We usually stay a few extra nights before or after to enjoy the city the cruise departs from or ends at.

There are drawbacks to cruising. You only get a 'taste' of the places you visit for a short time. Usually you will not be able to visit the port of calls during the evening when many places are so charming. You also need to be careful not to run up a large bill on board. Normally, many things are an extra charge such as drinks, photographs, shore excursions, airport transfers, onboard shopping, gambling, pricy telephone and Internet access, laundry, tips for the crew, some special classes, and spa treatments. Single women should be always be cautious, even on cruises, to avoid unwanted sexual abuse. Choosing other passengers to do things with is a helpful preventative measure… and more fun.

We include cruises on our travel adventures for many reasons. First, we like to have some downtime to relax and plan our future travel. Also, we will take a cruise that goes to a unique area we are not sure we would be interested in spending a lot of time exploring. On one of our trips through Asia, we included a cruise out of Singapore to see some of Indonesia and Malaysia. Sometimes a cruise to a unique area will entice us to go back. Our passion for the Greek Islands was sparked by a cruise (on our honeymoon).

Cruises can also take you to visit places that may be hard to get to otherwise. Our Baltic Sea cruise took us to Stockholm, Sweden; Helsinki, Finland; Oslo, Norway; St. Petersburg, Russia; Tallinn, Estonia; Berlin, Germany; and Denmark. It would be difficult and expensive to visit all these wonderful places any other way.

Repositioning Cruises

Because we have more time on extended travel, we have taken three cruises for one-way transportation (and fun). We took a trans-Atlantic Ocean cruise from Ft. Lauderdale to Rome visiting several places in Portugal, Spain, Monaco, and Italy. We also traveled to Asia on a trans-Pacific Ocean cruise from Vancouver to Japan. Our days pass quickly. Normally the cruise includes some interesting ports of call and while at sea, they schedule entertainment, interesting lectures, and special activities in addition to all the regular cruise features. We exercise, read, and visit with interesting people. The great thing is the cost of these 2-week cruises on sale was about the cost of flight to our destination and there is no jet lag. We went back to Europe again on a repositioning cruise from Miami to Barcelona paying just $599 per person plus taxes for a 5-star 14-day cruise!

Cruise ships need to be repositioned twice a year. For example, when the cruising season is over in the Caribbean, the cruise ships will be moved to Europe. Because most people do not have enough time for this type of travel and want to visit more ports of call returning to the same port they left from, repositioning cruises are often a bargain. You can research repositioning cruises on the cruise websites mentioned later in this section.

Ways to Save on a Cruise

Normally we opt for an inside cabin in order to get the best bargain for a cruise. We are active and do not spend too much time in our cabin. Once we walk out of our cabin, we have all the same benefits of the cruise that others have who paid much more for a larger cabin or one with a window. If you do opt for a window (good for scenic cruises), ask if it is just a porthole and if it is blocked or opens to an open deck with people walking by.

Requesting 'open seating' for dinner allows us to have dinner with new interesting people we meet on board instead of having the same table of people every night for weeks. Larger tables allow you to met more people. We prefer late seating because it gives us a chance to relax before dinner after returning from a day of exploring the port of call. You should try the specialty restaurants. They are usually worth the extra charge.

We do a little research and save money by finding most of our excursions once we get on shore because the cruise companies greatly mark up their excursions. Many ports have a visitor's center near the cruise ship dock. Often you can find other passengers interested doing this and you can team up with them to share transportation costs and have company. You do need to be sure you get back to the ship on time and some places may be difficult to get to without a cruise line sponsored excursion.

Cruise bargain hunters are excited when they find a highly rated cruise for less than $100/day per person, sometimes much lower especially for repositioning cruises. This varies for cruises in different parts of the world and for unique itineraries where a higher cost per day may be a bargain. You can sometimes find better bargains by being flexible with your dates, opting for older ships, lower decks, and cruising at the beginning or end of the cruising season for that area. Waiting for last-minute sales can yield great deals. Of course, you risk having the cruise book out and missing it. If the cruise you are planning to take is crucial for your travel plans, do not wait too long.

When you reserve your cruise, ask for special perks such as on-board credits, free airport transfers, cabin upgrades, and other perks such as a bottle of wine. Ask questions about your cabin assignment. Is it located above, below, or next to noisy areas such as elevators, discos or shows, or equipment rooms? Does it face out to open areas? If you are concerned about motion sickness, lower mid-ship is better.

Don't worry about the formal dress nights. Many men wear a suit or sports jacket, tie, and pants and women can look great in a semi-formal dress. A simple classy black dress accessorized with a striking brooch or beaded shawl will make you look elegant. Women should bring an evening wrap because the ship can be chilly at night.

We have found some very good cruise bargains using two cruise websites called **VacationsToGo (www.vacationstogo.com)** and **Cruises-N-More (www.cruises-n-more.com).** When the cruise companies anticipate that specific cruises may be hard to sell (often due to less popular dates), they offer them through cruise discounter companies like the two mentioned. Last minute (90 days or less from departure) can yield very good deals. Using these websites, we also do our research on cruise itineraries, prices, ships, and port of calls.

Other cruise websites include **CruiseDeals (www.cruisedeals.com)** and **Cayole (www.cayole.com).** Good websites for user reviews of cruises, ships, cabins, port of calles, excursions, and many other cruise-related topics are **CruiseCritic (www.cruisecritic.com)** and **CruiseMates (www.cruisemates.com).**

Preventing Seasickness

Most people do not experience seasickness on the large cruise ships because of modern stabilizers. There are several remedies for those who suffer from motion sickness. A prescription option is a patch worn behind the ear. Over-the-counter medications such as Dramamine and Bonine work well for many people. They often cause drowsiness and should not be mixed with alcohol. A natural option is powdered ginger root. If you forget to bring something, the ship's doctor or purser will probably have remedy available. Many people who do suffer from motion sickness get their 'sea legs' after a few days.

Finding Bargains on Car Rentals

To save money, we try to use public transportation as much as possible. Unlike most U.S. cities and destinations the trains, subways, and buses are often very good in other parts of the world. Also, having a car in major cities is often more of a bother because of parking and travel issues. Keep in mind you can usually rent a car for a day or so to explore more out of the way areas when you are visiting a city.

Sometimes it is more convenient and you are able to better explore certain destinations with a car. We have had wonderful driving trips in Chile, New Zealand, Germany, France, Scotland, Spain, Tuscany, California, Florida, Hawaii, and the U.S. Pacific Northwest. When we do rent a car, we normally choose the smallest car possible. They are fine for us to get around with our luggage. We do like to have air conditioning during warmer seasons. Many cars around the world only have manual transmissions. If you require automatic, be sure to specify.

Check with your local auto club or sources for the country where you plan to drive to see if special international driving permits are required. You should call your auto insurance provider and credit card company to see what coverage, if any, you have when driving internationally. You must book the car rental with the credit card to be eligible for any coverage. Also, keep in mind they drive on the 'other side' of the road in the United Kingdom and many countries related to their commonwealth (i.e. Australia, New Zealand, India, Pakistan, Singapore, Malaysia, Hong Kong, South Africa). Other countries that drive on the left include Japan, Thailand, Indonesia, and U.S. Virgin Islands and other Caribbean islands.

If you are considering a RV driving trip around America, see Appendix D ("Recommended Reading") for a good book on how to do it.

Finding a Good Deal on Car Rentals

Use the travel websites mentioned above to research car rentals. In addition, **AutoEurope (www.autoeurope.com)** is also good to use. Remember to wait for online bounce back offers. We have received great car rental deals this way. You may want to use an online auction to find an even better deal once you are familiar with what might be a good price. Some people say **Hotwire (www.hotwire.com)** is the best online auction website for car rentals.

Car rental companies operating either at or next to the airport often pay fees to the airport resulting in higher rental rates. Checking rates at a city location away from the airport can yield good bargains. Also, you may want to go opposite from the way most people go. For example, in New Zealand we started in Christchurch and went north to Auckland. Most people travel north to south. We were able to negotiate a great deal because they needed to get cars back up north.

You may want to consider waiting until you arrive at your destination to book your car rental. This can be a bit of a risk although we have found great car rental deals with local companies.

Many car rental websites and companies do not include all the costs when quoting you a price. Costs to ask about are: unlimited miles, taxes, insurance, fuel, automatic transmission, one-way, drop-off, underage driver, and fees for extra driver and extra equipment such as luggage or ski racks and GPS systems.

Paying the extra fee for a GPS system can be a good investment to assist you in finding your way from place to place in an region unfamiliar to you. We use **Google Maps (www.maps.google.com)** to plan routes, also available as a smartphone app on the Android, BlackBerry, iPhone, and iPad.

Before leaving the rental agency, take photos of any damage the car may have. This may assist if you are blamed for any damage. You may receive a car that may be unfamiliar to you and it may not work properly. Before driving off, test the controls, headlights, brakes, radio, and extra tire and changing tools.

Public Transportation

You name it and we have used it – planes, helicopters, trains, cog trains, buses, motor coaches, RV's, cars, taxis, subways, cable cars, funiculars, monorails, trams, trucks, motorbikes, tuk-tuks, ships, boats, sailboats, speedboats, yachts, ferries, barges, houseboats, canoes, rafts, hovercraft, peticabs, and rickshaws. One of our more exciting adventures was being biked down the middle of busy traffic in Hanoi, Viet Nam, in a peticab.

Many modes of transportation – ATV'n on the Greek Island of Ios.

Somehow the traffic parted way and we lived through the experience.

Public transportation is a good way to see some of the country's most breathtaking scenery and meet other travelers. In many parts of the world it is much better than we experience in the U.S. Subways and buses run in the cities and trains and buses can take you to many places around the country. Stations are located inside many airports and conveniently in town centers. There are buses in South America that serve you meals and wine. You can plan many of your trips solely using public transportation because many people overseas rely on it.

Often there are different 'classes' offering different services. If you want more legroom and sometimes a seat, you may want to consider upgrading to a higher class. First class buses are usually worth the price although trains often have less difference between classes. Overnight transportation can save you lodging costs. You may want to upgrade for a bunk bed if you are planning to use a train.

Your travel guidebook will have websites where you can research train and bus schedules. When you arrive at a new destination, ask for assistance from your hotel. They are usually very helpful in understanding the schedules and routes. The visitor's information center is also an excellent resource. If you plan to use trains often in a period of time, a rail pass may be less expensive. You can go to **Amtrak (www.amtrak.com)** for information about the U.S. and **Rick Steves (www.ricksteves.com/rail)** for information about European rail passes. For information on rail passes all over the world, go to **International Rail (www.internationalrail.com)**.

When using public transportation, it is important to be patient. In some places they don't always run on schedule (unless in Japan where you can set your watch to them). It is often important to have exact change.

Be careful to ask questions to determine the correct station, platform, or stop to get on or off. Many cities have multiple train and bus stations. Have the booking agent carefully write it out for you. Ask a fellow passenger when you get on to be sure you are on the correct train or other means of transportation. Keep your valuables with you in your carry-on bag when checking your luggage. Travel light - getting off and on public transportation with heavy suitcases can be a burden.

Bargaining

Bargaining is a way of life in many places of the world. When haggling for the best price, the golden rule is to keep a smile on your face. Don't get upset or let them intimidate you, take your time, keep the discussion light and friendly, and think of it as a game. They do. Never show a high

Pat practicing her bargaining skills with women of the hillside tribes in northern Thailand.

level of interest like holding the item up and saying, "Look at this" to your partner.

In order to get the best price you need to know what a good price is. This can be learned from fellow travelers, hotel owners, and tour guides. Since several vendors typically sell the same tourist items, you can shop around before purchasing. Often the vendor will ask how much you will pay for it. This is where your research pays off. Start by offering a price 30-50% below the market price and work up to just below the market price. You can be more convincing if you say you spoke to some locals and they told you not to pay more than the price you have offered.

Also tell them you are traveling on a budget and cannot offer more. Don't be swayed if the vendor tells you they are losing money. No vendor will sell you something at a loss. Be prepared to walk away. Often the simple action of walking away will get the vendor to reduce the price.

Sometimes it is important to keep in mind the price of the item and the exchange rate. It is probably overdoing it trying to get the last 50 cents out of a vendor who has a family to take care of.

Especially during off peak times, we also negotiate pricing for rooms and sometime other travel needs. This can often be done through e-mail. We politely tell them we are on a budget and ask what they can do for us or would they match a competitor's price. Sometimes they do. Sometimes a less popular room in the back or up some stairs will be offered at a big discount allowing us to stay in a better area while staying within our budget.

Local Deals and Other Tips to Save

Frequently the best source of information is found locally when you arrive at your destination. Ask people you meet and your hotel management. Check out tourist information offices to find unbiased information on the accommodation, excursions, and activities that work best for you. You can find them on the **Tourist Office Worldwide Directory (www.towd.com)**. It is harder to get recommendations because they are not supposed to play favorites. Be careful in countries where you feel the information might be biased. Look for promotions in coupon booklets and local media. Sometimes you will find discount coupons that will save you money.

Save money by taking home more good photos and movies of your travel adventure instead of souvenirs that weigh you down while traveling and clutter your life when your return home. See Chapter 16 ("Take Travel Photos Like a Pro") for tips on taking more interesting photos.

When deciding on different destinations around the world consider the exchange value of their currency. If the dollar is particularly strong in one country at this time, you may want to travel to other places when their currency exchange is better.

Finally, take advantage of contacts you may have at your destination, even if you do not know them well. Friends and family are usually glad to show off their city to visitors even inviting you to stay with them. To thank them, we always bring a gift such as a couple of nice bottles of wine and pick up the dinner tab.

In the next chapter, we discuss ways you can get more enjoyment from your travel adventures by being a good traveler. Also, how do you travel together with a partner sharing close quarters and a lot of time together and have the experience make your relationship even better? Turn the page to find out how.

Chapter 8

Being a Friendly Traveler and Good Travel Partner

In this chapter...

Don't Sweat the Small Stuff!

Being a Friendly Traveler Will Make Your Experience Better

How to Be a Good Travel Partner and Bring You Closer Together

How to Ease Your Partner into Loving to Travel with You

This may be the most important chapter of this book for the enjoyment of your travel experience and your life. When we become a friendly traveler and good travel partner other people become friendlier to us and our enjoyment of life and travel is greatly enhanced. Whole new experiences will open up for you.

Don't Sweat the Small Stuff!

"The way I see it, if you want the rainbow, you gotta put up with the rain."

~ Dolly Parton

Travel is fun but let's get it right out there. You are going to get lost, lose something, miss a travel connection, or get into a situation you may not like. Something will go wrong somewhere. It happens. Getting upset and angry at people usually does nothing to help solve the problem. It only makes your experience worse. If you remain upset, then they are controlling you. Lighten up, don't take life so seriously, and even laugh about things if you can.

Remember not all is bad. You are on a wonderful adventure visiting an amazing place. How does that compare to having to wait a few extra hours or having to change some plans. The best way to handle the unexpected is to make the best of it and continue to enjoy your travel day. Learn to relax your preferences and go with the flow. Evaluating the situation and coming up with the best alternative is better than making yourself crazy and upset. People around the world generally like travelers and will help you if you smile and act politely.

Sometimes problems have a silver lining. Working them out is a great way to meet people and have some experiences you did not expect. Our alternative plan has often turned out to be better than our original plan.

Being a Friendly Traveler Will Make Your Experience Better

"The world is like a mirror: frown and it frowns at you; smile, and it smiles too."

~ Herbert Samuel

Respect

Interacting with others will be a part of your travel adventure. Being kind and polite is a part of everyday life in every culture. One of the many joys of travel is to learn more about the different people living on this planet.

Make an effort to chat with local people. Start with a big smile, making eye contact, and saying "hello." Say or indicate something nice about them or their things (i.e. pet, meal, store, house, anything) or ask for their advice. It's a great way to get a conversation started. Be interested in them and ask questions. It is amazing what you will learn and how helpful to you they will become.

Good travelers have a sense of humility and do not treat anyone as inferior. Don't stare at locals behaving in a manner different from which you are accustomed to or treat them like sightseeing objects.

In Scotland, we visited a small pub and bought everyone a round of drinks (only about 5 people were there costing us about $15). That was the best 15 travel dollars we have spent. They bought our second and third rounds, arranged a private tour of the town church, and picked us up from our hotel for an excursion to visit the local professor who collected historical items. We also were able to get to know some locals very well – try three strong Scottish ales sometime.

Don't forget to stop and help others along the way. You can make new friends this way and possibly learn things making your travel experience even better. Little acts of kindness will bring joy for you and others. On a bus in Chile, a woman shared her loaf of fresh baked bread with us after we helped by putting her bag in the overhead. The bread was still warm!

When resolving disputes try to smile, offer a compliment, and ask politely. Saying 'please' will usually get you much further than any loud demands. Also, 'saving face' is very important in many cultures so it is important not to make others wrong when attempting to resolve a dispute or even asking for directions.

We have all witnessed tourists along our travels being loud and disrespectful demanding things done their way or behaving in an embarrassing matter. By being polite and respectful, good travelers are good ambassadors of their country.

Have an Open Mind

Travel is an adventure and a chance to enjoy yourself and learn more about yourself and other cultures. To get the full enjoyment of your experience you should embrace new ways of doing things, enjoy new foods, and appreciate people and beliefs different from what you already know. Try to understand and not judge the correctness compared to your beliefs. In doing so, you will learn more about yourself and adopt new attitudes that will enrich the rest of your life.

Look forward to changing your plans if something interesting comes along. We have been invited into people's homes for dinner, teamed up with people we have met taking unexpected excursions, and taken other people's suggestions - all creating an even better adventure than the one we had planned. Remember, this is a travel adventure.

Learn About Local Customs

"Travelers never think that they are the foreigners."
                                                      ~ Mason Cooley

Your enjoyment of traveling will be greatly enhanced by being respectful of the local customs and etiquette of the countries you are visiting. Some practices we find acceptable such as pointing with your finger or blowing your nose in public can be offensive in other cultures. Remember when President George Bush went to Australia? He gave the thumbs up gesture but in Australia it is their way of being flipped off.

You can increase your awareness with a little bit of reading. A very good place to start is **Wikitravel (www.wikitravel.org)** that contains a huge amount of information about countries all over the world. Good travel guidebooks will also have a section on local customs and etiquette.

Learn to Communicate with Locals

"If you speak two languages, you're bilingual. If you speak one language, you're American."
                                                      ~ often heard quote

English is commonly spoken throughout the world, especially in the travel industry. You will often find locals who speak English in your hotel, restaurants, tourist areas, information places, and in the markets. Because English is their second language, speaking slowly, simply, and clearly is important. Speaking louder or with an accent will not help people understand you. Compliment them on their English and they will be more likely to help you.

People are friendly all over the world – school girls in Indonesia.

In many parts of the world, young children may come up to you and practice their English. In Japan and China, we had fun interacting with the children and answering their questions. With adults we ask questions about their country. Most people are grateful for your interest and you can have a great experience and learn much at the same time.

Sometimes you will not have people around who speak English. Knowing just a few common phrases will go far. Even if you do not pronounce it well, you show respect to the people living there and they will be much more likely to help you. People around the world will appreciate you much more if you attempt to communicate with them in their language. You will have a much better time with the people you meet. Good travel guidebooks will have a section on the local language. Here is basic list of phrases you may want to learn if you're traveling to a foreign land with a different language:

- Greetings (good morning/afternoon/evening)
- Common courtesies (yes, no, please, thank you, excuse me, sorry)
- How much does it cost?
- I would like…
- May I have the bill?
- Please don't bother me/I don't need help
- Where is _____? (learn the word for bathroom)
- Do you speak English?
- How do you say _____? if you want to learn more.

Communications with someone when you cannot speak each other's language can still be done. You can get pretty far by being friendly and using gestures. We have usually done well by pointing to things with a big smile. Your travel guidebook and other travel literature contain pictures you can point at. Travelers make use of smartphone apps that do language translations such as Google Translate available on the Android, iPhone, and iPad. It is also possible to show photos you have taken of objects and landmarks on your digital camera. With a little patience and courtesy, chances are you will get your point across.

Hotel Etiquette

We sometimes forget we are surrounded by many other people while in our hotel room. A good traveler will try to keep the noise to a minimum. When you watch TV or listen to music, turn the volume so your neighbor will not hear it. Also, ease the door shut when you come in and out. Keep in mind water and energy are precious in most parts of the world. Try not to overuse water and turn off the lights when you leave.

A good traveler is courteous to the people who work in the hotel. When you do so, they will often go out of their way to help you and make your visit at their hotel or city much more enjoyable. Be nice to the check-in staff and if you do have a maid or a doorman who give you good service, offer a tip. Also be nice to restaurant staff. They will be grateful and often stop and talk with you. You can learn much about what is going on and what is fun to do from locals you meet.

Other Helpful Tips

Carry a bunch coins and some denomination bill. They make good quick tips and will create new helpful friends along the way. Having a few coins in the local currency comes in very handy when you are faced with pay toilets.

How to Be a Good Travel Partner and Bring You Closer Together

> *"I have found out that there ain't no surer way to find out whether you like people or hate them than to travel with them."*
> ~ Mark Twain

One of the reasons we were inspirited to write this book was because we met so many people along our travels considering extended travel to further enjoy their dreams. Because of our extensive travel experience we were able to answer long lists of questions. One question made us think. A British man we met in Crete asked "How do you get along with each other on a long trip?"

Many people travel solo and meet up with people along the way who become good friends. Others prefer a travel partner like a lifetime partner, good friend, or family member. A good travel partner can provide motivation, support, and be someone to share the ups and downs (hopefully many more ups than downs).

How do you travel together with a partner sharing close quarters and a lot of time together and have the experience make your relationship even better?

Gratitude

> *"Good company in a journey makes the way seem shorter."*
> ~ Izaak Walton

First, start with tremendous gratitude that you have a partner that shares similar feelings. Don't take it for granted because not everyone has a partner who would like to share a travel adventure with him or her.

A growing body of research suggests an attitude of gratitude can improve your psychological, emotional, and physical well being. Gratitude forces us to overcome our tendencies to dwell on problems and annoyances. Gratitude is good for your health and can boost feelings of happiness and romance in your partner.

Showing your partner gratitude every day will greatly enhance your relationship. Take notice and thank them for the things they do – even the small things. A warm word of appreciation can provide a positive stimulus for your relationship for the rest of the day. Also, acknowledge them publicly.

You can show you are grateful by doing something nice. Without expecting anything in return, do something nice for your partner. Get them a drink or make a cup of coffee for them. Offer to fix something or go with them to get something they need. Be attentive and regularly think of what your partner likes, wants, or needs, and try to do something (even something small) to help or be kind to them.

You can also show your partner gratitude by supporting and encouraging them to achieve their long term goals and dreams. Pay attention to what they are doing and telling you and give genuine positive encouragement and compliments. Help them in achieving their desires in any way you can, even if it is just positive feedback.

Look at Your Own Navel First

"Your net worth to the world is usually determined by what remains after your bad habits are subtracted from your good ones."
~ Benjamin Franklin

At times we believe the issues in our lives are caused by the behavior and actions of others. Sometimes it is true. At other times, especially when 'everything' is going wrong in our lives, it is often our behavior and actions that are pushing others away from us. To evaluate any situation it is best to 'look at your own navel first.' That is, think about what you are doing that may be causing your life to not go the way you would like it to go.

If you are experiencing problems with your partner and having

issues attracting the kind of people you want to have around you, then
you should start with an honest self-analysis of your personal behaviors,
hygiene, reactions, and importantly what you say. Be truthful with yourself
when reading the following questions. It only takes couple of these negative
behaviors to turn people off.

- Do you have personal habits that may be unpleasant to others?
- Are you upbeat every day or do you have moods that may be
  hard to be around?
- Do you have pleasant conversations with nice things to say
  or are you argumentative, withdrawn, or constantly play with
  electronic gadgets?
- Are you curious to learn more, listen, and react courteously to
  what others have to say or are you opinionated, interruptive, and
  always have to be right?
- Do you get excited about what others are doing, ask questions,
  and learn from them or do you feel the need to impress others
  about you?
- Do you see the positive in people and activities or do you
  complain or find and point out faults?
- Are you friendly, supportive, and show gratitude or are you
  judgmental, critical, and look to blame others?
- Are you flexible and willing to try new things others may want
  to do or do you insist on controlling and doing what you want
  to do?
- Do you show compassion and want to make others around you
  happy or is it about you?
- Are you excited about life and regularly suggest fun activities to
  do others around you would like to do?
- Do you often give compliments and make others feel good
  about themselves?
- Are you enthusiastic and laugh regularly? Are you fun?

There is a basic law of attraction among people. You attract what you
put out. If you want lovely, active, interesting, positive, supportive, and fun
people in your life, then you need to be lovely, active, interesting, positive,
supportive, and fun.

If you are unhappy and having troubles with others, you may need to ask yourself if you want to continue doing what you are doing or should you work on some changes in yourself so you can have a loving supportive partner and have people want to be around you.

Communication and Working Together

Knowing often gets in the way of learning. Good communications is essential in all relationships. It becomes even more important when spending more time with each other. Become familiar with the needs of your partner by listening carefully to them. Encouraged them to express their feelings by kindly acknowledging and responding to them. Also, respectfully communicate your needs to your partner. Don't make them guess what you are thinking.

Some people get grumpy when they do not eat regularly. Some people need more sleep or need a break for rest. Some want to see sights. Others want to time to shop. Some people have ADT (Another Darn Temple) syndrome while others can't get enough of history and major sites. Try to laugh and have fun working through your concerns. Remember, this is an adventure and you are supposed to have fun.

In happy relationships partners do not try to manipulate each other. When planning your trips and the activities of each day, be considerate of your partner's needs and wishes and work closely together finding the right compromise that satisfies both of your needs. It is rare during weeks of travel both you and your partner will always want to do the same things at the same time. We learned a good way to deal with this. Give in on things very important to the other even though you may not consider it very fun or interesting. Nobody wants to travel to a place and miss out on something they looked forward to doing.

Of course, this goes both ways. One day you may visit that famous temple during the day to satisfy the history buff and in the evening have a romantic dinner. One week you may sail on a cruise ship while the next week you explore Roman ruins. A wonderful way to satisfy many travel dreams is to include a few days at a resort at the beach, river, or mountains after visiting several amazing but hectic cities.

Make sure your relationship satisfies the needs of both partners. Don't try to impose your wishes or beliefs of the best way of doing something on them. A controlling or know-it-all type of person can make a relationship difficult, especially when traveling. Dissatisfaction results when one person makes all the decisions without taking into consideration of what their partner may want to do. The other partner feels unimportant and does not get to do the things they want to do. They will be less likely to want to travel with you.

As best as possible, try to avoid being critical, accessing blame, and making your travel partner feel guilty. If something goes wrong, instead of expressing criticism and finding blame that may hurt your partner's feelings and your relationship, think of all the things your partner has done well. Hey, they are with you! Focusing on blame causes resentment and will make your partner want to do less so they will not risk making a mistake. Studies show using negative and derogatory words can negatively affect your mood. Stay positive and learn from any mistakes. Move forward in a constructive manner. Your relationship and your health will become stronger.

Be Positive and Appreciative

"Most folks are about as happy as they make up their minds to be."
~ Abraham Lincoln

Always be as positive as you can. Be appreciative of the opportunity to have a travel adventure. As you travel to new places you may never see again, remember to fully enjoy it now. Wake up and greet the day with joy and gratitude. It's time to have fun. Be thankful you are alive and have the wonderful opportunity of this travel adventure!

Fill your head with positive thoughts, express thanks and encouragement aloud, and look for something for which to be grateful. Avoid negative talk and criticism and try to see the best in every situation. An optimistic and upbeat attitude will attract the same type of people to you greatly enhancing your enjoyment of your trip and your life. It will also enhance your partner's experience and they will enjoy spending even more time with you.

Be Flexible

Active travel can wear you out and create tension in your relationship. When you plan a longer trip, you have time to leave flexibility in your schedule for relaxation. There will come times when you are more energetic and want to have a more adventurous time filled with activities and other times you will want to relax and let the day evolve.

A good way to handle this is to plan more days in any particular place leaving you time to be busy and time to relax. Make a list of the things you want to do during your stay at a particular place. Have it ready each day so you can plan the day you both want to have. Don't try to do it all in one day. Based on how you feel on a given day, you can go down the list and decide what is best for the both of you.

One day you may want to walk miles exploring the town visiting famous sites. The next day you may want to slow down and have a long leisurely lunch on the water. Any particular activity usually does not have to be done on any given day (unless certain events are happening or are closed on some days of the week). This lets you better fulfill both you and your partner's wishes on a day-to-day basis.

Pull Your Own Weight

Traveling takes planning as well as effort moving luggage around. A good travel partner does not let the other do all the work. You should 'divide and conquer' the tasks based on what each other most likes to do. One partner might prefer researching particular matters like booking the right hotel, cruise, or daily event while the other does a lot of reading to lay out the overall itinerary of travel over several weeks and what activities to do once you are there.

On day-to-day events, one might take care of clothing while the other updates your travel blog or Facebook posts. One partner may plan meals while the other researches daily activities. Don't expect your partner to do the heavy lifting of the luggage all the time. If you cannot handle your own luggage, take less.

How to Ease Your Partner into Loving to Travel with You

Travel can be stressful especially if you are having some relationship issues. First carefully read this chapter especially the previous section "How to Be a Good Travel Partner and Bring You Closer Together". Stop and think about the ideas presented. By incorporating them in your behavior your partner will want to spend even more time with you and you will derive much more pleasure from your travel experiences and your life.

Learn Your Partner's Core Desires

Your travel partner may have other reasons to be reluctant about traveling. They may have fears, have already traveled a considerable amount for work, or may not share your visions of a wonderful travel experience. Start with finding a core desire your partner would like to try. This could be something they longed to see or have a great interest in. Maybe it is romantic, relaxing, food or sports related, historic, active, adventurous, visiting relatives or a particular place, or other. Now you have something, a small spark, to work with. Just like a spark in a fire, if you fan it too hard at first it may go out. To have your partner's spark grow into a flame start your travels slowly.

Start Out Slowly

Before you go out on long trips on your own and travel to off-the-beaten path places, start your travel adventures together slowly. You should first learn to have fun together and work out mutually beneficial travel plans. Communicate well and learn what each other enjoys doing and what special needs they may have. Take some time to build your experience of the requirements of travel (hopefully this book will give you a jump start).

First, go for a long weekend and then out on a week trip together. Take longer but easier trips to more popular destinations using organized tours and cruises breaking off the tour to have a short travel or living away experience on your own before returning home. Before going completely independent, you may want to consider trips offering independent travel that organize the flights and hotels. Then go out on your own for longer periods of time planning things both of you enjoy. Leave the more adventurous destinations for later in your travels.

You will be glad you did because you will have much more fun together when you know more about each other's travel needs and wishes as well as what it takes to enjoy travel when you are on the road for a longer time.

Schedule Downtime

Once you do plan a longer trip be sure to schedule some downtime. Traveling too fast and trying to see too much is one of the top traveler mistakes. Traveling to new places with different schedules, things to do and see, customs, foods, noises, and transportation and sleeping arrangements can wear you out. Schedule periodic downtimes like a snorkeling beach resort, villa in the mountains, cruise, or longer stays in a wonderful place. You may want to start your trip this way for a few days to recover from jet lag and acclimate to the new culture.

The length and regularity of your scheduled downtimes depends on your fortitude and enjoyment of relaxation. You can recharge your batteries and enjoy the place even more, have time to research the rest of your trip, or just relax and read a book. We have had some wonderful experiences during our 'downtimes' because we have been less hurried and were able to take in the experience as it comes to us. After our downtimes we are much more excited and energetic to enjoy travel with a more full schedule of activities and touring.

Downtime can become such an enjoyable part of your trip it is sometimes hard to move on. When we did our Greek Island hopping adventure, we started on the beautiful island of Santorini. We planned to stay for three days. We loved Santorini so much that after 7 days I told my wife my wife this was our Greek Island 'hopping' trip and we should move on to experience other islands.

Give Each Other Some Space

Spending all your time together for weeks can at times be overwhelming. Occasionally split up and go your separate ways for a few hours or a whole day. One might want to be active and explore while the other needs a rest and wants to read a book. One partner may want to go shopping while the other explores another museum or has a drink with friends. Meet up later at lunch or dinner. You will find your conversations lively as you share your adventures with each other.

For You Lovers

"Love implies generosity, care, not to hurt another, not to make them feel guilty, to be generous, courteous, and behave in such a manner that your words and thoughts are born out of compassion."
~ Krishnamurti

You are especially fortunate when your travel partner is also your lover. Cherish this opportunity. It will forever change your life. A travel adventure is a time to be playful, unburdened with the pressure and stress of jobs, raising children, maintenance of house and possessions, and all the responsibilities of the real world.

Sexy tango dancers on the streets of Buenos Aires, Argentina.

Extended travel is wonderful for lovers because you can stay longer at each place giving time for you to include leisurely romantic days and nights where your love can flourish under joyful circumstances. Take time to be intimate and fall in love with each other all over again in exciting and beautiful places in this wonderful world.

Conclusion

No one has all the secrets to establishing good human relationships. This chapter provides some guidelines to assist you. Always remember when you give you receive more in return and you can learn much from everyone around you. Look for ways to enjoy and help others while you travel and your travel adventures will be more enjoyable and meaningful.

When in doubt about how to be a friendly traveler and good travel partner, here are some enlightened words on the subject:

> *"Everyday, think as you wake up, 'Today I am fortunate to have woken up, I am alive, I have a precious human life, I am not going to waste it. I am going to use all my energies to develop myself, to expand my heart out to others, to achieve enlightenment for the benefit of all beings, I am going to have kind thoughts towards others, I am not going to get angry or think badly about others, I am going to benefit others as much as I can.' "*
> ~ Dalai Lama

When you are on the road for an extended period of time, how do you pay your bills and manage your accounts? The next chapter will help you better understand how to do this.

 *Chapter 9*

Paying Your Bills While You Are Away

In this chapter...

Paying Your Bills Automatically While Traveling

Eliminate Junk Mail

Modern Internet technology has made managing your finances much easier while you are away from home. This chapter explains how you can pay your bills, make deposits, review your credit card and checking accounts statements, and manage your investments through the Internet.

Paying Your Bills Automatically While Traveling
Auto-pay

Instead of writing checks each month to pay your bills, automate your bill paying by paying your bills using your credit card and making use of your credit card and bank checking account autopay feature to allow you to set up automatic payments for your bills. You will still receive a full statement (online and/or mailed to you) each month detailing all your charges.

First, we charge to our credit card as many of our bills as we can in order to receive airline frequent flyer points – nice to have when you are traveling the world. Examples of these bills are our cell phone, health insurance, and other utilities. You can call each company's customer support and they will tell you how to do it – usually a form needs to be completed and mailed back or done online.

We then authorize our credit card company for autopay transferring funds from our checking account each month to pay our credit card bill. For bills not payable by credit card, we use our checking account autopay to pay them.

There are two ways to do bank autopay. One is where you set a certain amount of funds to be transferred when a fixed bill is due such as your mortgage. This type of autopay can be set up with your bank to have your checking account pay on a certain day of the month or one-time transfers.

The other type of autopay is when the bill varies each month like your credit card charges. This type of autopay needs to be arranged with the company the charge is coming from to authorize them to automatically transfer funds from your checking account for the payment.

Most major companies and banks encourage autopay for no charge because it significantly reduces their costs of paperwork and handling checks. It also helps them by insuring they get paid on time. You will need to contact each company in order to do this. This usually can be done with a simple phone call to the customer support number to learn the way to do it. If your current bank does not offer autopay and online banking, you may want to find one that does.

Auto-deposit

Sign up for auto-deposit of all your incoming funds such as rental income, pensions, Social Security, and distributions from investments. This can be done by calling the organization, giving them your checking account information, and following their procedures.

Odd Bills

We used autopay for several years without any problem for our monthly bills. Unfortunately, we had one bill (our property tax) that gets paid once a year that we forgot about and had to pay several hundred dollars of extra late fees. Before leaving on a trip, review your checking account payments for the past year to see if you have any odd bills that need to be dealt with while you are gone. You may have to pay it early or have a reliable friend or relative mail it in for you on a certain day. It can also be auto-paid with future dates or you can add someone to your checking account to pay these bills for you.

On-line Accounts

We have set up online accounts with passwords with our bank, credit card companies, and other companies we need to review statements so we can check our statements online while we are traveling in case we suspect a problem. This also allows us to periodically check our checking account and credit card and cell phone statements for unauthorized charges.

Make sure you have plenty of funds in your checking account to cover your anticipated monthly bills. We have all our banking accounts online so we can check the level of our checking account and transfer funds from higher interest paying money market accounts when needed in order to maximize our interest income from our accounts.

Getting Started

You should start setting up and using your new online bill paying several months before you leave in order to work out any issues while you can still benefit from toll-free customer service. You can start setting up these accounts slowly over a few months as your bills come in. It was not difficult for us to set up these online accounts and we have had excellent service when we called the customer support numbers.

Eliminate Junk Mail

We reduced our mail from about 10 pieces a day to just 1 or 2 per day (with just 1 or 2 pieces of unwanted mail per week). This is pretty much just the items we want.

Junk mail fills our mailboxes and after a trip it takes a time to sort through. You can help save some trees and yourself some time by registering with ***DirectMail.com's National Do Not Mail List***. Because direct mail is expensive to send out, many direct mail marketers check this list and will remove people from their mail lists who do not want to receive unsolicited mail. Removal from lists takes many weeks. We noticed a significant reduction in our junk mail after a couple of months after registering.

Go paperless. You can request statements from your bank, credit card, cell phone, investments, etc. not be mailed to you. This is called 'paperless' and if you have an online account with the company you can view your statements online. Many companies will send a notification to you by e-mail when a new statement is available.

Another method we used to significantly reduce our mail from many vendors was to send them a note asking them to remove our address from their mailing list. We tear off the label of our name and address and write on it "Please remove from Data Base" and mail it to their address listed on the mailing.

By doing this over time we stopped receiving most of our unwanted mail.

We can be much safer while traveling when we follow the tips laid out in the next chapter.

Chapter 10

Security - Staying Safe on the Road

In this chapter...

Travel Insurance

Avoid Becoming a Target

Keeping Your Money and Important Items Safe

The majority of the people of the world are generally friendly, honest, and will regard you with hospitality and respect. There is no need to be overly paranoid about safety so not to enjoy your travel adventure. Unfortunately, there are a few people who attempt to prey on the unaware traveler. This chapter gives you some tips to provide extra safeguards for yourself and your money and important items. These tips will help you use common sense and keep your wits about you instead of being lulled into a false sense of security.

Travel Insurance

Travel insurance is insurance covering different parts of your trip. This could be the cost of your trip if you are required to cancel it, your health care while you are traveling, your luggage, or some other aspect of your trip. You do not have to search very hard to find stories of people needing to cancel trips that have been paid for and who were stuck with bills of $40,000, even $100,000, for emergency medical evacuations.

You may be wondering whether you should purchase travel insurance. This decision is difficult because there is always the likelihood you will not need the policy. When you are traveling overseas, cancellation or interruption insurance should be considered. When traveling out of the country, your personal medical insurance may not cover you so a travel insurance policy will ensure you have medical care if you need it. You also put your personal belongings at higher risk of loss or theft. Cruises and overseas flights can be unexpectedly canceled.

Travel Insurance Options

There are a variety of options to consider when purchasing a travel insurance plan. Trip cancellation and interruption is one of the most common types of coverage. This will cover the cost of your trip if it is unexpectedly canceled or interrupted. Another type of coverage is medical expense and transportation that covers the cost of medical care or an evacuation (medevac) when you are traveling out of the country. Because travel medical care insurance is commonly reasonably priced for a year, it is often a good value for those who take extended trips. Lost or stolen baggage is another option.

Although many situations overseas may not be covered by your existing insurance policies and credit card coverage, it is still wise to check your coverage before purchasing travel insurance. Your health and car insurance policies may have some coverage for expenses. If you purchase your trip by your credit card, canceled tickets and lost luggage may be covered although situations such as bankruptcy will probably not be covered.

If you decide you need travel insurance, have your travel agent purchase an insurance plan for you or shop online. You will also find a wide selection of insurance companies on the Internet where you can get a policy quickly such as **Travel Guard (www.travelguard.com)** and **USI Affinity Travel Insurance Services (www.travelinsure.com)**. **InsureMyTrip (www.insuremytrip. com)** and **TravelInsuranceCenter (www.worldtravelcenter.com)** will show you comparisons of the fees of various travel insurance companies. Make sure your travel insurance provider offers 24-hour hotline customer service. Do not purchase trip cancellation insurance from the same tour operator that may be responsible for the cancellation. For example, the trip insurance you purchase from a cruise company may also become invalid if the cruise company is bankrupted.

If you do bring your expensive items be sure they are covered by appropriate insurance. You may need to purchase supplemental insurance because most homeowners' policies will not cover jewelry, computers, and cameras if they are lost or stolen while traveling.

Make sure you understand what is actually covered before purchasing a travel insurance policy. For instance, a medical travel insurance policy may not cover the cost of injuries while skiing or scuba diving. The types of cancellations or interruptions covered vary greatly in different trip cancellation policies. Be sure to read and understand all exclusions and exemptions and make sure your trip expectations are covered before you purchase a policy.

Avoid Becoming a Target

The likelihood is low you will be a target of a crime. You do not need to be paranoid but it is wise to be smart and alert. To reduce the chances even more here are 14 tips to help you avoid becoming a prime target of a thief, pickpocket, purse snatcher, or a taxi or travel scam:

1) *Be deliberate, confident, and walk with purpose.* Looking confused, reading maps, or acting like a tourist may bring unwanted attention to you.

2) *Use your common sense.* Do not enter questionable streets or buildings especially at night. Staying in well lighted areas where other people are is usually a better option even if you have to walk a little further. Ask your hotel manager or other locals you meet to mark dangerous areas on your map.

3) *Get into the habit of checking over your shoulder to see if you are being followed.* Walk closer to the street to avoid hiding places in doorways. Cross the street if you do see a questionable person. Jump into a taxi if you feel uncomfortable about the area. They can take you back to your hotel or to a local landmark with which you are familiar.

4) *Pickpockets and purse snatchers often use distraction in order to catch you off guard.* Be extra cautious if someone drops something in front of you, touches you, or comes near you in a crowd with something like a jacket over their arm. Be particularly aware when using public transportation, in crowded areas, or when you are distracted watching something. Use a money belt under your clothing instead of a purse or wallet in your pocket or bag. Items hung over the back of chairs, placed on the floor, or left

unattended (e.g. at the beach) are particularly vulnerable. When eating at sidewalk cafes, keep your bag under the table with the strap around your leg.

5) **Do not flash cash around.** Go to a discrete place and take the amount you need out of your money belt without letting people see. Use extra caution when using ATM cash machines.

6) **Leave your expensive jewelry, watches, cameras, etc. at home.** If you do bring them, use the hotel safe. A pricey mobile phone or camera can be a target for thieves.

7) **Carrying multiple suitcases indicates a novice traveler who is more of a target.** Pack lighter in one travel suitcase as suggested in Chapter 13 ("How to Pack Lighter and Still Be Prepared").

8) **Carry a business card or postcard of your hotel.** Alternatively, write down the name, address, and phone number to hand to taxi drivers. Remember to do this for your first hotel when you arrive. This is very useful in countries that English is not commonly spoken.

9) **Emergency-dial numbers may be different from 911.** Learn the number for the area you are visiting.

10) **Be aware of travel scams.** Always stay alert and use common sense. Stay clear of any get-rich scheme. Be alert to any distraction that diverts you, even someone who offers help. This is the mode of operation of most thieves. Men with fake police badges may try to accost you for money. Never hand over your passport or money. Ask them to accompany you on foot to your hotel or police station.

11) **Always count your change.** Do this for all transactions to be sure you are not shorted, even in banks and cash exchanges.

12) **Ask taxi drivers what the charge will be before you get in.** Be sure the price includes you and your luggage. If metered, check the meter when you get in to make sure it is at the starting rate. Say no if the driver suggests taking you somewhere else. They are probably getting a commission.

13) **Because of cultural differences, women can attract unwanted attention.** To avoid this attention from men and sometimes other women, being extra alert and more conservative in dress, behavior, and body language is important in some parts of the world.

14) *Always respect the laws of the country you are visiting.* For example, possession of illegal drugs is a serious crime in many countries.

Keeping Your Money and Important Items Safe

Here are eighteen ideas to keep in mind to help keep your money and important items from being lost or stolen:

1) *Use a money belt for your security wallet.* Wear it under your clothing around your waist, hung around your neck, or stashed away in a leg of your pants. See Chapter 13 ("How to Pack Lighter and Still Be Prepared") for a checklist of what should be carried in your security wallet.

2) *Fanny packs worn outside are a magnet for pickpockets.* They should not be used as money belts.

3) *Carry things in your daypack you can live without if lost.* Do this for things such as guidebooks, maps, extra clothing, snacks and any other item you might need for the day. If you are carrying semi-valuable items in your daypack, wear it on your front or tuck it under your arm when you are in crowded places.

4) *Keep track of your things.* You are more likely to unintentionally lose your bags and possessions than to have them stolen. Always check behind you before you leave any place or type of transportation. On every trip we discover each other's processions such as sunglasses on dining tables, checking the hotel before leaving (shake out the bedcover), or by carefully searching our seats or overhead storage when taking public transportation.

5) *When tired, confused, or using public transportation you are especially vulnerable.* Take turns with your travel partner watching the luggage. Always be in close physical contact with your possessions. Be extra cautious anytime in crowded areas or if there is a disturbance because it is often a cover for a theft.

6) *Tourist cars can be targets for thieves.* Judge the safety of a parking place by the amount of broken glass indicating broken car windows. Paying to park in a garage with an attendant can be a good investment. Take everything, especially valuables and suitcases, out of your car when you leave it.

7) ***You should hide your cash in more than one place.*** Use your suitcase, daypack, and money belt to help insure it is not lost all at once.

8) ***To be extra cautious, pick up an inexpensive wallet.*** Fill it with expired cards like expired or old gift cards, fake money covered with a few one-dollar bills, etc. Since most thieves are anxious to get away quickly, they may be fooled. You can also insert a little cash beneath the sole of your shoe. If you do lose your cash, you will have enough for a cab ride back.

9) ***Before traveling internationally call your ATM and credit card companies' toll free number.*** Advise them of the countries you will be using the card and the dates you are traveling.

10) ***You and your travel partner should each carry different ATM and credit cards from separate accounts.*** In case one of you gets their cards lost or stolen you will still have an ATM and credit card to use until they are replaced.

11) ***Users of ATM cash machines can be targeted.*** Extra care is prudent. Here is some advice given by the ATM companies: "Make sure no one waiting behind you can see you entering your PIN number. Be sure to take your ATM receipt with you. Be aware of your surroundings. If the machine is poorly lit, or is in a hidden area, use another location. Don't count your cash or rummage through your personal items while standing at the ATM. If you are using an indoor ATM that requires your card to open the door, avoid letting anyone come in with you that you do not know. When using a drive-through ATM, lock your car doors. When walking up, never leave your car running or unlocked. If you lose your ATM card, immediately contact the financial institution that issued it."

12) ***Don't use an ATM machine that has a thin piece of plastic hanging out of the slot.*** They may be attempting to steal your card information.

13) ***If you have a cell phone, enter an emergency contact.*** Use it in case you need assistance or your cell phone is lost. Store the contact with the word "ICE" (In Case of Emergency). Also enter emergency numbers such as your bank and credit card companies' lost card number as well as your travel insurance, travel agent, tour, etc. companies' numbers with an identifier in the memo field like "MC and the last four digits of the card" or other. Also keep your

credit card company's fraud number stored in your cell phone. If a purchase is denied you can quickly call and sort it out. If you live in the U.S. and are traveling internationally make sure to get the international non-toll free number. Many places outside the U.S. you cannot dial a U.S. toll free number.

14) **Make copies of your passport front photo page, visa(s), passport photos, paper tickets, traveler check receipt, and any other important papers.** Store copies somewhere in your suitcase as well as leave copies with a relative or friend at home. To have a printable backup in case your important documents and copies are lost, scan and store them in an e-mail attachment sent to your personal e-mail address. Also do this with your list of emergency contacts (i.e. emergency contact person, 24-hour travel agent, home, medical and car insurance, and any other important contacts along with a list of doctor and lawyer names and numbers, allergies, medical history, special medication).

15) **If lost, cancel debit and credit cards within two days.** Do this to avoid liability and order replacements. Keep the necessary contact phone numbers and card details in your emergency contact list. To help insure bank and credit card numbers are more secure you may consider recording them with a special code. For example, take the last 8 digits and put them in the front, and the first 8 becomes the last numbers.

16) **Carry your passport in your money belt or keep it in the hotel safe.** Keep a copy of it in your luggage. As soon as you realize your passport is missing, contact the nearest police authorities or U.S. embassy or consulate. For emergencies, contact the National Passport Information Center (NPIC) at (877) 487-2778 to reach an operator Monday through Friday from 8 a.m. until 10 p.m. ET.

17) **Make sure the doors and windows of your hotel room are locked.** Do this when you leave and when you are in your hotel room. Windows are often overlooked.

18) **For security tips for your luggage, see Chapter 13 ("How to Pack Lighter and Still be Prepared").** To help insure your luggage is not lost or delayed, try to avoid late check-ins and tight connections. Also, head directly to baggage claim once getting off your flight. If your luggage does not show up at baggage claim, be sure to file a

claim immediately at the airport and give them your hotel address and phone number. Often, the airlines will bring your luggage to your hotel once located. Be sure to learn how to check on the status of your luggage. In the case your luggage is lost, an itemized list is helpful to back up your claim.

Staying healthy is an important way to enjoy your travels. In the next chapter, we offer many ideas to assist you in staying healthy and having the vitality to fully enjoy your travels.

Chapter 11

Staying Healthy

We have all overindulged while traveling. Many of us believe that following a healthy lifestyle is not important. Hey, "we are on vacation!" We should realize when on an extended trip traveling or living away for a month or more, it is more like living abroad than a vacation and establishing healthy habits is important.

Healthy Lifestyle – Some Tough Love

It is estimated that two thirds of Americans are overweight (half of these are obese!) and 20% smoke indicating a lifestyle with a lack of attention to healthy living. Many of these people are experiencing lack of mobility, energy, and often zest for life. It is sad to see so many experiencing serious health issues at an early age setting themselves up for a shortened life marred by health issues and becoming a burden to their love ones. When they talk about their weight, they often say life is short and they want to enjoy it. They are referring to eating more food than their body needs and practicing unhealthy habits.

It's fun to be active – climbing Franz Josef Glacier in New Zealand.

When we exercise regularly, eat healthfully, get plenty of sleep, and manage stress, vitality and energy flows from our bodies. Regular exercise, rest, minimizing stress, and consuming a diet including fresh fruit and vegetables improve health, increase vitality, and make weight control manageable.

Our doctors say we are their worst customers - rarely, except for checkups, do we see them. In my mid-50's, I was able to climb thousands of steps to the top of the Great Wall of China with 20-year olds and free dive with just a snorkel 35 feet below the ocean surface with a young village chief in Fiji. How does that compare with eating more cheeseburgers and French fries? We wonder who is truly enjoying life to the fullest?

Healthy Habits While Traveling

Water

Always drink plenty of clean bottled water. In some areas of the world, tap water is not safe to drink. Even in areas where water is safe, we take precautions because there may be other things in the water your system is not used to. Bottled water is usually available. Be sure to carefully check the seal before purchasing and carry a bottle with you in your daypack. An immersion heater, a lightweight electric coil, will boil water and make it safe. If you are going far off the beaten path, you may want to consider taking chemical purifiers or a filtering device.

When in doubt about the local water, you may want to eat only freshly cooked food and avoid salads, fruits, and vegetables unless they are cooked or pealed. Do not swallow the water when you are in the shower. Brush your teeth and rinse your toothbrush with bottled water. Do not drink bottled water or sodas in a glass with ice cubes unless you are sure the ice cubes were made with safe water. Even a small amount of contaminated water can cause you problems.

Eating Healthy

We highly recommend trying local foods including pastries and desserts with all things in moderation. Make mealtime an enjoyable not hurried time. Studies show you eat less feeling satisfied if the meal is spread over time (at least 30 minutes). Avoid fast and junk foods and anything fried. Eat smaller portions – we often share one appetizer and one main course. Eat whole grains and stay away from processed grains low in nutrition and fiber and high in calories. The basic rule is nothing white.

Also avoid sugar and saturated fatty foods. Substitute fish and skinless chicken for red meat. Try other forms of protein such as nuts, whole grains, tofu, and beans. Include fresh fruits and vegetables. Be careful in areas where the water is not safe to drink where perhaps you should not have raw fruits and vegetables. Numerous studies have confirmed the health benefits of the 'Mediterranean diet' high in monounsaturated fats such as olive oil and relying on whole grain cereals, fruit and vegetables, fish, and low consumption of animal fats.

We also take a daily vitamin just to be sure. We take Airborne before every flight or other means of longer transportation.

Once you properly nourish your body good things will happen. Your weight becomes manageable, energy will increase, cravings of sugar and stimulants like coffee will diminish, and feelings of hunger will come under control.

Habits to Change

Habits take time to change. Start slowly with one thing at a time like cutting back on sugar or red meat adding more healthy choices such as fruits and vegetables to your diet. Other healthy changes you can start with are:

- Water instead of soda
- Grilled, sautéed, or stir-fried instead of fried
- Raw nuts and dried fruit instead of snacks and candy

- Whole grains instead of processed white flour
- Yogurt instead of bacon
- Cutting out the bread and butter
- Vegetables or a salad instead of rice or French fries.
- Leave off the fatty dressing on salads

Be sure the vegetables are cooked in areas that the water is not safe to drink.

The good news is research has shown with repeated exposure you can retrain your taste buds to enjoy new healthy foods in as little as two weeks. Over time, new foods become familiar and start tasting good. In time, you will desire healthy and natural foods instead of a diet high in fat, sugar, and processed flour.

When traveling, be sure any meat you order is cooked and be wary of milk that may not be pasteurized, unpeeled fruits and salads that have not been washed in purified water, and shellfish.

OK, Now for the Fun Stuff

As the saying goes… anything in moderation. As you travel through this wonderful world, you will find amazing new foods to try. Wait until you try:

- Food and cheese in France!
- Free-range beef in Buenos Aires, Argentina
- Real pasta in Bellagio on Lake Como, Italy, or most anywhere in Italy
- Fish head curry and chili crab in Singapore
- Sukiyaki and Okonomiyaki in Japan
- Padang curry in Thailand
- The authentic version of fish and chips wrapped in newspaper in an English pub
- Lobster pizza in Bequia in the Caribbean Grenadines
- Greek food in the Greek Islands

Yum! We want to go back. Why wait? Want to go with us?

You should also try things you never had before. Sometimes it may not work out so well. Other times you will gain a passion for a type of food that remains for the rest of your life. On that note, it reminds us of another story of the dancing shrimp in Thailand.

There is a large lake in the middle of Thailand – a beautiful peaceful place. In this lake lives a small shrimp about 1/8 inch long. They catch these shrimp, put hundreds of them in a small paper cone with water, and add mild Thai spices. Get ready now... you swallow them alive and they die 'dancing' down your throat while you enjoy the Thai spices. Sounds awful but it was one of the most memorable and delightful things I have tried in the world. My wife passed.

Exercise

It is important to get plenty of exercise while traveling. Walking is a good way to do so. Walking is a great way to learn about the new places you are visiting and you will discover much more. Plan to take long walks every day you can. You can extend the area you discover by taking a walk one way and transportation back. To prepare for your trip start taking walks at home weeks before you leave.

Sleep and Rest

Traveling and discovering new things can be stressful especially when your body is deprived of sleep and it is unable to rebuild and recharge itself. Sleeping in a new bed or on a plane surrounded by new noises sometimes adds difficulties. Try to create a sleep-promoting environment that is dark, cool, and comfortable. Starting late afternoon, do not have simulates such as nicotine and caffeine (i.e. coffee, tea, soft drinks), do not eat or drink too much close to bedtime, and turn off the TV. A white noise machine helps many people. Exercise done early in the day can reduce stress and promote sleep.

Traveling can cause fatigue. Sleep patterns can also be interrupted when traveling making it harder for you to get enough rest. Blocking out the noise and light can help you sleep. The use of earplugs is helpful when the noise level is bothersome. Take them in your carry-on bag when you fly or take long train or bus rides. Some people also use a blindfold to create a sense of more darkness. When we do have trouble falling asleep, occasionally we use a sleep aid such as melatonin.

In addition to getting plenty of sleep each day, take a break from traveling and take a day or more to just rest. Arrange your travel itinerary to include a few days at a beach or other resort and do nothing but rest, play, read, and maybe plan the next leg of your trip.

Jet Lag

Jet lag results from the disruption of your normal sleep-wake patterns when traveling rapidly across time zones. It is more pronounced when you are traveling east. As soon as we get on the plane we reset our watches to our destination time and use the new time when deciding when to sleep even while on the plane flight. This helps us adjust our sleep patterns to our new time zone.

When we experience jet lag we attempt to quickly adapt to the local schedule of sleeping during the night. We try not to nap during the day even if we are very tired. Go outside because bright light can help reset circadian rhythms. Exercise and conversations with others stimulate your body and helps keep you alert. Eating high protein food tends to assist alertness where a diet of starch and sweets high in carbohydrates can induce sleepiness. The idea is to force yourself into the new time schedule as quickly as possible. If we need help falling asleep at night on the new time schedule, we do use a sleep aid.

Starting diet changes 3 days before your flight can also help. Make your breakfasts high in protein and dinners high in carbohydrates. When traveling west and it will be daytime when you arrive at your destination, try to sleep on the plane. If it will be nighttime when arriving, stay awake on your flight so you will sleep when you get there. When traveling east get up early on your travel day, eat as little as possible, avoid caffeine, set your sleeping patterns on your flight to the time of your destination, and avoid the urge to sleep on your first day at your destination.

Manage Stress

Just as poor diet, lack of exercise, and not enough sleep, stress and worry can rob you of your vitality and joy of traveling. It is important to deal with stressful events as they come up. Try not to get agitated when stressful events happen. Take a couple of deep breaths and relax your shoulders. Then put the stressful event in perspective by giving yourself an affirmation such as "will this cause us to die?" or "is our whole trip ruined?" Most likely the event is not significant enough to cause you to have a bad day, damage your health, or diminish the enjoyment of your travel experience.

If you can, try to laugh about it. Sometimes unexpected events create the best stories when you get home. Be flexible and create an alternative option. Many times our alternative plan turned out to be better than the original plan.

Sun

Exposure to the sun can lead to unhealthy sunburn and heat stroke. Long term exposure can accelerate skin aging and cancer. It is wise to use sunscreen every day and reapply after you have been swimming. It is also wise to regularly wear polarized sunglasses and carry a hat and sunscreen in your daypack. Clothing that shields skin from UV light is readily available and highly recommended. When selecting a sunscreen or special clothing, choose a one with a UPF rating of 25 or more (higher if you are light skinned). Drink plenty of water to avoid dehydration in hot climates.

Wash Your Hands Often

Good old soap and water can be a blessing to your health by making it harder on microorganisms that cause illness. In addition to washing your hands before meals and after using the toilet, try to wash them whenever you can such as on flights, when you get back to your hotel, and after touching things or handling anything like animals. Carrying and using a small bottle of hand sanitizer can also be beneficial.

Traveler's Diarrhea

If you take the precautions described in this chapter you are less likely to worry about diarrhea. Unfortunately, it may happen due to tainted food and general changes in diet. The best way to deal with it is to keep well hydrated, take Pepto-Bismol or other treatment, and eat bland foods (i.e. rice, bread, yogurt) for a few days. If it persists beyond 2-3 days, has extreme symptoms, or if there is blood in the stool, it is wise to see a local doctor. Other symptoms requiring prompt attention include fever, chills, and profuse sweating. Carrying your own antibiotics with you as described below is another option.

Medical

Putting together and taking the 'Medical and First-aid Kit' items described in Chapter 13 ("How to Pack Lighter and Still Be Prepared") as a precaution is very highly recommended. You may not be able to prevent every illness or injury but you can plan ahead to be able to deal with them. Most of the suggested items are often available most places but you will be glad to have them instead of going out looking for them when you are not feeling well. If you do need medical assistance, ask your hotel for directions to the pharmacy, doctor, or hospital. Other sources of advice for assistance can be found by calling your insurance company and credit card company or the local U.S. embassy or consulate.

You do not need to take whole bottles or packages of the suggested items. To consolidate space, fill your 3 oz. travel bottles of any liquids you plan to take. For the pills, take some of each out of the box leaving them in the original packaging so not to concern border control agents. Mark them well or write a guide of what color pill does what so you will know later what they are. Put them together in a sealable plastic bag.

Talk to your doctor about getting a prescription and discussion of best use so you can take some antibiotics with you. Although antibiotics are useful in a wide variety of infections, antibiotics are useless against viral infections (e.g. colds and flu) and fungal infections (e.g. ringworm).

Vaccinations

At least eight weeks before you travel you should familiarize yourself with vaccination requirements and other precautions. Most vaccines take time to become effective in your body and some vaccines must be given in a series over a period of days or sometimes weeks. If it is less than 4 weeks before you leave, you should still see your doctor. You might still benefit from shots or medications and other information about how to protect yourself from illness and injury while traveling.

You can learn the risks and vaccine requirements and recommendations for your destinations through **CDC (Centers for Disease Control and Prevention - www.cdc.gov/travel)**. Many cities have special travel clinics that can assist you.

Getting vaccinations for Hepatitis A and B is important, especially if you are visiting developing countries. Do keep in mind for protection lasting for ten years you need to plan six months ahead. Shorter-term protection can be had with the first shot.

Always check if malaria is a problem. Remember you must start taking anti-malarial pills two weeks before you leave.

What is the best way to handle money and credit cards while you are traveling? We offer suggestions in the next chapter.

Chapter 12

Money and Credit Cards

"When preparing to travel, lay out all your clothes and all your
money. Then take half the clothes and twice the money."
~ Susan Heller

It has been said money makes the world go around. We are not sure of
that, but we are certain it takes money to go around the world. Hopefully
by using the cost saving tips presented in Chapter 7 ("Finding Great
Travel Bargains") you can significantly lower your costs of travel. In this
chapter we offer guidelines on how to manage money while traveling.

ATM Debit Cards

ATM machines are generally the easiest and cheapest way to get cash

when traveling. You can receive good foreign currency exchange rates using your bank's ATM debit card, usually better than exchanging cash or traveler's checks. ATM cards have good security because they are usable only with a PIN (personal identification number).

Young monks in Laos live on the generosity of others – the rest of us need to take money.

Check with your bank about the international compatibility of your ATM card. If the ATM card from your home bank is not connected to the worldwide Cirrus or PLUS networks, you may want to look into getting a MasterCard or Visa debit card that does. While they look and can be used like regular charge cards, they actually debit your checking account the same way your ATM card does.

You should be aware many banks now charge a small foreign ATM fee for each transaction. Although usually better than the charges for use of credit cards and exchanging cash or traveler's checks, these fees can add up if you use your ATM card regularly. To minimize ATM transaction fees it is generally a good idea to take out as much money in a single transaction as you need or feel comfortable carrying, rather than making multiple stops at the ATM.

Because exchanging cash has higher fees, we normally take out only as much local currency as we need for that country so not to have foreign currency left over when returning home or traveling on to the next country. If we foresee having cash left over, we pay the last days' expenses (i.e. hotel, meals, airport departure tax) with our foreign currency.

You should be aware some ATM's overseas do not accept PIN's longer than four digits and no letters. Some travelers report that sometimes only numbers with no zeros are accepted and only the primary account can be accessed. If your PIN is longer than four digits or contains letters or zeros, contact your bank to have it changed to four digits of only numbers without zeros. Also, be sure your primary account has enough money and a high enough daily withdraw limit to cover you.

Finally, for security you and your travel partner should each carry different ATM and credit cards from separate accounts. In case one of you gets their cards lost or stolen you will still have an ATM and credit card to use until they are replaced.

ATM Locators

The location of ATM machines can be found using these websites:

- *MasterCard/Cirrus/Maestro (www.mastercard.com/atmlocator)*
- *Visa/PLUS (www.visa.com/atms)*

Credit Cards

Credit cards are convenient and accepted most everywhere in the world. Notable exceptions are budget hotels, some restaurants and shops, on board many public transportation options, and businesses in some more off-the-beaten-path locations that run their business cash only. In addition to credit cards, having access to local currency through ATM or cash exchange is important. MasterCard and Visa are the most accepted credit cards around the world.

We try to use credit cards whenever possible for large purchases such as flights, hotel bills, tickets, car rentals, etc. If we have problems with any charge, we can work it out later with our credit card company. Some local vendors such as restaurants and shops may charge a fee for credit card transactions.

Keep in mind most credit card companies add fees for foreign transactions that are usually larger than ATM transactions (sometimes as high as 3%). If you want to avoid these fees, *Capital One (www.capitalone. com)* is a credit card company that does not charge fees for foreign transactions. If you want to use your credit card for cash withdrawals, you will almost always get a better rate than exchanging cash or traveler's checks but be aware of any other fee your credit card company may add on.

Another way to avoid credit card transaction fees (and possibly any finance charges your credit card company imposes while traveling abroad) is to use your credit card for cash withdrawals by putting some money in your credit card account. Be sure to check first with your credit card company to learn how this is done and if it will save from paying fees.

Some companies such as rental car and hotels will put 'holds' on your credit card account as security deposits. Although not charges, these holds will be applied to your credit limit. Be sure your credit card as sufficient credit limits for your anticipated charges and holds.

Also keep in mind when problems arise about questionable charges you may not have as much protection overseas as you do at home. Although we have never experienced any issues, there are reports from travelers about being charged twice for the same item or for items they never purchased and credit card companies unwilling or unable to intercede on their behalf. Always watch merchants imprinting your card and keep your receipts. Online or after you get home, carefully check your credit card statement. If you see charges you did not make, call your credit card company and ask them to dispute the charges.

Contact Your Bank Before Leaving

For all the ATM and credit cards you plan to take with you, it is very important to call your banks before leaving on your trip. There is usually a phone number on the back of your card for customer support. Tell them when and where you will be traveling. Otherwise, foreign transactions may activate the security fraud alert and cause your bank to freeze your account. You may want to review the fees they will charge you for foreign transactions or cash withdrawals. Also ask for the international phone number you need to use in case your card is lost or stolen.

Why Taking U.S. Cash Is Necessary

Although increasingly available in many areas around the world, ATM machines offering your ATM service (i.e. MasterCard Cirrus/Maestro or Visa PLUS) can sometimes be hard to find in the place you are visiting, although you may be able to get a cash advance using your Visa or MasterCard (be aware of any finance charges). You can use the website resources listed above in the section about ATM's to determine if ATM machines are plentiful for your service in the areas you plan to visit.

Many places have ATM machines located on every corner that worked well for us. Other places such as in Japan we had to go to a post office and in Argentina our type of ATM was troublesome to locate. Some places have limitations on the daily amount you can withdraw. For example, in Cambodia we could only withdraw about $72 U.S. a day in Cambodian currency when we were there. When our hotel required payment in local currency, we were thankful to have some U.S. currency with us to exchange. In addition, new credit card systems with built-in chips for security are used in places such as Europe. A few places do not accept U.S. type credit cards.

It is best to take some U.S. cash or traveler's checks with you to exchange just in case. More if you determine ATM machines for your service may be difficult to find or have limitations, especially in second and third world countries.

Traveler's Checks

Traveler's checks have become less popular with travelers because electronic banking has made travel and paying for it much easier. As pointed out in the section above, taking some cash or traveler's checks can be important. Unlike cash, traveler's checks do offer some security if lost or stolen.

Getting the Best Exchange Rate

Between commissions, credit card and ATM fees, and other expenses, you will almost always have to pay a little extra when purchasing something in a foreign currency or exchanging cash or traveler's checks. The best way to know if you are getting a good exchange rate is knowing the current rate. Before you leave on your trip, go to *Oanda (www.oanda. com/currency/converter)* to learn what the current exchange rates are for the countries you plan to visit. If you are taking an extended trip, check the rate periodically to stay abreast of any significant changes.

Be aware of the exchange rate as well as any commissions. Some commissions are charged on each transaction while others on a percentage basis. Some moneychangers will post the sell rate for U.S. dollars rather than the buy rate, which is what you will want if you are exchanging U.S. dollars into foreign currency. Be very wary of black market exchanges, which can be a source of scams or counterfeit currency.

You will usually get the best exchange rates at banks, government-run post offices, and American Express offices (particularly if using their traveler's checks). Hotels are sometimes worth a try. Although occasionally you will get lucky, the change bureaus you see in airports, train stations, and tourist areas usually have the worst exchange rates. If so, you may want to get a little local currency and then take some time to shop around for a better exchange rate. Read the posted exchange rates carefully and ask for the net rate after any commissions and fees.

Sometimes you will be given the option to pay in U.S. dollars and the merchant may charge you a little extra for the convenience of paying in your own currency. Ask what the price is in local currency and do the math. Often paying in local currency works out better in your favor.

Doing the Conversion Math in Your Head

Carrying a small calculator or using the one on your smart phone is an easy way to convert local prices to prices you better understand.

We use a simple way to quickly calculate prices without using a calculator. For smaller items, I like to make a simple procedure in my head to quickly determine the approximate cost of items. For example, if I was traveling through Mexico with an exchange rate of 12 pesos to 1 U.S. dollar, I would take the Mexican price, move the decimal place to the left one place and then subtract 20% or 1/5 (rounding things off). So, 240 pesos become 24 less about 5 or 19 dollars. The actual would have been 20 U.S. dollars – pretty close for a ballpark estimate. If I were traveling through European countries using the Euro with an exchange rate of 1.37 dollars to 1 Euro, I would add about 1/3 to the price. So, something costing 30 Euros would be 40 U.S. dollars. The actual would be 41 U.S. dollars.

OK, I was a math major. If this is a bit too much, try this. Memorize what $5 and $10 U.S. would be in local currency. Using the examples above, in Mexico, $5 and $10 U.S. would 60 pesos and 120 pesos. Something costing 30 pesos would be half of $5 U.S. and something costing 240 pesos would be $20 U.S.

Previously we said we go out for months with just our 40-pound main suitcases. Did you believe it? Well read the next chapter to see how we do it and what travel clothing and gear is important to take.

Chapter 13

How To Pack Lighter and Still Be Prepared

In this chapter...

One of our most asked questions is: "How do you pack for a longer trip?" Traveling the world or living for a few weeks to a month or more does require different needs and more preparations for packing. This chapter presents detailed suggestions on how to pack lighter and still be prepared.

The checklists in the chapter are exhaustive so you will not forget anything. This is manageable because you will not need every item on each trip and you can miniaturized and share items with your travel partner.

Many of the items mentioned in this chapter can be purchased at travel stores or online travel stores such as:

- **Magellan's (www.magellans.com)**
- **TravelSmith (www.travelsmith.com)**
- **REI (www.rei.com)**
- **Rick Steves (www.ricksteves.com)**

Leaving It Behind

"The wisdom of life consists in the elimination of nonessentials."
~ Lin Yutang, Chinese writer and educator

"He who would travel happily must travel light."
~ Antoine de St. Exupery

More is not better when it comes to travel and luggage. Not a single traveler looks with envy at another traveler with lots of luggage to move around.

You want to make your adventure as wonderful as possible. Making strange animal sounds moving and carrying heavy luggage is not attractive. It also takes some of the fun out of travel especially when your travels take you to multiple places or adventurous and off-the-beaten-path destinations.

Monks in Thailand travel light – you may need a little more than this.

This chapter gives you a good way to be mobile as well as check-off lists of items that will help you look great and be prepared for weather changes, a variety of activities, and other potential travel needs without being overly weighed down by 'baggage'.

Most of us don't need half of what we bring on a trip. Many of us suffer from the "just-in-case" syndrome and/or feeling compelled to wear different fashions for every day or even time of day. Without knowledge and planning, this creates anxiety and convinces us to pack much too much. Remember you need to unhook from past behavior. And with modern innovations in travel luggage, clothing, and gear, traveling light has never been easier.

Traveling light gives you mobility and freedom and will save you time. It will allow you to be more adventurous in your travels and not wear you out moving heavy luggage. Also, without the fancy designer labels and expensive watches and jewelry, you are less of a target for pickpockets. You should make it a resolution to travel light – the pay offs are great.

"The more you know, the less you need."
~ old Aboriginal saying

Traveling light does require preparation. Packing less means planning more, especially when you first start out. It is often a choice of what not to take then what to take. Think about what you can do without – not what would be handy to have. Give yourself at least a month before leaving so not to be hurried. Following the suggestions in this chapter will make your planning much easier and will save you time and stress.

Choice of Suitcase

This is a very important decision. Taking some time to select your luggage will yield huge returns in your enjoyment of your adventure. Modern travel luggage is made of high-tech materials that are compact, sturdy, and light. The correct suitcase choice can lighten you load by many pounds. If you have not updated your travel luggage lately, this is a very worthy investment. Keep in mind, what may seem expensive may save you money and hassles in the long run.

There are many types of travel suitcases suited for many different needs. Take some time to think about your needs and investigate your options. Our preference is to take two bags each – one main suitcase and a much smaller daypack that can also be used as a carry-on and daypack bag.

Main Suitcase

We prefer to have a lightweight wheeled pullman-style suitcase with

an adjustable telescoping handle and big built-in wheels. It is very nice
to be able to pull out the handle and roll your suitcase around. Look for
sturdy thin walls made of water-resistant ballistic or Cordura nylon material
with double stitched finished zippers and seams (preferably lock stitched).
Consider waterproofing if your travel plans take you to outdoor, rainy, or
adventurous places. Corner protectors and plastic curb slides along the
bottom of your suitcase will add years to its life. Very importantly, your
suitcase should be comfortable to handle.

Make sure the telescoping handle is sturdy (rigid when rolling) and
the casing does not take too much room on the inside of the bag. It should
also be easy to open and close and lock in the open and closed position.
The wheels should big to make it easy to roll around and made of rubber
or urethane that are sturdy, widely spaced, firmly bolted into place, and
recessed into the suitcase's frame for protection.

Even with this remarkable convenience it is very important to choose a
lightweight bag with few structured compartments and extras. Open space
allows you to pack a little more and still weigh less. If you do need a divider,
a piece of cardboard can be used. It is still very important to not over
pack because you will need to carry your luggage from time to time lifting
it to overhead storage areas on trains and buses, across unpaved areas, or
even up stairs in smaller hotels. Look for both side and top carry handles
that are comfortable to handle and well riveted to the bag, either a single
handle or a flap design (two handle straps joined by material like Velcro).

We also prefer a simple non-rigid collapsible suitcase with a rigid
structured floor and adjustable tie-down straps on the outside. Too many
features such as pockets, pouches, or a frame add weight and can limit
the room you have to pack. Although we do like a foldable wet bag for
wet and soiled garments and one outside pocket for documents. Suitcases
with structured floors determine the way the bag is stored and are easier to
pack. A suitcase with non-rigid sides and adjustable tie-down straps allows
you to adjust the size of the bag (hopefully smaller) to the needs of your
trip. This helps keep your clothes from sliding around and wrinkling and
makes the suitcase easier to place in storage areas and overhead bins. Also,
a collapsible bag fits more easily under the bed giving you extra room in
small hotel rooms or cruise ships cabins.

You should consider a convertible backpack if you are considering hiking or walking on rough terrain. You should also consider a smaller carry-on suitcase if you plan a shorter trip with less luggage requirements. A carry-on sized suitcase is much easier to travel with and saves the hassles and potential extra costs of checking your suitcase. Check airline websites for acceptable carry-on sizes. Of course, you need to pack even less.

Carry-on / Daypack Bag

A second much smaller carry-on/daypack bag is very helpful. It should be large enough to be used daily to take things with you that you will need during your day and night (i.e. water, snacks, sunscreen, change of clothes, camera, guidebooks, umbrella) so you do not have to return to your hotel.

Your zippered daypack should be made of modern lightweight sturdy nylon material that will fold up into your suitcase when not needed. Modern travel daypacks fold down to almost nothing. It should be comfortable while worn on your back to leave your hands free. Keep it simple and avoid the heavier small backpack style with the many compartments. It is nice to have padded shoulder straps, at least one pocket on the outside, a handle at the top, and a place for a water bottle on the outside.

If you plan to take extensive camera/video equipment and/or a computer laptop or tablet/netbook with you (a laptop can be very useful) – see Chapter 15 ("How to Stay in Touch with Family and Friends"), different bags may be necessary. If you are traveling as a couple, one can have a computer bag as a carry-on and the other can use the daypack with the camera and other valuables inside it. Additional smaller camera bags can be useful for your camera and video equipment. Again, choose modern lightweight sturdy bags with padded shoulder straps. Whatever bag you select make sure it is large enough to do the job but not too large. Weight and mobility is vital to your enjoyment of travel.

Security Tips for Your Luggage

Luggage tags are mandatory for airline travel and very advisable for identification – include your name, address, e-mail address, and telephone number (mobile phone number is best so they can reach you while traveling). Use an address other than your home address (i.e. business or family/friend address) because your home address can be used to alert thieves while you are away. Also label your bags inside and out in case the tags are torn off.

Because luggage bags look so similar today, we also place several short brightly colored ribbons on three sides of our bags to assist us to easily identify our suitcases. This also helps in preventing your suitcase being mistaken for another.

Although rare, bags do sometimes get lost or delayed. You may want to include your destination phone number on your tags to increase the chance your lost bags will find you while you are on your trip and not be returned home. Be sure to identify it as your destination phone number. Including a copy of your itinerary (complete with destination contacts, flight numbers, and hotel and travel agent contacts) placed in each suitcase where it will be easily found (on top of your clothing or in an outside tag or pocket) may help lost bags find you. It may also be helpful to carry a photo of your packed suitcase to help locate it in non-English speaking countries.

Tiny luggage locks may be helpful. If you do use locks, the combination type avoids the worry of losing keys. If you plan to check your luggage on planes, use TSA-approved locks. If you don't want to use locks, plastic cable twist ties available at hardware stores will add some security. They need to be cut off at your destination. For extra security, bring a locking cable to secure your luggage in hotel rooms and trains.

When your main suitcases are not in sight while traveling (checked on planes, buses, etc.), be sure to place all valuables not in your money belt (i.e. cameras, computers, jewelry) in your daypack and take them with you. Watch your daypack closely because thieves in many parts of the world are very adept at opening your bag while you are distracted.

Travel Gear and Accessories

Every item taken on your trip must be chosen carefully. Only pack easily portable essentials evaluating each item on need, weight, and size. You do not have to pack for the whole trip because you can pick up things along the way. To travel light, you need to learn to make do, improvise, and, if necessary, purchase things along the way. Take manual items like lightweight toothbrushes and disposable razors instead of electrical devices. To avoid doubling up, share essentials with your travel partner. For example, only one small tube of toothpaste is necessary. This is true for many items.

When choosing your travel gear, think miniature. A wise investment would be to stock up on smaller travel items, sample sizes, and 3 oz. travel bottles available at travel related stores. Refilling hotel shampoo bottles with your favorite brands is a good option. When your large tube of toothpaste or sunscreen has at least enough left for two months, set it aside with your travel accessories, and start a new tube for home use. If you plan to carry on your suitcase, all liquids and gels must be in 3.4-ounce or smaller containers and all of these items must fit within a single, quart-size sealable plastic bag.

Because travel gear essentials do not change extensively from trip to trip, it is very helpful to put together small accessory kits that you keep separate and untouched. Keeping your travel accessory kits untouched between trips will save you time and stress in packing because you have less chance of forgetting things. You will only need to fill or replenish the small travel containers or pills in your travel accessory kits and not pack the larger versions you use around home.

According to your personal and travel needs you can assemble several separate kits (detailed below) in water-repellent, non-bulky, zippered nylon pouches for your toiletries, makeup, medical and first-aid needs, clothing care, 3 oz. liquid containers, electronic accessories, etc. There are many organizational pouches and organizers on the market. Heavier zip-lock plastic bags also work well. See-through packing cubes are popular. So you can quickly recognize the kit you need, purchase several different colors. Always choose the smallest pouch that will hold the items you take.

Before your flight, you can check with the **Transportation Security Administration (TSA) website (www.tsa.gov/travelers/index.shtm)** to learn the most recent rules on what is permitted and prohibited in both carry-on and checked luggage.

The following are some things you should consider taking (remember to get miniature versions). You may add or subtract items from the following lists (e.g. camping needs are not covered in this book) but always be selective so not to take too much.

Personal Hygiene Accessory Kit

☐ toothbrush (leave the electrical devices at home)
☐ toothpaste

- [ ] all-purpose travel soap
- [ ] hand sanitizer like Purell
- [ ] deodorant
- [ ] dental floss
- [ ] disposable razors
- [ ] comb
- [ ] small folding hairbrush
- [ ] small scissors
- [ ] nail clipper/file
- [ ] earplugs (nice for that noisy hotel room or airplane – take in carry-on bag)
- [ ] contact lens solution and/or sterilizer
- [ ] birth control and feminine sanitary items (take along enough for your entire trip because your favorite type may be hard to find)
- [ ] makeup (keep to a minimum like lipstick, lip gloss, lip pencils, mascara, and eyeliners or shadow, all-purpose moisturizer, makeup remover swabs – all in travel sized containers, lip pencils or sample size lip gloss are better for hot weather because they do not tend to melt)

Always put items that may leak in a sealable plastic bag. Because temperature and flight air pressure changes can cause bottles to leak, we also carry in separate non-leak sealable bags items such as:

- [ ] sunscreen and moisturizer
- [ ] insect and/or mosquito repellent (don't forget, mosquito repellent containing DEET is important if traveling to areas where malaria, yellow fever, dengue, and other mosquito-borne disease are possible, mosquito coils and nets may also be necessary)
- [ ] small containers of moisturizer and combination shampoo/conditioner
- [ ] any other container of liquid that may leak

Medical and First-aid Kit

You do not need to take whole bottles or packages of the following items. To consolidate space, fill your 3 oz. travel bottles of any liquids you plan to take. For the packaged pills, take some of each out of the box and put them together in a sealable plastic bag. Mark them well or write a guide of what color pill does what so you will know later what they are. Be sure to leave them in their original packages so not to create illegal drugs concern at border inspections. As necessary for your personal and trip needs, you should consider taking the following:

☐ any necessary prescription medicine in their original bottle in case questioned about it from authorities - also bring an original copy of the doctor's prescription in your name, including the generic name, in case you need to refill. Talk to your doctor about getting a prescription and discussion of best use so you can take some antibiotics with you. Some countries (e.g. Mexico) have requirements to have a prescription from a doctor from that country to legally possess certain drugs and medicines. Be sure to check with the country's consulate before going.

☐ motion and seasick medication (i.e. Dramamine tablets, Scopamine patches)

☐ vitamins

☐ pain/fever reliever (i.e. ibuprofen, aspirin, acetaminophen)

☐ for colds and flu: pills (both day and night time), decongestant tablets, throat lozenges

☐ jet lag remedy - more on this in Chapter 11 ("Staying Healthy")

☐ antacid

☐ temporary upset stomach and diarrhea relief (i.e. Pepto-Bismol tablets and Imodium)

☐ antihistamines for allergies

☐ laxative

☐ sleeping pills

☐ bandages (various sizes)

☐ antibiotic ointment (e.g. Neosporin)

☐ antiseptic wipes

☐ blister kit (e.g. Moleskin)

☐ antifungal or yeast infection creams

☐ hydrocortisone cream (counters the alien bacteria that causes itching or a rash, it is also good for insect bites and sunburns

☐ nail clipper and/or file

☐ tweezers

☐ thermometer (digital is best)

☐ antimalarial medicines, if necessary

☐ personal syringe kit, if necessary

☐ water purification tablets or equipment, if necessary

Clothing Cleaning and Maintenance Supplies

We pack fewer clothes by washing them along the way - more on how to keep clothes clean in the next chapter ("How to Keep Your Clothes Clean and Fresh"). We carry clothing cleaning supplies in a sealable bag such as:

☐ small container of cold-water detergent (liquid is easier to work with)

☐ stain remover (not bleach)

☐ 10 baby wipes

☐ baby powder

☐ universal sink plug

☐ small sewing kit

Other Helpful Items to Consider Taking

Use this list as a helpful reminder. Only one per couple of many of these shared items are necessary and some may not be necessary for your trip or for your needs.

☐ guidebooks (if traveling to multiple places, tear out or photocopy necessary sections and stable them together, leave them behind when you are done traveling through a country or place)

☐ maps and directions

- ☐ paperback book or magazine to read (or E-reader device, paperback books are nice to trade for others along the way – many hotels have book exchanges so you do not need to bring books for the whole trip)

- ☐ money belt for your security wallet wearable under your clothes (more on security in Chapter 10 ("Security – How to Stay Safe on the Road")

- ☐ watch and travel alarm (take an inexpensive watch you will not miss if lost, most mobile phones have a handy alarm and time keeping features avoiding the need for a watch and travel alarm)

- ☐ lightweight fast drying travel towel to use for swimming and hostels that do not provide towels, also great for picnics

- ☐ extra wire hangers from the dry cleaners (about 10, there are never enough hangers in budget hotels, remove all the paper from them except for two with the pants rollers)

- ☐ small flashlight with batteries

- ☐ small reading light to avoid disturbing your travel partner when reading at night

- ☐ combination wine cock-screw and capped bottle opener

- ☐ plastic knife and fork (useful for the wine & cheese picnics and snacks)

- ☐ sunglasses with covers

- ☐ extra eyeglasses with covers

- ☐ eyeglass repair kit

- ☐ pens

- ☐ small paper notebook (if you like to write or take notes)

- ☐ business/travel cards (note: you can have your personalized cards printed for free (except for a shipping charge) at **Vistaprint (www. vistaprint.com)**

- ☐ photographs of your family and home – nice icebreaker when meeting new friends along the way, you can also bring postcards of your hometown

- ☐ extra sealable (zip-lock) plastic storage bags of various sizes (always helpful along the way)

☐ large plastic bags from merchants or the newspaper – great to keep shoes from soiling other clothing

☐ large and small envelopes to organize travel documents

☐ small packet of tissues (also handy as toilet paper and toilet seat covers)

☐ toilet paper (take along a half finished roll because toilet paper is not always high quality and it may not be available when traveling to many places, always carry some in your daypack)

☐ safety pins (great for many 'emergencies' like clothing tears and bag security)

☐ small roll of duct tape for repairs (wrap some around a pencil)

☐ luggage locks or cable twist ties (cable twist ties can also be used to repair a broken luggage zipper or tag)

☐ small binoculars if you are planning to visit scenic places

☐ inexpensive small compass if you are direction impaired

☐ small calculator (handy for calculating foreign currency exchange)

☐ deck of playing cards – great icebreaker, people all over the world love to play cards

☐ camera/video recorder and card reader or computer cables and extra batteries and memory cards or film

☐ mobile phone

☐ music player (i.e. iPod, MP3 player)

☐ headphones– also useful if you plan to talk on Skype in Internet cafes

☐ computer laptop or tablet/netbook and USB memory stick for backup and copying files to share – also bring a larger external storage disk if you have large files (i.e. photos) to backup

☐ foreign electricity adapter plugs for each country you plan to visit. Many countries share the same adapter plug but you may need a couple of different ones if you plan to visit countries in different regions. Go to *Kropla (www.kropla.com/electric2.htm)* for information on what foreign adapter plugs you will need. Secure your adapter to your appliance's plug with electrical or duct tape to insure it will not get left behind when you pull out the plug.

☐ electrical three-way plug – helpful if you have several chargers to deal with. This allows you to bring just one foreign electricity adapter plug and some hotel rooms have limited outlets.

☐ power cords, chargers, cables (including camera to computer), and extra batteries for all electronic devices (rechargeable devices are nice because you do not need to worry about batteries)

☐ voltage converter and transformer adaptors, if necessary (note: to avoid the need for voltage adaptors you should purchase electronic devices that are "dual-voltage" (adaptable to 110, 220, and 240 volts), ask your appliance dealer or electronic or travel store what you will need if your electrical appliances are not adaptable)

☐ swimming accessories (goggles and ear and nose plugs), if necessary

☐ sleep sheet and travel lock - if planning to stay in hostels, dorms, and campgrounds with lockers (choose silk or cotton, also good for areas suspected of having bedbugs)

☐ travel jewelry and small case (bring just a few versatile pieces, a small case like a soap container can help keep your jewelry from breaking, pack jewelry in separate small plastic bags to help keep them from getting snagged together)

☐ hair accessories: comb, folding hairbrush, clips, hair ties, curling iron, hair dyer, etc. – check with hotels to see if you need a hair dryer

☐ compact mirror

☐ lightweight immersion heater to boil water

☐ hearing aids, if necessary

☐ shoe shine pads, if necessary

☐ extra lightweight fold-up expandable zippered nylon duffel bag, if necessary

Travel Documents and Money

Security Wallet

As relevant to your needs, the following items need to be put away in a money belt for your security wallet to be carried with you and worn under your clothing. See Chapter 10 ("Security – Staying Safe on the Road") for more tips about security.

- ☐ cash – both local and U.S. dollars to exchange (try to get much of it in $20 bills)

- ☐ credit cards (Visa and MasterCard are the most widely accepted, taking 2 different ones is helpful in case one has a problem, having you and your travel partner each carry one is helpful in case either of you loses theirs you still have one while the other is being replaced)

- ☐ ATM debit cards (for 2 different accounts)

- ☐ passport and visas, photo ID (e.g. driver's license), or if needed, birth certificate (passports need to be valid for at least 6 months after departure)

- ☐ extra passport-type photos in case you need them for entry visas that are becoming more common

- ☐ driver's license, student ID card, auto club card, and/or hostel card

- ☐ traveler's checks and records

- ☐ prepaid telephone card

- ☐ transportation passes and vouchers

- ☐ medical insurance card

- ☐ original doctor's prescriptions for medicine and eyeglasses/ contact lens

- ☐ list of credit and debit card contact information as well as any PIN and access codes you may need

- ☐ list of emergency contacts (i.e. emergency contact person, 24-hour travel agent, home, medical and car insurance, and any other important contacts along with a list of doctor and lawyer names and numbers, allergies, medical history, special medication) – make this easily locatable so it can be accessed in case of an emergency.

Note: Refer to Chapter 12 ("Money and Credit Cards)" for recommendations concerning money and credit cards.

Other Documents to Remember

- ☐ copy of passports – copies are good to have in case you lose your passport. It is also handy for hotel check-in so you do not give up your passport.

- ☐ tickets, vouchers, and confirmations (i.e. hotel, airline, bus, train, cruise, E-tickets) – also make copies in case they are misplaced
- ☐ itinerary
- ☐ immunization certificates (e.g. yellow fever or other)
- ☐ traveler's checks record
- ☐ membership cards (i.e. AAA, AARP, hotel/hostel, frequent flier)
- ☐ medical, auto, and travel insurance papers
- ☐ trip cancellation and health insurance policies
- ☐ health forms
- ☐ customs declaration papers and sales receipts for item to be declared
- ☐ copy of all other important documents like prescriptions
- ☐ list of addresses and phone numbers of hotels where you will be staying and family addresses, phone numbers, and e-mail address to send postcards and stay in touch through the Internet

Rather than risking losing them, leave behind items you will not be using (i.e. car keys, department store and membership cards). It is very important to remember only one of many of the above items is necessary so reminding once again is wise… don't double up with your travel partner on things you can share.

How to Make Your Travel Wardrobe Work for You

Instead of bringing loads of clothes for every 'just-in-case' and fashion circumstance, you need to make your wardrobe work for you. To avoid weighing you down, your selective choice of garments should be versatile to give you an assortment of outfits and to serve you in a broad variety of weather and social situations. They should also be easily maintainable looking nice after washing. Avoid garments designed for a specific function. Every item of clothing should have many different ways of wearing it and be worn many times.

Here are some guidelines to help you minimize the size of your wardrobe while greatly expanding your choice of outfits:

Choose One Neutral Color Scheme

Neutral color items (not necessarily just one color) can be more easily mixed and matched. With less clothing you can mix and match to create many different looks without the need to bring loads of accessories like shoes, belts, etc. Solids, rather than prints, work better and can work for both casual and fancy. Solid black and white garments match well. Darker colors show dirt less. You can make use of brighter accessories to enhance your look.

Select Compact and Easily Maintained Fabrics

Clothing made of the modern attractive, quick-drying, wrinkle-resistant materials will give you much more use of each item and reduce the time maintaining them. Being able to easily wash your clothes along the way and have them look good after drying makes traveling light much easier because you can take far fewer garments. The following chapter offers useful tips about maintaining your clothes while traveling.

Think Layers

Instead of bulky coats and sweaters, pack thinner clothing that can be layered (unless you are going to a very cold climate). Several complementary lightweight layers will be useful because you can add or take off layers to be comfortable storing them in your daypack when the day warms up. Layers also gives you many more options for different outfits.

Pack Separates

Separates are comfortable, easier to pack, and will give you more options in mixing and matching. Try to choose casual/dressy separates to serve more purposes.

Bring with You Comfortable Clothes in Versatile Simple Classic Styles

You are on you way to enjoy an adventure, not to impress people. You will get more use from simple classic styles that lack bulk. Loose fitting clothes are more comfortable and will better accommodate your money belt. To make cleaning easier, avoid any clothing that are dry-clean only.

Bring Comfortable Shoes that are Cushioned and Broken In

To fully enjoy the wonders of this beautiful world you will probably be doing more walking than you normally do. Comfort is a top priority. Tired feet and blisters are not a good way to enjoy yourself. Many shoe manufacturers make stylish comfortable shoes with springy composition soles with good traction. Leather soles are usually too hard, smooth, and less water-resistant for rainy days.

Choose a shoe or sandal with an adjustable lace or strap to accommodate different thickness of socks and because your foot size and need for socks will change during the day. Also make sure they match the color scheme you have chosen for your wardrobe. Open styles allowing your feet to breath are more comfortable for warm and tropical weather. Take into account water repellency when selecting your shoes. You will have a much more enjoyable trip if you spend some time in choosing your travel shoes. Do this a month before you leave so you have time to break them in.

You Need to Dress Modestly in Many Countries

Modest dressing is especially important when visiting religious sites and in Asian and Muslim countries. This particularly true for women to not only to adhere to cultural norms but also to not attract undesired attention from men. Modesty means to not wear revealing clothes (skimpy tops and short hemlines showing bare arms, knees, and midriffs) and sometimes head, shoulders, and legs need to be covered. Women should substitute skirts, capris, and pants that cover the knees. In your daypack, women can bring a scarf to cover your head and shoulders as well as black socks and leggings to cover your legs and feet if needed. Also, women should wear nontransparent cover-ups for swimsuits when you are away from the beach. A good idea for men is pants with zip on and off legs described later under men's wardrobe.

Total Weight

We plan to take up to 25 pounds each in our main suitcase if we plan to go carry on for shorter and less demanding trips and about 40 pounds each for check on for longer or more demanding trips. This will keep you under most airline weigh limits with the ability to take a few souvenirs without shipping them home. Some international flights and smaller planes have limits of 20 kilograms for check-on luggage, which is about 44 pounds. Carry-on security rules may limit you on liquids and other items you can carry on airplanes. Check with your airline before leaving because requirements do change.

Our suitcases have weighed 50 pounds (OK, a little more) and they did become more difficult to manage – 10 extra pounds makes a big difference.

Also, as airlines tack on more fees, you risk extra charges if your luggage is too heavy.

If you use the guidelines above, the following wardrobe suggestions should provide a good baseline for your travel needs. Every person and each trip has special requirements so your final list may vary.

Suggested Travel Wardrobe (Women's and Men's) – Take Less and Have More

"The finest clothing made is a person's skin, but, of course, society demands something more than this."
~ Mark Twain

The following wardrobe suggestions are a baseline you should work to as you become a more experienced traveler. At first you may believe more is necessary. If you follow the guidelines in this chapter and begin to realize you do not need all the items you are use to taking and that traveling light is more enjoyable, the lower limits of this baseline will become easier to achieve.

This suggested selection of clothing is for a trip that has many different social and climate situations. For shorter trips and more simple trips like beach resorts or hiking, much less clothing is necessary. Special needs such as cold or tropical weather are addressed below.

The clothes you wear on the flight count as part of these guidelines, not in addition to them. You can wear your heavier and more bulky clothing and shoes on flights to lessen the weight of your suitcase.

Example Women's Wardrobe

- ☐ underwear (panties, bras, hose) and socks (casual and dressy) – bring a few pairs of each and wash them along the way, pantyhose are light, cheap, warm, and disposable, a sports bra is nice to have for active adventures

- ☐ silk long thermal underwear (tops and bottoms) – 1 pair is very compact and nice to have to layer for cold times, also nice to sleep in on cold nights

- ☐ leggings or tights (black works best)

☐ nightgown or large T-shirt (large T-shirt can also be used as a beach cover-up)

☐ swimsuit (quick drying, one piece may be more appropriate in some places, an optional second one is handy if you plan to be in the water a lot)

☐ sarong – for cover-up

☐ 3-5 shirts/blouses/tops (one lightweight long sleeved for sun protection, cotton/polyester blend is best)

☐ T-shirts/Tank tops (take only a couple of various styles but do not pack too many – you can purchase them along the way for great souvenirs)

☐ 2-3 shorts or capris (one pair of walking shorts with pockets, remember modesty is important in many countries so loose fitting knee-length may be appropriate)

☐ 2 skirts (knee-length may be more appropriate)

☐ 2 long pants/slacks (one dressy and one casual lightweight and loose-fitting, black and khaki is best, jeans are too warm for summer travel)

☐ 2-4 sweaters, jackets, button-up cardigans, or sleeveless vests (at least one sweater) - not bulky, remember lighter layers, lightweight fleece is nice and darker colors don't show wrinkles or stains as well

☐ dresses – a classic short versatile black wrinkle-resistant cocktail dress that can be dressed up or down with accessories will work for many situations including dressy events, light sundresses are convenient for warm days, a long dress may be necessary if more formal nights like cruising are in your plans)

☐ two-piece dress – gives you more options with other items

☐ 2-3 scarves/shawls/wraps – one lightweight, one heavier, one shawl-sized. A scarf can beautifully accessorize an outfit. Choosing patterns or brighter colors for your scarves is nice to be able to dress up your outfits – make sure they match the color scheme you have chosen. Scarves/shawls are also great for layering for protection from the sun or warmth substituting for a sweater or blanket on a plane or train. Also, in certain more religious areas a shawl-sized scarf is good for covering shoulders and heads.

- [ ] compact workout sports clothing
- [ ] 2 belts – day and evening in classic styles that match all your outfits
- [ ] 2 pairs of shoes (don't overdo this) – one dressy that matches all garments (e.g. low pump) and one for walking or running shoes if necessary
- [ ] 1-2 pair of sandals (one for walking and hiking)
- [ ] slippers (heavy socks work well in most situations)
- [ ] hats – sun and rain (get the collapsible travel type so they look good after being packed in you luggage)
- [ ] gloves or mittens, liners
- [ ] ear warmers
- [ ] 1 handbag (make it small and packable, simple and elegant styles also work for dressy occasions, consider one with a removable long shoulder strap for security)
- [ ] watch
- [ ] jewelry (earrings, necklaces, bracelets, pins, etc.) – to minimize the number choose basic styles in one color (gold or silver works best) and bring only those that can be used with many outfits, also do not risk being a target for thief or losing something valuable by taking anything flashy or of monetary or sentimental value, bring clip-on decorations to dress up pumps, remember showing conspicuous wealth can make you a target for thieves so keep it simple
- [ ] small travel umbrella – having a small travel umbrella in your daypack will allow you to continue your plans on a rainy day
- [ ] compact hooded raincoat or poncho – purchase a travel raincoat that folds down to a small package

Note: one thin hooded Gore-Tex jacket can substitute for several items above (raincoat and jacket). It is waterproof, wrinkle-resistant, and great for a range of temperatures because it is breathable. It also has internal zippered pockets for your security wallet and other valuables.

Example Men's Wardrobe

- [ ] underwear, undershirts, and socks (casual and dressy) – bring a few pairs of each and wash them along the way

☐ silk long thermal underwear (tops and bottoms) – 1 pair is very compact and nice to have to layer for cold times, also nice to sleep in on cold nights

☐ pajamas or large T-shirt

☐ swim trucks (quick drying with pockets to carry keys, etc., an optional second pair is handy if you plan to be in the water a lot)

☐ 3-5 shirts (one lightweight long sleeved for sun protection, cotton/polyester blend coarser-weave polo-type shirts work well in a variety of circumstances and wrinkle less easily)

☐ T-shirts (pack only a couple – you can purchase them along the way for great souvenirs)

☐ 2-3 shorts (one pair of walking shorts with pockets)

☐ 2-3 long pants/slacks (one dressy slacks and one casual lightweight and loose-fitting, khaki is best, jeans are too warm for summer travel) – a great idea is to have one made of washable material with legs that zip on and off. You can start your day with the legs on and then zip them off when the day warms up. They can also be used as shorts carrying the legs in your daypack in case you need them for entrance to more formal or religious sites or if the evening turns cooler.)

☐ 2-3 jackets or sweaters (at least one sweater) - not bulky, remember lighter layers, lightweight fleece is nice and darker colors don't show wrinkles or stains as well

☐ windbreaker

☐ dress jacket, shirt, tie, and cufflinks, if necessary

☐ compact workout sport clothing

☐ 2 belts – casual and dressy. Purchase a reversible black/brown dressy belt. Along with a casual belt, these two belts will give you many options.

☐ 2 pairs of shoes – one dressy that matches all garments and one walking (one pair of all-purpose walking/dress shoes often works well unless needed for hiking or running)

☐ 1 pair of all-purpose sandals for walking and hiking

☐ slippers (heavy socks work well in most situations)

- ☐ hats – sun and rain
- ☐ gloves or mittens, liners
- ☐ ear warmers
- ☐ watch
- ☐ small travel umbrella – having a small travel umbrella in your daypack will allow you to continue your plans on a rainy day
- ☐ compact hooded raincoat or poncho – purchase a travel raincoat that folds down to a small package

Note: one thin hooded Gore-Tex jacket can substitute for several items above (raincoat, jacket, windbreaker). It is waterproof, wrinkle-resistant, and great for a range of temperatures because it is breathable. It also has internal zippered pockets for your security wallet and other valuables.

Special Wardrobe Needs for Both Women and Men

For cold weather needs, remember layers are better than packing bulky sweaters. You may consider reducing some of the items above and adding or substituting the following:

- ☐ remember the silk long thermal underwear (tops and bottoms)
- ☐ pantyhose are light, cheap, warm, and disposable
- ☐ wool or fleece socks and sock liners
- ☐ substitute a pair of heavier pants like jeans for the shorts
- ☐ turtleneck instead of T-shirt
- ☐ substitute a wool or micro fleece shirt or sweater for the light long-sleeved shirt
- ☐ warm shoes
- ☐ warm hat and gloves
- ☐ heavier sweater or coat

For tropical and hot climate travel, you should choose lightweight, loose fitting, and quick drying clothing that will protect you from the sun and insects. A trip to your outdoor clothing store will yield great benefits of enjoying your trip to tropical and hot climate areas. Remember to eliminate and substitute items to the above list, not add to the list.

For more active trips like camping and hiking, other special needs may be required.

Important Packing Tips to Make Your Trip More Enjoyable

We have learned many lessons the hard way. These 22 additional simple planning and packing tips can make your travel adventure even more enjoyable:

1) **Start planning your packing list a least a month before leaving.** This will allow you time to shop for the things you will need. Selecting your travel clothing and setting up or replenishing your travel kits takes much longer than packing. Get the clothes you plan to take cleaned and mended. Use the suggested packing lists in this book to make a shopping list of the things you will need. Note: it is a good idea is to take an inventory after every trip taking note of the things you needed or did not use to be better prepared or lighter packed for your next trip.

2) **Determine what activities you will be participating in and consult weather information.** The Internet is great for good weather websites on your planned destinations to help you determine what you will need to bring. Try **The Weather Channel (www.weather.com)**.

3) **Before packing your suitcase, make piles of everything you plan to take.** This gives you the opportunity to eliminate a few more items as well as recheck your check-off lists. Sometimes you forget what you put in when you pack directly into your suitcase and will be tempted to throw in a few more things.

4) **Consider using space-saving vacuum packing bags.** These will organize your clothing and remove the air so they take up less space and can be more easily located. They are also be used for your wet and dirty laundry bag. These packing bags can be convenient but be sure not to fill up the extra space in your suitcase with more things because you still need to be concerned about weight.

5) **Before you leave on your trip, pack your luggage and walk with it for 20 minutes.** Also, carry it for short periods of time. If you can, carry it up some stairs. If you find it uncomfortable, eliminate items.

6) **Pack the items you will need most last in your suitcase.** They will be accessible first when you open your suitcase. This changes as your

trip evolves from cold to warm areas or city to outdoors. To protect fragile items, pack them in the middle of your suitcase surrounded by clothing. To conserve space and to keep things from moving, fill spaces with rolled t-shirts, leggings, swimsuits, nightwear, shoes, accessory pouches, etc.

7) **Pack travel gear, accessory kits, and other accessories in the same place.** This includes your raincoat, umbrella, gloves, pouches, etc. and do it every time you repack. This helps us locate those things quickly when we need them.

8) **If you are traveling to humid or rainy destinations, you should consider packing your clothes and water sensitive accessories in a large garbage bag before placing them in your suitcase.** This will help insure they stay dry even if your suitcase is left out in the rain in transit.

9) **Leave behind anything you would hate to lose.** Consider taking inexpensive watches and costume jewelry leaving behind expensive clothing and electrical gadgets.

10) **Consider taking older clothes you are about to discard.** Leave them behind as you go. This leaves space for new clothing items you purchase along the way. If you know you are going to purchase a new item (e.g. hat) at your destination, don't bring one from home.

11) **Cover each pair of shoes with a plastic bag. Larger plastic bags are available from stores or the newspaper.** This keeps the rest of your clothes clean and helps prevent scuffs on your shoes during transit. Also, if your shoes do not pack down, stuff socks, underwear, and appliances in them to conserve packing space. Wear your heaviest pair of shoes on the airplane to conserve space and weight in your suitcase.

12) **Pack the heaviest items at the end of your suitcase.** Do this near the wheels at the end that contacts the ground when it is standing. This will help stabilize your suitcase from toppling over when you need to stop. This will also help keep the heavy items from crushing the other items when you are rolling your suitcase.

13) **Take a lightweight foldable wet bag.** This is very useful for garments that need to dry or to be laundered at your next designation. This is a big help in keeping the rest of your clothes fresh.

14) **Air pressure and temperature changes can cause liquids to leak.** To

avoid a mess in your suitcase, pack all liquids and creams in high-quality bottles (preferably smaller 3 oz. travel bottles). Squeeze out the excess air each time you close it and do not completely fill the bottle. Place the bottles inside plastic sealable bags and then place these bags into your organizer pouches.

15) **Some items needed for a specific portion of your trip can often be purchased or rented when you arrive.** Items such as sports equipment (i.e. snorkel gear, tennis rackets), beach mats, wide bream hats, etc. can be left behind when you leave saving you the packing space and effort of carrying them for your whole trip.

16) **Avoid extra luggage fees for heavy suitcases.** Wear or pack in your carry-on/daypack bag heavy items such as shoes, belts, jackets, paper items, etc. Keep putting on or packing more things in your carry-on until your suitcase is under the weight limit. If you are allowed a second check-on suitcase, you can take with you an extra lightweight fold-up expandable zippered nylon duffel bag in your suitcase. Put items in your duffel bag and repack later. An extra duffel bag is also handy for those who like to collect souvenirs. A better way is to follow the suggestions of this chapter and take less.

17) **Always carry all valuable documents in your money belt under your clothes.** Do this for items such as passports, cash, credit and debit cards, traveler's checks, tickets, prescriptions, and other important documents that will be hard to replace or cause you great inconvenience or cost if lost.

18) **Suitcases can be targets for theft when left unattended.** When your main suitcases are not in sight while traveling (checked on planes, buses, etc.), be sure to place in your daypack all remaining valuables not in your money belt (i.e. cameras, computers, jewelry, travel documents) and take them with you. Watch your daypack closely because thieves in many parts of the world are very good at opening your daypack while you are distracted. Also, unattended luggage in public transportation stations, especially airports, can create a serious security alert so keep close watch on them.

19) **Take your small daypack with you each day.** Include items you will need during the day and night (i.e. sweater, change of clothing, camera, literature, etc.) so you do not have to return to the hotel to

enjoy your next activity. Clean out your daypack every day to make it ready for the needs of the next day. Carrying the weight of things you do not need will make you fatigue quicker.

20) ***Airplanes, trains, and buses can be chilly.*** Take a light jacket, sweater, and/or scarf with you in your carry-on daypack when traveling.

21) ***Checked suitcases sometimes get lost or delayed.*** It is wise to take a few necessary items with you in your carry-on bag. Take a few items that will make your stay at your initial destination a bit easier until your bags catch up to you or you have time to replace things. Good items to consider are basic toiletries, toothbrush, medications, glasses, bathing suit, causal cover up, light sweater, etc. If traveling with a partner, you may consider packing a few essential items in each other's suitcase in case just one of your suitcases is lost or delayed.

22) ***Take a small medical and first aid kit in your daypack/carry-on bag.*** You will be able to quickly address physical issues as they may arise. In case you may need them before you can get to your main suitcase or if your main suitcase is lost or delayed, carry half of your prescription medicine along with a small portion of vital items, for instance pain reliever, antacid, antihistamine, band aids, toilet paper, hand sanitizer and cream, plastic bag to protect your camera in case of rain, and whatever you may need. Place these items in a zip-lock bag so you can remove it when going through airport security. See a doctor if symptoms last for more than a couple of days or unhealthy symptoms occur.

Conclusion

We hope you enjoy using these suggestions to make your trip more enjoyable. Every person and every trip has unique requirements. Your travel list will likely include items not mentioned in this chapter. Remember other than being clean and presentable, how you look and wearing different clothing every day has little to do with the enjoyment you receive from traveling. The joys of travel are to have fun, enjoy this wonderful world, learn more about different people as well as yourself, and bring back wonderful memories.

Taking less clothing means you are going to wear them more often. The next chapter offers instructions on how to keep your clothes clean and fresh.

Chapter 14

Keep Your Clothes Clean And Fresh

In this chapter...

Looking nice and keeping your clothes clean and mended is important. When we took shorter trips we could collect our laundry and do it when we returned home. This chapter explains how you can stay looking good while on a trip or stay and do it with fewer clothes.

Laundry Options

In order to take fewer clothes and keep them clean and fresh, we do a little laundry like underwear and more soiled or smelly items about twice a week or more often depending on how active we are. We collect these items in a sealable wet bag so not to add odors to the rest of our clothing.

Washing and drying your clothes in a self-service coin-operated laundromat is a good way to maintain your wardrobe. You can also send your clothes out to be cleaned at your

These guys have their self-cleaning tuxedos on in Chile – a penguin wedding?

hotel. Using a laundromat is time consuming and often they are not easily available. Send-out laundry services on the road can be expensive although it is sometimes a nice indulgence.

You will find you will often have just a few items that are of need of cleaning so finding a laundromat or sending them out is not worth the time or effort. Often, we find it is much easier to maintain our clothes in our room. It may feel at bit strange at first if you are not familiar doing it this way. If you follow the fairly easy and quick clothes washing procedure described below, you will become accustomed to doing it this way and it will save you a lot of time and expense.

Easy Procedure for Washing Your Clothes

1) It is important to take wrinkle-resistant fast-drying travel clothing. Avoid taking clothing with special cleaning needs (e.g. dry clean only). Do treat yourself to a trip to the travel/outdoor clothing store near you or visit the online travel stores listed at the beginning of the previous chapter.

2) Before you start, check the labels on your clothes for specific instructions. Some are to be cleaned in cold water only or need to be dry cleaned.

3) If you only have underwear, socks, and light clothing to wash, you can rinse them out in the shower. Using a little shampoo or detergent is an easy way to take care of it. Be sure to rinse them thoroughly to get out the shampoo or detergent. You should avoid using hand soap because it can build up a residue in your clothes.

4) Otherwise, fill the sink or bathtub with lukewarm water. This is where your sink stopper comes in handy (often missing from hotel sinks and tubs) that you should bring along. Add some shampoo or cold-water detergent.

5) Pretreat stains with your stain remover. More about stains later. Before you use your stain remover on delicate garments test it on a place of the garment that does not show (e.g. inside seem or the hem) in case the color of the garment is not stay fast. Do not use bleach.

6) Put your laundry in the water and actively swirl it around. Do not squeeze or twist so not to cause wrinkling of your garments. Gently rub the stained and extra soiled areas. Then gently squeeze the soapy water through garments like sweaters.

7) Let soak in the water for about 10-15 minutes. If very soiled or stained repeat the above step (#6).

8) Let the water drain out and refill the sink or bathtub with cold water and rinse the garments thoroughly. Swirl the garments in the water. Get all the detergent out otherwise it may discolor the garment. You may have to repeat this step.

9) To remove excess water from thicker items or if you want to quicken the drying process, lay the garments on a towel flat pulling out the wrinkles and then fold the towel over the garment. Press lightly. Again do not directly squeeze or twist your garments so not to cause wrinkling. Some garments can be rolled in your towel and lightly squeezed. Underwear you do not care about wrinkles can be twisted and squeezed to remove water.

10) Hang your garments to dry in a place where water dripping from them will not harm anything. Towel racks, shower or curtain rods, or a clothes cord work well. You may want to place a hotel towel under the wet garments. If draped over, remember to reverse them after awhile to get the other side dry. We often use clothes hangers (plastic is better but some of our dry cleaner's wire hangers work well if nothing else is available) and hang garments from places in our room where air can get to them from both sides – near an air vent or open window is best. For pants, use the hangers with the pants roller to avoid placing a wrinkle. Always straighten out any folds in the garments when you hang them so not to cause wrinkles.

This will look a bit funny at first but you will get used to it and who is going to see it but you and the maid. It is best if you have the opportunity to hang the garments outside on a warm day. Don't leave them out in the direct sun too long or they may fade. In high humidity areas it may take a couple of days to dry so do not start doing laundry unless you will be there for a while.

Other Clothing Maintenance Tips

Special Needs

Wool takes time to dry and delicate garments like some sweaters are best to lie flat on a towel to dry to avoid stretching. We prefer fleece and travel sweaters and jackets that are easier to care for.

Clothing in Luggage

It is important not to leave wet clothing in your wet bag for more than a day. Wash and/or hang them out to dry as soon as you can. If you are planning to stay at some destinations for more than a few days, you should regularly hang up most your clothes to air out along your trip. Even in your suitcase, clothing collects smells and moisture. The extra wire hangers from the dry cleaners come in handy here.

Open your shoes as best as possible every time by putting the 'tongue' up and out to let them air out and dry inside. It is a good idea to take all your shoes out of your suitcase whenever you can and let them air out.

Removing Wrinkles

Removing wrinkles can be less of a worry if you take wrinkle-resistant travel clothing. Often all it takes is hanging up tomorrow's outfit the day before and many of the wrinkles will diminish. You can minimize wrinkles in your clothes by properly folding or rolling each item of clothing well every time you repack. Rolled items are less likely to wrinkle. Pack formalwear in plastic dry cleaner bags to help prevent wrinkles.

A good trick to remove some wrinkles is to hang your clothes near the shower and take a hot shower with the bathroom room door closed. Wet your hand and moisten the tougher wrinkles. Let the garment hang in the steamy bathroom. Then let the garment dry before wearing to prevent placing wrinkles back in.

Because of we use these techniques, we do not take a travel iron with us. If needed, irons can be borrowed at most non-budget hotels and can be helpful in making your clothing (especially formalwear) look sharp. Travel steamers can be used to get many wrinkles out and weigh less than irons. Spray-on fabric wrinkle remover (e.g. Downey Wrinkle Release) is also available.

Stains

Stains do not need to be a big worry if you know how to take care of them. When you stain your clothes, immediately wet the stain with cold water and blot out the stain. You may have to repeat this several times. Put a towel on the back of the stain so not to wet and possibly stain the rest of the garment. Try to get the stain out as best you can before using heat (i.e. hot water, dryer) because heat may set the stain. Try using baby wipes or baby powder as described in the following paragraphs. Then use your stain remover, as suggested above, when washing the garment. To save some time, you may only need to wash the area of the stain.

Baby wipes make a good stain remover for many fabrics and other travel gear. The use of baby wipes to remove a stain can save you having to wash the entire garment. One traveler told us they used baby wipes to remove red wine stains. Baby wipes have many other uses such as wiping handles and toilet seats, getting makeup off, or even giving yourself a nice clean up during long flights or while you are away from your hotel. You should consider taking about ten or more along with you.

Oil stains often resist normal cleaning procedures. We carry a small bottle of baby powder to remove oil and make-up stains (also nice for smelly shoes). To prevent setting the oil stain, before you wash the garment lightly rub a little baby powder over oil stain. Be sure the garment is dry before you start. Let it sit for a few minutes and then rub the baby powder off with a towel. You may need to repeat this several times for best results.

Removing Lint

Scotch tape rolled backwards around your hand makes for a good lint remover.

Mending Your Clothes

Sometimes your clothes will require a little mending. You should bring a compact travel sewing kit. Many hotels have these in the room you can take for your next trip. You can make up your own travel sewing kit by including a sewing needle and various colors of thread matching your wardrobe wrapped around a small piece of cardboard. Other items that may be helpful are a thimble, straight pins, safety pins, and some standard buttons.

In other to maintain your relationships, staying in touch with friends and family is important when you are away. The next chapter offers cost-saving tips on many ways to stay in touch.

Chapter 15

Staying in Touch with Friends and Family

Traveling or living away from home can create a feeling of isolation from your friends and family. Good friendships and family relationships should be nurtured while you are away so you can return to your life with these relationships intact. Modern technology has made it much easier to stay in touch and maintain relationships with friends and family. In this chapter we review how you can stay in touch inexpensively.

Ways to Save Money Staying Connected by Phone

Having a cell phone (often called 'mobile' phone) with you while traveling can be a huge convenience. You can quickly make a hotel reservation, catch up with traveling partners or interesting locals you have met, handle a crisis, or stay in touch with folks back home. Smartphones with Internet connection have many more uses. You should always be aware that using your cell phone could be one of the more expensive ways to stay in touch. Warn your friends not to call you while you are traveling unless there is an emergency. Later in this chapter we review much less expensive ways like Skype, e-mail, social networking, and blogging.

Most major U.S. cell phone companies give you an option to choose plans that allow international calls. Sometimes they offer temporary service for a short time. The rates vary and can be expensive. For the best coverage around the world, take a cell phone that is GSM compatible and issued within the last 2 years. Different countries use different frequency bands so a triband or quadband phone may be needed.

Before leaving, be sure to visit or call your cell phone provider and carefully appraise your phone and your plan to be sure you are covered in the countries you plan to visit. You should be aware that cell phones, especially the new smartphones (e.g. iPhone, BlackBerry, Android) can run up huge bills for calls and accessing data from the Internet when you travel abroad. Check with your provider to see what features (i.e. data roaming, fetch new data) should be turned off to avoid these charges. It probably is best to do your Internet searching elsewhere.

In many of the countries you are visiting, local prepaid options can be a fraction of the cost you will pay with your cell phone company. Your cell phone must be unlocked to be able to take advantage of this. An easy way to see if your cell phone is unlocked is to put another SIM card in it and test it. Contact your cell phone provider before you leave on your trip to learn how to unlock your phone. It is relatively easy to grab a SIM card with prepaid minutes from most convenience stores or mobile service vendors. You will have a new phone number requiring you to tell everyone who may call you or use call forwarding. Some features you may be used to using may not be available.

Alternatively, if you are unable to unlock your phone or it is not compatible, you may be able to purchase or rent an inexpensive basic cell phone locally and use a local SIM card with prepaid minutes. A calling card is another option where you can be make less expensive calls from any phone. You can find more information about international calling cards at **CallingCards (www.callingcards.com)**.

Remember to store your phone numbers in the phone itself, rather than on the SIM card or you'll lose access to them when you switch SIM cards. When storing phone numbers, include the plus (+) sign and the country code so your calls will go through, regardless from where you are calling.

Talk Cheaply with Skype

Another much less costly option is using an Internet Voice Over Internet Protocol (VoIP) service such as **Skype (www.skype.com)**, where you can make calls and send instant messages through the Internet. The cost is free for Skype users to each other and often just pennies per minute for other calls around the world. You can even share video images of each other if you have compatible devices. Just go to Skype and download their software. Internet cafes sometimes will have Skype available for your use. You can set up an account with a minimum investment. Skype is available as a smartphone app on the Android, BlackBerry, iPhone, iPad, and Windows Phone 7.

Remember if you use your smartphone to use Skype, you may still need to have an international plan, or even better use Wi-Fi, to avoid large data charges. Another VoIP service is offered by **Google Voice (www.google.com/googlevoice/about.html)**.

E-mail and Social Networking

In most places in the world, connecting to the Internet through Wi-Fi or other connection is available for free or low cost through your hotel, a local restaurant, or an Internet store (cybercafe). You can locate cybercafés around the world using **Cybercafes (www.cybercafes.com)**.

E-mail is a wonderful way to remain in touch. You can send messages to friends and family or even send updates to a group list of names. We use e-mail to contact hotels and other companies to learn about availability and negotiate prices. We use **Google's Gmail (www.mail.google.com)**. It is free, feature rich, logged into directly without using webmail, and works well everywhere we go.

Social networking sites also allow you to stay connected with your friends and family. We use **Facebook (www.facebook.com)** and post regular updates and photos of our adventures along the way. We also stay in touch this way with people we meet.

By making regular use of e-mail, Facebook, Skype, and our travel blog, it is very easy and very affordable to stay in touch with our friends and family. When we arrive back home, many who have followed our adventures are already caught up and excited to learn more. Some of our friends are excited about our travel updates and tell us they live vicariously through us.

Bringing Your Computer Laptop or Tablet/Netbook Along

We bring a lightweight laptop along with us on our travel adventures. Modern computer tablets/netbooks can do many of the things we do with our laptop with much less weight to carry. It is wonderful to conveniently connect to the Internet in our hotel room eliminating the need to find a computer or Internet store. We remain much more connected this way. Also, there are many other things having a laptop on our trip allows us to do we cannot do on the Internet. We use our laptop computer conveniently connecting to the Internet Wi-Fi in our hotel room for many reasons listed below:

- Send and receive e-mail
- Stay connected through social networking sites such as Facebook
- Do research for hotel rooms, flights, and other reservations
- Research things to do and what's happening locally
- Learn more about the places we are visiting
- Update our travel blog
- Check the weather to plan our days
- Stay in touch with world news
- Check our bank, credit card, and investment accounts

Other things we use our laptop for that cannot be done at Internet cafes:

- Connect with Skype (not always available at Internet stores because it requires a microphone)
- Store, edit, and organize our photos
- Show slideshows of photos – you quickly become popular
- Create Word documents of our trip notes, updates, and blog

postings – nice for a permanent record and to be able to quickly download if you must pay for Internet connection

- Play music and watch movies
- Store e-mail, articles, and books (even travel books)
- Have reference articles on the places we are visiting
- Save contacts, account information, and important documents
- Read a book
- Write this book

There are downsides to carrying a laptop computer. They do add weight, can be stolen, and need to be easily accessible when going through security. With advancements in technology, computer tablet/netbooks and smartphones can do many of these functions and require you carrying much less weigh. Also, a flash drive can store a large amount of data if you plan to use Internet cafes. If you do plan to take some device with you, evaluate your needs and shop around to investigate the option best for you. Ask lots of questions, especially about the after purchase costs such as international data and voice plans.

Tape a business card or a piece of paper with your contact information on the bottom of your electronic device. With the new airport security and making travel connections, some devices do get left behind.

As a reminder, the following are things to remember to bring along with you when planning to bring electrical devices:

- Smartphone or computer laptop or tablet/netbook and USB memory stick for backup and copying files to share – also bring a larger external storage disk if you have large files (e.g. photos) to backup

- Foreign electricity adapter plugs for each country you plan to visit. Many countries share the same adapter plug but you may need a couple of different ones if you plan to visit countries in different regions. Go to **Kropla (www.kropla.com/electric2.htm)** for information on what foreign adapter plugs you will need.

- Electrical three-way plug – helpful if you have several chargers to deal with. This allows you to bring just one foreign electricity adapter plug and some hotel rooms have limited outlets.

- Power cords, chargers, cables (including camera to computer) and extra batteries for all electronic devices (rechargeable devices are nice because you do not need to worry about batteries)

- Voltage converter and transformer adaptors, if necessary (note: to avoid the need for voltage adaptors you should purchase electronic devices that are "dual-voltage" (adaptable to 110, 220, and 240 volts), ask your appliance dealer or electronic or travel store what you will need if your electrical appliances are not adaptable)

- Headphones – also useful if you plan to use Skype in Internet cafes or play music

Blogging Made Easy

A blog, short for web-log, can be used to share your travel adventure and serve as a permanent memory of your experience. Text, photos, and videos can be shared and you can receive comments.

We use Google's free blogging tool, **Blogger (www.blogger.com)** for creating and hosting our blog. It is powerful and easy to use for producing uncomplicated blogs. There are other blogging tools you pay for offering more features so you may want to investigate other options if you think your requirements are more complex.

To get started with Google's Blogger is straightforward. Create a Google account, choose a name for your blog that will be displayed when published, and then select a template for your blog's design. You can change templates at a later date if you want to. Google will host your blog for free on blogspot.com. Once your blog is set up, Blogger has a basic editor that works like a word processor so you do not need to know fancy Internet language (although those who do know HTML can also use it). Click on "New Post", enter a title of your blog posting (e.g. "Jerusalem, Israel"), and then write your blog posting.

Blogger's editor allows you to boldface, italic, and check the spelling of your text. A nice feature is adding links to other websites. We use this to direct viewers to our Flickr travel photo website to view more photos on each place we visit. Now it is time to upload photos and videos and post them to your blog. Just click on the 'Add Image' or 'Add Video' icons to do so.

Your blog is ready to post now. You can preview it, save it as a draft, or just go for it by clicking "Publish Post". You can go back and edit any post by clicking on "Edit Posts" after selecting the 'Posting' tab of your Blogger interfaces.

Other things you can do are:

- Review your viewers' comments ("Comment")
- Give your blog a title and description among many other things ("Settings")
- Edit the layout of your blog ("Design")
- Make money with Google AdSense ads ("Monetize")
- Check how many people are visiting your blog ("Stats")
- Create a profile page ("Dashboard")

You can do some online research and learn more about using Blogger. Also, review other blogs and see what they are doing. When you get more familiarized with using Blogger, play around with these features to create an even more interesting blog.

Here are some tips we use to help organize our blogging. Create separate documents and files on your computer laptop to write and edit your blogs and collect photos. This is helpful for several reasons. You can write each blog posting and collect the best photos over time. You can also quickly download the posting and photos to the blog, your photo website, and Facebook when ready and connected to the Internet. From our separate photo file, the top three or four photos go on our blog and many more (about 10-25) go on our Flickr photo website. Before posting, be sure to edit the chosen photos and downside them so they will download faster – viewing photos on the Internet does not require high resolution.

When writing your blog posts keep in mind most people do not have the time to read long posts. Include the most interesting highlights and stories. I am a history bluff so you will see a lot of history and why this place is significant in our blog.

Please view our ***travel blog (www.UnhookNow.com)*** for a simple example using Google's free Blogger tool and our online ***travel photo files (www.flickr. com/photos/unhooknow/sets)*** using Yahoo's Flickr tool.

Conclusion

In addition to these modern technologies, your friends and family will enjoy a simple postcard from exotic places. The local stamps are also interesting.

Staying in touch with your friends and family is important and relatively easy to do with modern technology. New ways will surface as new technology becomes available. Remember to enjoy yourself and not get too involved sitting in front of computer screens (large and small). The world is your 'screen' – enjoy it.

Taking home memorable photos can be better than souvenirs. In the next chapter, we reveal the secrets of the pros so you can take magical photos of your travel adventures.

Chapter 16

Take Travel Photos Like a Pro

❚n this chapter...

"To me, photography is an art of observation. It's about finding something interesting in an ordinary place... I've found it has little to do with the things you see and everything to do with the way you see them."

~ Ansel Adams (American Photographer, 1902-1984)

We have all seen them. Trying to hold back our yawns, we view photo after photo of our friend's boring snapshots of people standing in front of famous travel sites. The photos you bring back from your trip will be your lasting memory of the trip. Having interesting and heart-warming photos to enjoy for years to come and be proud to share with your friends and family are better than most souvenirs. Developing photography skills make you a more observant and perceptive traveler. Not loading up on souvenirs saves you money, avoids weighing you down while you travel, and helps eliminate clutter at home.

This chapter is targeted to the amateur and intermediate photographer offering tried and true methods to help you make your travel photos more interesting and memorable. More advanced photographers may also find some new interesting tips as well as many good reminders.

Choice of Camera

You do not need expensive cameras to bring back great photos. Although, on our trips we do take both a larger more expensive DSLR camera as well as our compact point-and-shoot camera, many of our best photos are from our small pocket size 'point-and-shoot' camera. For the amateur photographer, learning more about how to take a good photo, as explained in this chapter, will do more for the quality of your photos than hauling around expensive bulky camera equipment. Once you do become more familiar with photography techniques, better gear does have its advantages.

Because camera technology has advanced so much, you do not need to buy expensive photo equipment. Today $150 will purchase a nice pocket size compact 'point-and-shoot' camera including some of the extra accessories suggested below. To get a point-and-shoot camera with even better features, you may want to budget $200-350 for a camera with more advanced capabilities and an extra battery, a couple of memory cards, and small case.

Before purchasing a camera, go to a camera store that carries a wide number of different cameras. Hold them in you hands and play with the controls. It should feel comfortable and be easy to adjust the controls so you will make use of the additional features. Some of the top brand manufacturers for compact point-and-shoot cameras are Canon, Nikon,

Panasonic, Fuji, Pentax, and Casio. You should do some research on the Internet before purchasing to see what is offered and what users say about different cameras.

The capabilities of compact point-and-shoot cameras are advancing rapidly offering more features at better prices. For the amateur photographer, at the time of writing this book, a camera with the following features will serve you well:

Go Digital (Over Film) for Many Reasons

Professionals shoot digital now because digital quality is very good. Digital also has many advantages over using film. Going digital allows you to experiment more and learn faster because you can view your photos immediately. Your photos will be easier to manage, send to friends through the Internet, create blogs, and send to printing services. Wonderful photo editing programs are available for digital photos so you can enhance your photos. Also, your digital camera's photo storage devices are not harmed when going through security screenings where extra care must be taken for film.

Compact Pocket Size with Built-in Flash

Being able to have your camera with you all the time is very important to take advantage of all photo opportunities as they come up. When it is pocket sized, you will more likely carry your camera at all times of the day and night. Being inconspicuous in your pocket or daypack draws less attention to you for security reasons.

6+ MP (Megapixels)

Too much emphasize is often placed on megapixel rating (photo data storage capacity). 6 MP is more than enough if you plan to display photos on the Internet and make standard sized prints. Larger megapixel capacity may be helpful to avoid the photos appearing grainy if you plan to make large size prints. Also larger megapixel capacity is nice to be able to crop and blow up sections of your photos. The megapixel capacity of modern cameras is increasing so getting a new camera with 10 or more megapixels is not uncommon or overly expensive. Do keep in mind that more megapixels take more storage on your memory cards.

Large LCD Screen

It is helpful to have the largest LCD screen you can because it is where you view potential images you plan to photograph as well as playback photos for review, analysis, and sharing. LCD screen sizes are measured diagonally. A good minimum is 2.7 inches (larger is even better).

At Least 3X Optical Zoom Lens (Larger Even Better)

The word 'optical' is important because optical zoom physically moves the camera lens to zoom in on a subject. Extra 'digital' zoom is often available but it just magnifies the image without capturing more information. Focusing in too much with the digital zoom feature of your camera often produces grainy (less clear) photos. We find our 14X optical zoom camera on our point-and-shoot camera very handy in capturing full detail for distant images.

Pre-programmed Scene Modes

Pre-programmed scene modes are described in the next section. They are useful to be able to quickly and easily capture great images. Having a dial on the outside of your camera to access the basic pre-programmed modes is very helpful and highly recommended.

Image Stabilization (IS) or Vibration Reduction (VR)

This feature gives you the ability to get clearer photos reducing the problems of motion and vibration caused by you holding your camera.

Ability to Turn the Flash Off and On

Very helpful feature explained in more detail later in this chapter.

AF (Auto Focus) Lock

Continues to focus on your main subject while pressing the shutter release button halfway. How to use this feature is explained later in this chapter.

Self Timer

This feature takes your photo after a short delay – Usually with options from 2 to 10 seconds. In addition to allowing the photographer to be in the photo, the self-timer feature has other benefits (also explained later in this chapter) to improve your photos in low light and other situations.

Rechargeable Battery

Not being required to bring or purchase batteries is a blessing, especially on a longer trip. You should ask about battery life (length of operation) because not all batteries are created equal. It is good to purchase one extra rechargeable battery to be able to have a backup battery on those days when you use your camera for a long time or in the case you forgot to recharge your battery. You do not want to miss any of those precious photos – we know because it has happened to us. Try to select a camera with a charger that supports dual-voltage so you do not need a voltage adaptor when traveling overseas. It is always good to remember to recharge your camera batteries every day.

Extra Large High Capacity (High Speed) Storage Memory Cards

Fast download capability is good to have. 8 MB (megabytes) is nice, 16 MB or more is better. Large storage capacity is necessary if you do not plan to bring a laptop computer on your trip. A good rule of thumb is to bring twice what you think you will need. The high-speed download capacity frees up the camera quicker for your next shot. A couple of seconds will seem a long time when capturing the best shot. If you plan to shoot a large number of photos and movies, take even more memory cards with you. You can buy them along the way but you may find it troublesome to find the right type (e.g. high-capacity for fast downloading). Tip: Every day we view our photos on the camera and delete the redundant and obviously bad ones to free up space on our memory cards.

Video Capability (Movie Mode for Shooting Movies)

Video capability (HD is nice) is also good although not necessary. Movies capture sound and motion and are fun to watch. Many modern cameras have this feature. We enjoy watching the movies produced from our 'point-and-shoot' camera and they are very popular with our friends and family.

Other Accessories

A small lightweight camera case is valuable to have to help protect your point-and-shoot camera. We also take a USB card reader. This makes transferring photos easier and eliminates needing the camera to computer cable. Having a card reader is also handy to share photos with other fellow travelers. Having a tripod as an accessory is helpful for more advanced photography although a tripod can come in handy from time to time for amateurs. Smaller travel tripods about 4-6 inches tall can be taken along and set up on walls or other supports. Some tips on how to get great photos without using a tripod are presented later in this chapter.

If your adventures are rugged, take you to areas with lots of water, or you want to take photos underwater, consider an adventure (underwater) camera that is waterproof, shockproof, and freeze proof. This takes away a lot of the worries of keeping your camera safe from the elements and rougher treatment. Some of the better waterproof cameras have most of the features mentioned above.

Using Your Camera's Pre-programmed Scene Modes to Get Better Photos

The pre-programmed (pre-set) scene modes that appear on the outside dial (sometimes in menus) of modern cameras are extremely helpful to amateur photographers. These modes automatically adjust settings (flash, focus, shutter speed, aperture, ISO, and white balance) in your camera to enable you to take better photos in specific scenes and different circumstances. As you become a more experienced photographer you will want to experiment with your own manual adjustments of these settings that are available to you on most cameras. Until then, you can make use of your camera's pre-programmed modes to improve your photos.

To better understand the operations of the pre-programmed modes a brief description of a few photography terms is important. Very simply, your photos are exposures of light coming from your image through the lens of your camera. The aperture is the size of the opening of the shutter and the shutter speed is how long the shutter stays open when the photo is taken. ISO is a measure of sensitivity to light.

Using a combination of aperture, shutter speed, and ISO settings determines the exposure and depth of field of your photo. Exposure is how much light from your image is recorded and depth of field is how deep (distance from camera) your image will be in focus. A wide depth of field is good for landscapes while a narrow depth of field, with backgrounds blurred, better emphasizes your main subject like portraits of people. Other factors also come into play such as white balance, focus, and flash that are further explained in this chapter.

Fortunately for us amateurs all this is controlled pretty well using the camera's pre-programmed modes. All you have to do is choose the right mode for your circumstance. Before purchasing your compact point-and-shoot camera spend a little time playing with the controls to see if you are comfortable using them. You should read the operation manual for your camera to help you understand the best use of your particular camera. The following is a brief review of some of the more popular and useful pre-programmed modes:

Automatic Mode

A Good results in many conditions can be had by setting your camera to auto mode and leaving it there. This mode is normally marked in a special color like green and is called "AUTO" or "A" on your camera. Most digital camera owners use automatic mode and for good reason. Auto mode allows your camera select the best shot it can. With some cameras auto mode lets you override flash or change it to red eye reduction. In other cameras you may have to use program mode marked P" in order to do adjustments such as flash, image size, ISO, focus, etc.

You should keep in mind when using auto mode you are not telling your camera any extra information about the type of photo you are taking so your camera will use its best guess as to what you want. By giving your camera more clues of your circumstance, some of the other modes described below may give you even better results.

Program Mode

P Some digital cameras have a program mode, marked "P" on your camera's dial, in addition to auto mode. In the cameras having both, program mode works similar to auto mode but allows you more control over some other features such as the flash, self-timer, ISO, white balance, exposure, micro, etc. Turning the flash off and on and using the self-timer (more about both of these is presented later in this chapter) are important capacities with which you should familiarize yourself. You should read your camera's manual to learn how the program mode differs from auto mode for your camera.

Low Light, Indoor, or Party Modes

These are amazing modes to allow you to get those tricky indoor and dimly lit photos, especially when you are required to not use flash. We have gained the admiration of many fellow travelers during our travel adventures by showing them just this feature of their camera. You owe it to yourself to experiment using the low light, indoor, and/or party modes when taking photos inside buildings, in dim environments, at parties, you are required to turn your flash off, or whenever you have a low light situation. The indoor and party modes adjust for artificial indoor light and candlelight. When no flash is allowed you can still get very good photos by turning off your flash and switching to the low light modes. Try taking photos with both your auto and low light modes and see what works. Some tips on how to get great photos in low light situations without using a tripod are presented later in this chapter.

Landscape Mode

The landscape mode makes sure as much of your scene as possible will be in focus by giving it a wide depth of field. It is great for capturing photos of spacious scenes with points of interest at several different distances from your camera. In the landscape mode hold your camera steady because your camera may select a longer shutter speed in order to obtain the wide depth of field. You can also set your camera on a support and use the self-timer or consider using a tripod.

Portrait Mode

Portrait mode is usually marked with a face on your camera dial. It is best used when you want your subject to be the main interest in your photo. When you switch to portrait mode your camera will automatically bring your subject into focus and keep your background out of focus (blurred) with a narrow depth of field. Portrait mode works best when you are taking a photo of a single subject, usually the head and shoulders. Get in close enough to your subject either by zooming in or walking closer. If you are shooting into the sun or find shadows on your subject, you might want to move to a different angle or turn your flash on to always flash to add some light onto their face.

Night Portrait Mode

Night portrait mode is for taking photos at dusk or nighttime and will force your camera use the flash to better light subjects in the foreground. It sets your camera to use a longer shutter speed to help capture details of the background but it also sets the flash to light up the subject in the foreground. In the night portrait mode you need to hold your camera steady because your camera may select a longer shutter speed. Although sometimes a somewhat blurred background gives your photos an amusing look. Night portrait mode is also handy for parties and lower lit environments when you have a subject near your camera.

Sports Mode

Sports mode (also called 'action mode' or 'kids and pets' in some cameras) is ideal for taking photos of any fast moving subjects including people playing sports, pets, children, cars, wildlife etc. Sports mode attempts to freeze the action with a faster shutter speed and reduced focus time. Sports mode is best used in bright light. When taking photos of fast moving subjects you can increase your chances of capturing them by panning (moving) your camera along with the subject as it moves along or by pre-focusing (holding your shutter release down halfway) your camera on a spot where the subject will be. Another good way is to set your camera to take several continuous photos in order for you to have a better chance of capturing the best photo. This helps avoid having to wait between photos because of photo download time to your memory card.

Movie Mode

Movie mode is great because you capture motion and sound without extra video equipment. The movies we have taken are a big hit with our friends. Keep in mind movie files take up significantly more space on your memory storage so plan to take extra storage cards if you plan to take a lot of movies.

Macro Mode

Macro mode (often shown with a flower on your dial) is good for close up photos of small objects such as flowers and insects and allows you to get within inches to produce spectacular photos. It sometimes takes your camera a while to focus properly.

There are many other modes seen on some digital cameras. Some are:

- Night Scene – pre-programmed to use slow shutter speed to photograph nightscapes, use a tripod or the low light tips explained later in this chapter

- Backlight – automatically fires the flash to eliminate dark shadows when light is coming from behind a subject or when the subject is in the shade

- Sunset Mode – optimizes white balance to get the vivid colors of a sunset

- Beach/Snow Modes – for beach, snow, and sunlit water scenes to help prevent your photo from appearing washed out

- Fireworks Mode - for shooting skyrocketing firework displays, pre-focusing your camera is helpful

- Museum or Aquarium Mode – assists in getting a proper flash-free exposures to minimize the reflection of light off windows

- Fisheye Mode – can be use to achieve the classic fisheye photographic distortion without a fisheye lens

- Panoramic/Stitch Mode – for taking several shots of a panoramic (very wide or tall) scene to be joined together later as one image

- Underwater Mode – for use with an underwater camera - underwater photography has it's own unique set of exposure requirements

For more advanced photographers, most modern cameras also include some semi automatic modes such as aperture priority mode, shutter priority mode, and manual mode. These modes allow you to have more control over the aperture and shutter speed. They can be very useful in better managing depth of field, motion, and low light situations. For example, you can get a photo of trails of car lights by setting a long shutter speed in the shutter priority mode and keeping your camera still when taking the photo. The semi-automatic modes do require more experience and knowledge in order to best take advantage of them. The amateur photographer does not need to worry about these semi automatic modes. Great photos can be made using the other pre-programmed modes.

How to Use a Histogram to Improve Your Photos

Histograms can help better understand whether your photo is over or under exposed. Simply, a histogram is a graph of the pixels (recorded information) of your photo from dark to light tones (shades) from black on the left to white on the right. A histogram with lots of dark pixels will be skewed to the left and one with lots of lighter shades will be skewed to the right. An easy way to remember this is to think of the phrase "black and white" – black first on the left going to white on the right.

Because of different circumstances as well as what 'feeling' you are attempting to achieve, there is no such thing as the perfect histogram. For example, taking a shot with snow in the background will have large peaks on the right end of your histogram. Taking a silhouette shot with a darker background and well-lit subject may yield a histogram with peaks at both ends and with little in the middle. In general, you will most likely want a fairly balanced histogram graph with a nice spread of tones to both edges of your graph. Most well exposed photos have a histogram looking like a bell curve with a peak somewhere in the middle tapering off to the left and right.

By checking your histogram, you can better tell if your photo is over or under exposed (spikes of darker shades to the left could mean underexposed and spikes of lighter shades to the right overexposed). You can then adjust your settings (i.e. flash on or off, use a different pre-programmed mode like low light, night, portrait, or landscape) and take another shot. You should experiment with several different settings. After awhile you will learn to choose from a few settings of your camera that achieve the best results for you.

Consult with your camera's user manual to learn how to be able to view histograms on your LCD screen. Adjust your camera while in playback mode to view the histogram as well as the photo. This will enable you to see both the photo and the histogram when reviewing photos. Some cameras will allow you to view a small histogram on your LCD screen before you take a photo while you are viewing potential images. This helps you to better determine what angle to shoot from or what setting to adjust your camera to.

Using Basic Composition Rules to Make Sensational Photos

"A great photograph is one that fully expresses what one feels, in the deepest sense, about what is being photographed. You don't take a photograph, you make it." -
~ Ansel Adams

We can all learn from one of the world's greatest photographers. There are some rather simple composition guidelines that can greatly enhance your photos. Here are a few tried and true examples:

Get to Know Your Scene

"A good photograph is knowing where to stand."
~ Ansel Adams

You have spent time and money to be able to enjoy the fascinating scene you are about to photograph. First, enjoy yourself. This is why you are traveling. Walk around viewing the scene from many angles. Sit for a while and take it all in. This gives you time to enjoy the experience as well as think about your photo without herding people in front of it and taking a snapshot. What makes this scene memorable? Is it beautiful, majestic, tranquil, busy with energy, funny, emotional, character revealing, etc.? Think about how you can capture that feeling. Focus your photo on the portion of the scene that captures the emotion you are feeling without attempting to photograph the whole scene.

We are also big fans of discovering different angles to capture more interesting photos. Move around the scene. Is there an angle or distance (closer or further away) that gives the scene a unique perspective or better captures its beauty? Get above your subject and shoot down or crouch down, even laying down, and shoot up. Try getting closer and fill your frame with the image or moving back to include more.

Think about other aspects that make for a good photo. Is there a rock, tree, or building that you can use as a border? Is there an interesting person or object that may accent the scene or bring the size of the main subject into perspective?

Look all around your scene. Sometimes the best photo is behind you. For example, when a crowd is gathering for a beautiful sunset, a photo of the crowd can be interesting.

If you are using digital, you can take many different shots from many angles and perspectives using different settings of your camera. You will impress your viewers and have much more interesting photos by taking some time and effort in capturing photos of your travel adventures.

Rule of Thirds

Creating a good photo does not mean always centering your subject. Using the rule of thirds will often produce more remarkable results. To do this, imagine the image you see in your viewfinder divided both vertically and horizontally by two lines cutting each into three areas for a total of nine sections. Position the main subject one third up or down and/or one third from the right or left of the edge of the image. By placing your subject or points of interest along these lines your photo becomes more balanced.

When viewing photos, studies have shown people's eyes tend to go the intersection points of the rule of thirds instead of the center of the photo.

A variant of the rule of thirds is the golden rule where the main subject matter is placed on the lower right side of the image. This works because we are taught to read top to bottom and left to right ending at the bottom right where we pause the longest to move to the next page (or photo). The Chinese and Japanese may have a different interpretation of the golden rule.

When using the rule of thirds with people or moving subjects, it is better to have them look or have their motion going into the photo rather than to an edge.

Don't worry about exact placement. Just remember centering does not always create the best photo. The saying "rules are meant to broken" applies well to photography. Many photos like portraits of interesting faces look great centered. Finally, keep the rule of thirds and the golden rule in mind as you crop and edit your photos.

Locking the Focus

Because point-and-shoot cameras tend to center focus, using the rule of thirds to create more interesting photos sometimes presents a challenge. Subjects off center could be less focused especially when shooting with a wide depth of field when your camera attempts to focus somewhere in the distance. For example, you have a group of friends you want to capture when taking a photo of a beautiful landscape. Having your friends over to one side is great to better capture the view and make use of the rule of thirds. When taking this photo, your point-and-shoot camera may focus in the center of the photo on a point in the distance and your friends will be slightly out of focus. What to do?

Fortunately, there exists a simple and powerful solution – locking the focus. Pressing your shutter release half way down will focus your camera without taking a photo. Holding the shutter release halfway down will lock (retain) that focus. To take your photo, first do whatever repositioning of yourself and zooming you want to do. Then center focus on your subject and press the shutter release half way down. Don't move your zoom or body's position. Continue to hold the shutter release half way down while shifting your camera to reposition your subject to the place where you want it in your photo. Then press the shutter release down the rest of the way to take your photo.

You can lock the focus any time your desired composition does not place the subject in the center of your photo. You may need to use this technique when you have two subjects (like two people) on each side of the center of your photo and your camera focuses off in the middle somewhere between them. Locking the focus also works with vertical photos to move your subject up and down. Locking the focus is a very effective technique and with a little practice you will find it becomes easy to do.

Framing

In this section, we generalize the term 'framing' as what you see in your LCD screen and where and how you subject will be placed. This

determines what your photo will be. The following are some things to consider.

Avoid repetitive and boring "same old" tourist shots. Include local people to add excitement and color in your photos.

Award winning photo! The simple background emphasizes the subject - farming with water buffalo in Thailand.

Emphasize your main subject by keeping the background simple and clutter free. The more objects you remove from your photo the clearer and sharper your subject and what you want to convey will be to the viewer. If your subject tends to blend into the background or doesn't pop out of the scene, move around to choose an angle with less in the background. This can also be done by repositioning your subject to make it closer, larger, taller, or in sharper focus than other objects. Other times waiting will help. Letting the tour group or that guy with the large belly get out of your photo is well worth the wait. For moving subjects, selecting the right moment to take the photo is important.

We had the privilege to travel several weeks through Egypt and Jordon with David and Anna Smith, a professional photographer and his wife, who were from Vancouver, Canada. They are fun! One of the best lessons he taught us was to turn your camera vertical (sideways 90 degrees) much more often. He told us professionals take almost half their photos this way. Turning your camera vertically is better for many photos. Too many amateur photos are done only horizontally. Shoot vertically when you have tall subjects to emphasize height. Shoot horizontally to emphasize width. When in doubt, shoot both and decide later. This was an amazing tip that has greatly improved our photos. So, turn your camera and start shooting like a pro.

Perspective is another way to emphasize an image's size, depth, and distance. A familiar subject such as a person standing next to a building or tree, for example, can demonstrate its size. A river that gets progressively reduced in size as it becomes increasingly distant shows distance.

Objects in the foreground add depth and a three-dimensional look to your photo and bring out the subject in the background more effectively. To enhance your photo a simple rule is to include objects in your scene at about one-third the distance from your camera.

Look for ways to add nature to your composition even in the city. Look around for natural elements like earth, water, or plants to include in the frame. A pond, colorful flowers, or a hanging branch of a tree can make your picture more interesting.

Symmetry makes for a simple and balanced composition and is pleasing to the eye. Adjust your framing to establish symmetry and balance with lines, shapes, objects, and color. Repetitive objects make great subjects. A series of similar objects repeated over and over, like the poles of an ocean pier, columns of a building, or multiple tightly packed subjects, never fails to impress and create a unique photo.

One interesting framing technique is to create a sense of infinity. This technique has no borders or horizons and appears to be without limits having no beginning or end. For example, a field of flowers showing just the flowers appears to go on forever where they could just be a garden shot. This technique works well with landscape and ocean photos when you do not show the horizon. Infinity framing can often be achieved by shooting from slightly above.

Leading Lines

A classic way to compose your photo is with leading lines, usually diagonal, to direct your viewer's attention towards what you want to emphasize in your image. It could be the main subject matter or just off to the horizon showing the vastness of your scene. Typical examples are roads, rivers, fences, and landscape lines like mountains. Make sure your horizon line is level.

Lighting Secrets Revealed

Photography is all about the light. Even the best professional photographers will tell you that getting the proper lighting is one of the hardest things to do. Things to be aware of about light are time of day, direction, color, soft or bright, and natural or artificial. Here are some ways to help you to take advantage of light.

Sunlight

One very basic lighting rule is to try to keep the sun (or other source of lighting) at your back with the light of the sun falling on your subject. When shooting people, having the sun come from the side may be better to avoid making your subjects squint. Try to avoid taking photos in the middle of the day. The harsh light of midday can overexpose and can hit your subject straight down leaving dark shadows. Otherwise your subject may be underexposed (dark or in a shadow). Natural shade and clouds can soften the harsh sunlight, reduce shadows, and create a more even light situation.

Golden Hours

The golden hours (sometimes known as the magic hours) are approximately the first and last hour of sunlight just after sunrise and just before sunset. The magic of this lighting is it is softer and warmer with longer less dark shadows. Lighting in the golden hour can make your photos take on a warmer golden quality. Beautiful colors in the horizon will accent your photo. Do yourself a favor and take photos during the golden hours whenever you can.

Use of Flash

Often your compact point-and-shoot camera will determine that your photo does not need extra light from your flash, especially during the day or in the shade, leaving subjects close to you underexposed or with unwanted dark shadows. If this is the case, turn your flash on and retake your photo. At night, use the night portrait mode to achieve this.

Learning when to turn off the flash is also a valuable lesson. Where soft natural light occurs you can achieve warmer more natural results by turning off your flash.

When controlling the flash (you may have to switch to program mode in order to do this), you usually have the following options you can scroll through: auto flash (lets the camera decide), flash off (never flashes), and fill flash (always on). You may also have red eye reduction. Because the flash of a compact camera is next to the lens, the red blood vessels on the retina of the eye reflect back to the camera. Red eye reduction uses a double flash. Editing software also can solve the red eye issue.

You should remember the light from your point-and-shoot camera's flash will light up subjects in the range of up to 10-15 feet from your camera. You need to stand within this range in order for your flash to be effective. Also, the use of your flash can be annoying to other people. If you are taking photos of subjects in the distance beyond this range your flash will be ineffective, be polite and turn your flash off. If you need better exposure for distances larger than 10-15 feet from your camera, make use of the low light, indoor, party, or night modes of your camera.

Taking Great Photos in Low Light Situations
Low Light Situations Without the Use of a Tripod

Making use of the low light, indoor, and/or party modes of your camera's pre-programmed modes can help you capture very good photos in low light situations. When doing so (also when using the landscape and night portrait modes) your camera will be sensitive to movement that may cause your photo to be blurred or unclear. Holding your camera as still as you can and having a camera with image stabilization or vibration reduction will help you better capture some tricky low light images without the need of a tripod.

On our adventure through the rain forests of Costa Rica, we were fortunate to meet up with a senior photographer from "National Geographic Magazine". She taught us some fantastic simple tricks to get better photos in low light situations. Unwanted camera movement from your body is your enemy and here is how to minimize it. To help you steady your camera you can act like a tripod by placing your elbows next to your chest and spreading your feet apart. To remove even more motion, lean against a wall or tree (also you can kneel on one knee with an elbow on the other knee), pre-focus by pressing and holding the shutter release halfway down, hold your breath, steady your body as still as possible, and then take your photo by very carefully pressing the shutter release all the way down. We sometimes press our camera against or set it on a wall, table, or other support when taking a photo.

Even better, to eliminate any motion caused by your body, you can place your camera on a support like a wall or table and use the self-timer to avoid even the movement caused by pressing the shutter release button. Now you know the secrets, you can have your low light photos look like a pro. Maybe you will be the next National Geographic photographer.

Inside Lighting

Inside lighting varies greatly. Use your low light, inside, or party modes on your camera's pre-programmed modes to adjust for inside lighting. Some cameras have white balance settings (i.e. cloudy, tungsten, fluorescent), usually found in the menu, that will compensate for 'unnatural' light that cause your photos to look more yellow or blue. The inside or party modes help adjust for this. Some of these problems can also be adjusted with photo editing tools. When taking photos of people indoors, have them move away from any walls because your flash will create a shadow causing a 'halo' effect around them.

Night Photos

Probably not what you would normally think, better night photos can be had by turning your flash off and using the night or low light modes. An exception to this would be when you have a subject in the near foreground where using the night portrait mode that uses the flash to illuminate the subject. Keep your camera steady using procedures explained above. A trick used by pros is to revisit the scene during the golden hour at dusk when colors and details are easier to capture.

Taking Memorable Photos of People

"It is one thing to photograph people. It is another to make others care about them by revealing the core of their humanness."
~ Paul Strand (American Photographer 1890-1976)

Traveling is about people as well as visiting famous sites. Adding remarkable portraits of the people you meet and see to your photo collection will greatly enhance your recorded memories of your adventures. Taking snapshots of people is easy. Achieving an image that will evoke the interest of your viewer takes a little effort and a bit of cleverness. In addition to typical snapshots of people, try some of these ideas to achieve more memorable photos of people.

Some people are very interesting showing beauty or wisdom, wearing local attire or native costumes, or having wrinkled faces as evidence of the life they lived. Taking their picture looking into your camera can make for a magnificent photo. Zoom in or get close to the person to capture details of their face.

Most portraits are shot from eye level. More interesting photos can be had by getting up high and shooting down or getting low and shooting up.

Capture Your Subject Doing Something Interesting

Even ordinary people can provide opportunities of memorable photos. Instead of having your subject posed looking at the camera, take their picture focusing their attention on something else. Your photo will now appear more candid. It is even better if you can catch (or entice) them engaged and loving the moment or in an emotion so the viewer is intrigued by what is making your subject laugh or look interested. Get in closer to the person and show something interesting off to the side or in the background to get a sense of the place.

Waiting for the right timing is key. Also, your subject can be enticed into doing something interesting. This can be as easy as asking people to do something interesting such as lifting their glasses at a party or just leaving it open for them to decide what to do. After taking a photo of a group of people, take

People having fun make for more interesting photos – school children in Hiroshima, Japan

another photo asking them to do something fun on the count of three. Personalities come out making for more interesting and fun photos.

Alternatively you can have your subject look at something or someone. A mother with a child, a local person performing an activity unique to their region of the world, or your travel companion doing something interesting adds interest to your photo. One of our interesting photographs was taken in Viet Nam of a woman plowing a field with a water buffalo. It has been chosen for a travel book.

Parades and festivals are wonderful places to capture interesting photos of local people. They are usually more relaxed and dressed in local costumes.

A great way to have fun with people, especially children, is to take their photo and then show it to them on your LCD screen. The laughs are precious. We have handed our camera to children and they photograph each other and you. Great fun and you might get an unexpected special photo.

Get Permission First

You should always ask people for their permission first before taking a photo of them. Some people do not like to be photographed and in some regions in the world, taking ones photograph is against their beliefs. Gaining permission does not have to be difficult. Be patient. Take photos around your subject and get them use to you being there. Always respect other people and approach politely with a smile. Say something nice to them about their town or clothing and ask politely "may I?" pointing to them and your camera. Sometimes all it takes is to lift up your camera and nod to them.

How to Care for Your Camera and Photo Accessories

Take special care of the lens of your camera. In order to keep it clean and scratch free, do not touch it directly with your fingers and cover or close your lens when not taking photos. If your lens becomes dirty, you should use a small soft cloth designed to clean lens.

Here are some other considerations of which to be aware. Handle and pack your camera and photo accessories with care because they have delicate components. Storing your camera in a small camera case is a wise idea to protect it from the traumas that occur in traveling. Be careful not to have your camera experience temperature extremes. Leaving it out in the sun or out in the cold may cause damage. It is also a good idea to remove the battery if you plan to store your camera for a long time.

Make sure you keep your camera dry. Carry a zip-lock plastic bag in your daypack in case you are caught in a rainstorm or plan to be around water. We make it a practice to keep our point-and-shoot camera in a waterproof bag (zip-lock plastic bags work well) even when we carry it in our pocket or bag. You never know when something may be spilled on you or your camera.

There now exist increased security measures throughout the world. Digital is best because X-ray machines and metal detectors do not affect digital memory cards.

If you plan to use film, do not pack film in checked luggage because the machines used to screen checked bags are much more powerful than machines used at security checkpoints. X-ray machines at screening stations can damage film after a few screenings so it is best to have hand inspection if you are using film. Some screening stations do not allow hand screening. It is best to bring along special film bags for this purpose.

Take note that the magnetic fields of metal detectors can cause damage to computer and videodisks. When transporting your video and computer equipment put these items through the X-ray machine and not the metal detector. Ask for hand inspection around the metal detector if that is the only option available.

Organizing and Editing Your Photos

"Dodging and burning are steps to take care of mistakes God made in establishing tonal relationships."
~ Ansel Adams

As spoken by one world's great photographers, photographs can be improved with editing. You do not need to be influenced by the purists who say only photos direct from the camera without editing are worthy. Modern photo organizing and editing tools go far beyond the older methods of dodging and burning used by past masters.

Computer photo editing programs today have very good tools for cropping and reframing images so they fit within the composition rules described previously. They also have tools to rotate, straighten, retouch, and sharpen your photo, remove red eye, as well as to adjust exposure, contrast, color saturation, sharpness, noise, etc. Make duplicate copies and experiment with some of your old photos.

Unless you plan to use your photos professionally, the "jpg" format is a good one for saving your images because it compresses the file size. Try to do all your editing on jpg files at one time because each time you save, it compresses the photo file and you loose image quality. Just because you have the ability to make splendid changes to your photos while editing try to not over adjust making your photos appear unnatural.

How to Organize Your Photos

Organizing photos on your computer is very important. Otherwise you may have hundreds, possibly thousands, of photos in one large file and it will be time consuming locating the ones you want to view. We organize our photos into files (files will be called folders, albums, or directories depending on your program). To easily locate photos later, we give the files a descriptive name and date of the place or event and then make files of files. For example, on a trip to Italy we would have a master file named Italy709 containing sub-files of photos named Bologna709, Verona709, LakeComo709, etc. We also create a 'good' file for each of these for our Internet blog - more on that in Chapter 15 ("Staying in Touch with Friends and Family").

This method of organization of your photos can also be used for personal events. For example, for parties you can create a master file named 'Our Parties' containing files of photos named Christmas1208, NewYears109, AsianParty209, FarewellParty309, Christmas1209, etc.

It is helpful to take reference photos of signs and descriptions of places for you to remember site names later.

Tagging (labeling) your individual photos is a nice feature. For example, you could tag every photo that has you or your travel partner in it. When you want to see photos of yourself, your program will find all the photos of you regardless of where they are located.

Here is a great tip for those who take a lot of photos. Go to your camera's menu and set photo numbering to 'continuous'. Otherwise, when it reaches a certain number, the numbering system of your photos will start over and label new photos with numbers that you may already have in your computer causing confusion and potential troubles. While you are in your menu, turn off the date and time stamp so nothing is permanently imprinted on your photos. This information can be found for any photo using other techniques.

On longer trips we organize, edit, blog, etc. our photos along the way. Having hundreds, maybe thousands, of photos to organize at the end of a trip is overwhelming and too often never gets done. In order to minimize the number of photos, we delete the bad ones on our camera's memory card before downloading to our computer. After you have downloaded your photos to your computer or other storage device and confirmed they are there, keep your memory card as backup. If you do erase all your photos from your camera's memory card, you should format your memory card. This helps avoid corrupted memory cards and loss of photos.

Back Up Your Photos Regularly

Remember to backup your photos regularly. It would be a shame to lose your photo memories if your camera or memory cards are lost or damaged. CD's, DVD's, and flash drives are inexpensive and have large storage sizes. Flash drives have much more if you have that capability. There are services that will do backups for you. Because we travel with our laptop computer (more on that in Chapter 15 – "Staying in Touch with Friends and Family"), we take an external hard drive to backup all our files including our large photo files. We also take smaller USB flash memory to regularly back up our writing and other smaller files.

Having an Internet photo file using one of the popular photo organizing and sharing programs (see below) provides for another backup of your photos.

Photo Organizing and Editing Software Programs

Better photo software is available from third parties than what comes with your camera. Popular PC and Apple computers are offering decent photo management and editing tools such as Microsoft's Digital Image Suite and Apple's iPhoto. For more features, Adobe's Photoshop Elements is a powerful and popular photo-editing program. Classes are available for Photoshop. There are other good photo editing programs available for purchase such as Jasc Paint Shop Pro and Ulead PhotoImpact. Google offers a very good (currently free) photo managing, editing, and sharing program called Picasa.

Sharing Your Photos - Sending Large Numbers of Photos

Sharing your photos by e-mail or a social network website like Facebook is an easy and wonderful way to stay in touch and let your friends and family enjoy your adventures with you. We share our photos on Facebook using its photo album feature with a write up of each place as well as what we did in the description. We also maintain a travel blog (more on how to do a blog in Chapter 15 – "Staying in Touch with Friends and Family").

With new digital cameras with higher megapixel capacities capturing more data, the size of photo files has become large. Sending a sizable number of photos by e-mail can present a problem with limits of e-mail programs of less than 10 MB (some as low as 3 MB). On a hiking trip above the Salmon River in California, the guide told us for every problem nature presents you it also supplies the antidote within 100 yards. What may be true in nature is surely becoming true on the Internet. The e-mail limit problem on the Internet is also solved on the Internet with a solution... *YouSendIt (www.yousendit.com)*.

You can sign up for YouSendIt's "Lite" program and be able to single files (one photo) up to 50 MB for free. To facilitate sending multiple photos and files, they offer low-cost paid programs. To send your photos, go to YouSendIt and send the photo file(s) to the e-mail address of whomever you want to receive it. The recipient receives an e-mail notification. They can then select the YouSendIt link in their e-mail and download the file(s).

You can also make use of free photo organizing and sharing programs that allow you to upload photo albums and determine who can view them. A couple of popular ones are *Smugmug (www.smugmug.com)* and Yahoo's *Flickr (www.flickr.com)*. Flickr is free for a limited number of photos and videos with a small yearly fee of $25 for much more. Flickr is available as a smartphone app on the iPhone and Windows Phone 7. We use Flickr and it is easy to use and versatile. For an example, see our *travel photo file (www. flickr.com/photos/unhooknow/sets)*.

How to Get Started Taking More Memorable Photos

"Every artist was once an amateur."

~ Ralph Waldo Emerson

The photography guidelines and techniques presented in this chapter may seem a little overwhelming at first, especially for beginners. We would like to offer a word of encouragement. Only a few years ago our travel photos were not much better than your typical tourist snapshots. A little effort and learning (numerous helpful ideas summarized in this chapter) has yielded wonderful results. Our travel photo file on Yahoo's Flickr receives hundreds of downloaded views every day and several of our photos have been accepted for travel books and Internet travel sites. What is even more enjoyable for us is that our friends request photo slideshows when we return from our trips and we have a heart-warming reminder for years to come of our many adventures.

There is an old saying: "How do you eat an elephant? – One bite at a time". Our advice is at first to take a few ideas from this chapter and work on them. A good place to start is getting to know your scene before taking just snapshots, making better use of your pre-programmed scene modes, shooting vertical more often, the low light suggestions, and the framing ideas using the focus lock. Then come back later and reread this chapter and practice some more ideas.

With a little effort your photos will look more like a pro!

In the next chapter we offer a step-by-step guideline on how to help you realize your travel dreams.

Chapter 17

Getting Started on Your Travel Adventure

– A Step-by-Step Guide

In this chapter...

Transform Your Dreams into an Action Plan

Five-Month Planning and Preparation Guideline

Transform Your Dreams into an Action Plan

The following is a step-by-step preparation guideline to help you transform your travel dreams and goals into an action plan to make them happen. Following this guideline will allow you to better organize your tasks in a practical and efficient manner. Every trip or stay is unique so yours will probably include some additional items to these listed below.

Five-Month Planning and Preparation Guideline
Five Months Before Leaving

☐ *Choose your travel adventure.* Make a destination wish list based on your interests and priorities. Then based on your research and best time to go, prioritize your countries and cities list, outline your itinerary, and set a budget. For many more ideas and helpful planning Internet website resources, see Chapter 6 ("How Planning Can Enhance Your Experience"). Do research by going to your travel bookstore and picking up some travel guidebooks for your selected destinations. Also, go online and research various destinations and pricing options. Order travel brochures for escorted tours for planning or even booking options. Some travel options do book out many months ahead so the sooner you make plans the more options you will have.

☐ *If you plan to rent your home, give yourself plenty of time to find a suitable tenant.* See Chapter 5 ("What to Do with Your House and Possessions"). When rented, acquire a PO Box and mail forwarding, arrange for gardening and other maintenance, and change utilities to the renter. Also, install a watering system.

☐ *Start selling and downsizing your stuff.*

Four Months Before Leaving

☐ *Apply for or renew your passport.* If you have a passport, check to see if it will have six months of validity left at the end our your trip. Many countries require this for entry so you may have to renew your passport early. Also, make sure it has several blank pages. The Post Office usually has the necessary forms. Contact the *U.S. Department of State (www.travel.state.gov)* if necessary. Don't wait until last minute because the typical processing time is 4-6 weeks. Pay for the expedient fee if you have a close timeframe.

☐ *Research and apply for any necessary visas.* Many countries do not require visas for entry. Some you can obtain a visa when entering (often for $20 fee). It is wise to take a few passport photos with you in case local visas are required. Some countries require you to obtain a visa prior to entry. Get a 'multiple entry' visa if you plan to leave the country and return to it. If you are planning to work or stay longer than 90 days in any country, research the long-term stay and work permits/visa requirements. Don't wait to the last minute to apply for required visas because some can take a couple of months to obtain. For information on visa requirements of the countries you plan to visit, go to the *U.S. Department of State's website (www.travel.state.gov)*. For a visa processing company in the U.S., go to *Travisa (www.travisa.com)*.

Plan and take a shorter trip (even locally) to implement the principles laid out in this book. Make the necessary adjustments you learn before starting any extended trip.

Three Months Before Leaving

☐ *Finalize your basic travel ideas.*

☐ *Vaccinations* – Go to **CDC (United States Centers for Disease Control - wwwn.cdc.gov/travel)** for a list of vaccination requirements for the countries you plan to visit. Many areas in the world require no vaccinations although some are recommended and wise to have. Most vaccines take time to become effective in your body and some vaccines must be given in a series over a period of days or sometimes 8 weeks. If it is less than 4 weeks before you leave, you should still see your doctor. You might still benefit from shots or medications and other information about how to protect yourself from illness and injury while traveling. Many cities have special travel clinics available to assist you. Be sure to keep your proof of vaccination forms.

☐ *Acquire credit and debit cards or check with your existing companies to be sure they work well for the international areas you plan to visit.* Check the expiration dates. Make sure you have two different debit cards and two different credit cards in case you lose one. You may want to acquire a no fee international credit card. Before leaving, validate and use all new debit and credit cards to be sure they work. Check with your bank to adjust daily limits on your ATM withdrawals. See Chapter 12 ("Money and Credit Cards") for details.

☐ *Set up online banking to review all accounts* (i.e. checking, savings, investments, credit and debit cards). See Chapter 9 ("Paying Your Bills While You Are Away").

☐ *Set up autopay for your bill paying and auto-deposit for any deposits.* Starting early allows you to work out any issues while you can still benefit from toll-free customer service and you can set up these accounts over a few months as your bills arrive.

☐ *Check with your e-mail provider to learn how to connect with your e-mail when traveling* (e.g. webmail) or set up a new account with a more universally accessible service such as Google's Gmail (see Chapter 15 – "Staying in Touch with Friends and Family"). If you get a new e-mail address, inform everyone to use the new one.

☐ **If necessary, apply for work permits, student cards, hostel cards, or an international driver's license.**

☐ **Register with DirectMail.com's National Do Not Mail List to reduce your unwanted junk mail.** See Chapter 9 ("Paying Your Bills While You Are Away").

Two Months Before Leaving

Most of the items listed above can be accomplished in two months so it may not be too late if you have only two months to plan. Don't wait any longer on these items because you may not have enough time.

☐ **You should have your travel plans and itinerary firmed up and have or be reserving any tours, cruises, flights, places to stay you wish to do.** Book the place you plan to live for a while or some of your accommodations if you plan to travel. Even when we are traveling independently on our own, we like to have at least a reservation for accommodations at our first destination. You should be researching ideas of what you want to be doing while you are there possibly arranging local tours, events, and activities.

☐ **Review your insurance (i.e. medical, home, auto, other) and credit card policies to see if you have coverage for the trip you are planning – complete coverage is unlikely.** Seriously consider purchasing travel insurance as outlined in Chapter 10 ("Security – Staying Safe on the Road").

☐ **Purchase any necessary suitcase and other travel bags and start planning your packing list.** This will allow you time to shop for your travel clothing, gear, supplies, and accessories you will need. Purchasing necessary travel clothing and gear and setting up or replenishing your travel kits takes longer than packing. Get the clothes you plan to take cleaned and mended. Use the suggested packing lists in this book (see Chapter 13 - "How to Pack Lighter and Still Be Prepared") to make a shopping list of the things you will need.

☐ **If you plan to take a smartphone, computer laptop, or tablet/netbook, give yourself time to investigate options, acquire the necessary software, and learn how to use it before you leave.**

☐ **Give your resignation to any organization you have made a commitment to so they will have plenty of time to replace you.**

☐ *Begin exercising, especially walking, to get in shape for exploring sites and cities. Break in any new shoes you plan to wear on the trip.*

☐ *Order business/travel cards.* You can have your personalized cards printed for free (except for a small shipping charge) at *Vistaprint (www.vistaprint.com)*. See sample in Appendix B.

One Month Before Leaving

☐ *Get a medical checkup, visit the dentist, get any prescriptions filled for the complete time away, ask your doctor for a prescription for antibiotics, and order backup glasses and extra contact lenses, if necessary.*

☐ *Check with your cell phone provider to see if you will have coverage in the areas you plan to visit. Also, set up a Skype account.* See Chapter 15 ("Staying in Touch with Friends and Family").

☐ *Research and select a camera and accessories for your trip.* Read the user manual and get familiar with its features by taking photos at home. To help you select the right camera for you, see Chapter 16 ("Take Travel Photos Like a Pro").

☐ *Make a list of all important contacts including a list of friends and family addresses, phone numbers, and e-mail addresses to send postcards and stay in touch through the Internet. Also make a list of emergency contacts* (i.e. emergency contact person, 24-hour travel agent, home, medical and car insurance, and any other important contacts along with a list of doctor and lawyer names and numbers, allergies, medical history, and special medication). Make the emergency list easy to find in your luggage.

☐ *Designate a friend or family member to check your mail and contact you if something important needs to be addressed.* You may want to have it forwarded to them while you are gone. This person can be the contact you can ship back any extra clothing or souvenirs you can't live without. You may want to set someone up with 'power of attorney' to take care of legal documents in case something happens to you.

☐ *If driving, take in your vehicle for a complete road-safety check up.*

☐ *Purchase a telephone calling card, if necessary, and learn to use it.*

☐ *If you plan to do a travel blog or online travel photo file, set them up before you leave so you will not be stressed to learn new programs while you are traveling.* See Chapter 15 ("Staying in Touch with Friends and Family").

☐ *Inform your family and friends of your travel plans and give them the dates of your travel.*

☐ *Set up dinner dates with family and friends you will not see while you are gone.*

Two Weeks Before Leaving

☐ *For the period you are leaving, if not promised to your tenants or house sitter, cancel newspaper, magazines, and other subscriptions.* If you are planning to be gone for a long time decide what you want to do with utilities (i.e. cable, TV, electricity, phone, water). Many companies will put your plan on hold for the period of time you will be gone. Also cancel or suspend accounts and memberships you will not be using (i.e. gym, clubs)

☐ *Carefully review your itinerary and reservations looking for any discrepancies making sure the names on your tickets match exactly the names on your passport.* Double check the dates, times, and destinations.

☐ *Get some cash and maybe some traveler's checks.* See Chapter 12 ("Money and Credit Cards").

☐ *Take care of any veterinary needs for your pet before dropping it off with a caretaker.*

☐ *Load your favorite music onto your computer laptop or music player.*

☐ *Start taking anti-malarial pills if you are heading immediately to a malarial region.*

One Week Before Leaving

☐ *Call your credit and ATM debit card companies and inform them of your itinerary and dates you will be traveling and what countries you are visiting.*

☐ *Start gathering the things you will be taking with you.* Review the check-off list in Chapter 13 ("How to Pack Lighter and Still Be Prepared"). This will give you some time to pick up the things you overlooked.

☐ *Leave friends or family an envelope with photocopies of your* documents (i.e. passports, visas, credit card, prescriptions, essential travel documents, etc.) that can be sent to you in case of an emergency.

☐ **Look up forecasted weather information for your planned destinations to help you determine what you will need to bring.** A good weather website is the **The Weather Channel (www.weather.com).**

☐ **Arrange for your mail to be checked by or forwarded to friends or family.**

☐ **Get your hair cut and any other personal items (i.e. waxing, nails) done before you leave.**

☐ **Get cash from your bank.**

☐ **Do last minute laundry.**

Three Days Before Leaving

☐ **Pack your luggage.** Try to stay under 40 pounds for your main suitcase. Walk with it for 20 minutes and carry it for short periods of time. If you can, carry it up some stairs. If you find it uncomfortable, eliminate items.

☐ **Confirm your flight and arrange transportation for your departure.**

☐ **Traveling can be stressful so get plenty of sleep and eat nourishing meals before leaving.** Go easy on the alcohol because it will worsen jet lag.

☐ **Begin the jet lag diet and preparations described in Chapter 11 ("Staying Healthy").**

One Day to Departure

☐ **Print your flight boarding passes and all other reservations.**

☐ **Do last minute cleaning of your home (i.e. refrigerator, trash, dishes). Unplug all appliances and electronics you will not be using.**

☐ **Make any last minute phone calls and charge all your batteries (i.e. camera, computer laptop or tablet/netbook, music player). Don't forget to pack your chargers.**

☐ **Go over this check-off list once again as well as the packing list in Chapter 13** ("How to Pack Lighter and Still Be Prepared"). Pack your carry-on bag taking any valuables with you. Especially double check and organize passports, tickets, and other important personal and travel documents.

Day of Departure

☐ *Drink plenty of water.* Travel and flights can dehydrate you. Follow the jet lag suggestions in Chapter 11 ("Staying Healthy").

☐ *Get excited for your upcoming adventure! We are excited for you and wish you the best of luck.*

Chapter 18

See You on the Road

It has been our pleasure to share our travel experience and research with you. We wish you all the best in your life. We hope your travel adventures will bring you as much joy, excitement, and perspective, as well as giving your life more meaning like it has for us.

It's a wonderful world out there. We look forward to seeing you on the road… we will be the ones with the big smiles!

Appendix A

Travel Advice From Experienced Travelers Who Have Traveled the World and Changed Their Lives

We have been blessed to meet many interesting people while we were traveling and have good friends who love to travel. They have shared some thought-provoking ideas and perspectives with us that have helped us improve our lives and our travel experiences. We sent many of them a list of general questions related to this book and asked them to offer advice and share their experiences of world travel and living alternative lifestyles. From all around the world and from ages 27 to 81, we are excited to share their diverse viewpoints, travel secrets, and love for travel with you.

Sarah Gamber

Background: Sarah is a Senior Travel Counselor with Airtreks (referred to in this book for international flights). She has traveled all over the world and now has a family in San Francisco. Because of her vast worldwide travel experience, Sarah gave us great service on a couple of our trips helping us to better fine tune our itinerary to have more time in places where we needed it as well as adding interesting stopovers. She offers some thought provoking travel wisdom:

Hello Wayne and Pat,

Thank you for contacting me. How exciting that you are writing a book!

Mainly - Less is More.

Spend longer periods of time in less destinations. Allow yourself to slow down and really soak up the culture of the countries you visit. Try to see several cities/villages in one country to give yourself a rounder, more fully developed picture of the country you are visiting. Eat local cuisine! Stay in guesthouses! Don't isolate yourself with other tourists. Pack light - simplify. Be a gracious guest. Do NOT compare everything to your home (i.e. the U.S.). Find the beauty and pleasure in everywhere you go.

Happy Travels!

Sarah Gamber

David & Anna Smith

Background: We believe we share kindred spirits of travel with our new good friends David and Anna Smith. Our travel paths have crossed four times – we met on a trans-Atlantic Ocean repositioning cruise, a trip through Egypt and Jordan, their visit to our hometown San Diego, and we stayed with them in their home in West Vancouver, BC, Canada. This interesting couple are travel photographers, writers and key note speakers who follow, teach and share their passions of world travel, photography and fabric arts after completing their respective business careers and becoming empty nesters. This is what they write about themselves and their love of travel:

Dream Travelers – Capturing the World One Smiling Face At A Time

Anna and David became engaged in Paris 42 years ago and soon after they followed traditional family and career paths without offshore travel for 30 years. An impromptu anniversary trip to Europe in 1999 changed that and they have now visited 6 continents and over 50 countries since. The only reason they come home now is to change clothes and visit their 5 grandchildren.

Their inspiration to travel internationally came from their teen years when high school or family trips took each to Europe and by developing friendships with world travelers. Experiencing foreign countries and ethnic cultures and photographing local people is their love and breaks down all of their preconceived notions of other races, religions and beliefs. Their motto is: "Smile and the world just might smile back at you!"

A successful travel lifestyle as a couple requires extreme patience with each other and the rest of the world. If you don't get along at home, you will definitely not get along while travelling. You must trust and let people you meet, whether locals and other travellers, guide and help you along. Sure, escorted tours are easy but independent travel enables you to meet locals and smell the local spices.

Be sure to research destinations and places to stay and do and what previous visitors say online so there are no surprises.

Have a safety net that includes extra copies of all documents, important phone numbers, and credit card information and do not write down but memorize PINS. Carry valuables in a money belt when visiting busy cities and popular travel destinations, pickpockets abound. They each use a money belt for passports, tickets, cash and credit cards in all crowded tourist destinations without exception as they have met many travellers who have had their travels and plans ruined by a pickpocket. A backup camera, lots of memory cards, batteries and charger and several different cash accounts at different banks to thwart ATM issues are mandatory for the Smiths.

Their favorite destination is always their last one. However their many trips to the Greek Islands (there is no "bad" Greek island) and anywhere in Italy indicate European favorites and they intend in returning to Thailand soon to savor Thai food, people and stunning beauty. More of Muslim countries like Morocco and Egypt are also in their travel future. An evening gondola ride in Venice with an opera singers tenor voice and mandolin echoing off the canal walls, beach massages on the island of Koh Samui, Thailand, and dining Brazilian style at the Porcao restaurant in Rio de Janeiro are just some of their memories they cherish.

The best part of world travel is the travelers and local people you meet along the way. Eclectic Wayne and Pat Dunlap (authoring this book!) are a great inspiration to unhook from routine life and go for it; effervescent Irini and her family, proprietors of the Hotel Hellas in Santorini for their love and enthusiasm anytime we visit there; and the lovely Zeena of Sydney Australia for keeping us travel energized with her phone calls, e-mails and Sydney tours after meeting her in Rhodes 6 years ago are just some people David and Anna have had the fortune to meet. Their friendships and travel tales can literally fill a book, which they will do someday.

They use **Tripadvisor (www.tripadvisor.com)** frequently to research places to stay and what others say about an activity or location. They can easily select a quality level and budget for each destination then contact properties directly online or by phone to confirm details and current prices. With today's weak world travel economy direct phone contact can save lots of money versus published online rates. They prefer 3-star family run hotels versus luxury chain hotels not just to save money but to meet locals and experience family life and ethic culture. They will splurge on fine dining in view restaurants but share a main course.

A mini laptop with Wi-Fi and Skype permits free video calls to other Skype users and very inexpensive landline calls. It is faster, easier and cheaper to find a Wi-Fi hot spot and make computer calls than to seek phone cards and figure out how to use them in foreign lands. Besides, Skype video calls lets their grandchildren remember what they look like.

Watch out for the faux guides in Morocco and North Africa, they have many ways of manipulating their stories for you to become their friends only to find it will cost you big time at the end of the day. Watch out for photocopied money in Buenos Aires, we were at the Sunday market and were given some only to find out the next day at the deli they could tell it was fake from across the counter. Discover Japan and possibly other destinations using the local Good Host Guide program, what a remarkable rewarding experience and you make new friends.

Take taxis when there is limited time. It is so worth it and perhaps share a cab makes for a fun filled day. Local buses are easy and people are so willing to help you get to your destination.

Please remember to be courteous even if you don't understand. It only takes a smile and a nod of the head to try and communicate kindly. Try to learn a few words before you go. Take lots of small denomination bills for tipping, it can make the world of difference to someone and not hurt you in the least. Buy local handmade crafts (avoid the middleman) wherever you go - there is always a story behind every piece of artwork. Take pins or small souvenirs from your hometown to give away - make someone's day extra special.

Finally, make your Bucket List and Just Go For It - Remember life is not a dress rehearsal - we go this way once!

The Smith's are addicted to world travel. Visit their **Interface Images web site (www.interfaceimages.com)** *and follow them on their* **Blog "Images – Connecting the World" (www.interfaceimages.com/blog)** *to see why. They are truly dream travellers capturing the world one smiling face at a time.*

Good Luck and we look forward to your astonishing book publication. Keep us up to date and hopefully we will see you sooner than later.

Bob & Susan Kovitz

Background: Bob and Susan live in Tucson, Arizona. We met them on a Panama Canal cruise. They are an interesting and fun couple. They are easy to be with and thought provoking at the same time. Bob is a musician and actor and Susan teaches Jazzercise at the famous Canyon Ranch Spa Resort. Bob tells us:

The questions you've asked have (and will) continue to fill up travel guides for years to come. Obviously, every traveler's experience is singular, filtered through his or her own experiences and expectations.

In a perverse way, the Internet has helped and hindered travel - helped by providing us with comparative views of a place, a tour, a ship, a lodging; at the same time, it takes some of the excitement out of traveling to somewhere that is virtually unknown to you. There are times that you can do so much research that the reality of a trip becomes an afterthought.

Our cardinal rule for travel: If you think that you like (love) someone, travel first to some place where neither of you have been before and where neither of you has an advantage (e.g., language, family background). In Barcelona, after my then-girlfriend complained that I ate tangerines too loudly and after I found her wig washed out and drying on the shower stall handles, we could both see that this was not a perfect match. Needless to say, I didn't marry her.

On the other hand, too much togetherness is too much of a good thing. When teaching in China, Susan insisted on organizing an aerobics class at 6 a.m. for her fellow teachers. I just wanted to roll over in the (hard) bed and grab an extra hour of sleep. She came back with her endorphins on fire, and I got my sleep time in - win/win.

Or, better yet, see how your fellow traveler reacts in a situation: When I was bitten by a sea lion while SCUBA diving in Mexico, Susan didn't panic. She just kept sending down to the front desk for more tequila! And when Susan ended up in the decompression chamber on Roatan, Honduras, all I could do was to wave to her through the little porthole type window in the decompression capsule. And yet, we survived - and with good stories to tell, too.

I used to be put off by my fellow American travelers who would say, "that looks like _____ (fill in the blank - some place back home)." But now I realize that everyone needs a point of reference. When I was in Honolulu, my first wife's parents couldn't get over the fact that they were in Hawaii. Growing up, they were told that when something was far away, it was in "Honolulu." By the same token, we learn to say "Timbuktu" as a faraway place. But my in-laws were from the Middle East, a place much closer to Timbuktu than Hawaii. Where you end up depends so much on where you start.

Finally, if you run into the Dunlap's, stick out your hand and say "hi." You never know when they might hit you up for some travel experiences!

Susie & Steve Ladow

Background: Susie and Steve are relatives of ours living in San Diego, California. They are about as lovely of a couple you can image. Steve is a general contractor building luxury homes and Susie is a former teacher. They have raised three children. They have tried new ways of living and traveling. Susie shares with us:

Dear Wayne and Pat,

Can't wait to read your book. I know it will spark a lot of ideas for adventures. Steve claims we live our lives in reverse. We are carefree and adventurous when we are young and as we age we become more timid and fearful of change and afraid to take risks. Shouldn't it be the other way around? The older you get you are always getting closer to the end and it does come to an end for all of us. Why not go doing things you love or grow from? Traveling is experiencing life outside of your comfort zone. I love to try to enjoy the place and culture as if I was living there, not as a visitor. The people you meet are the real highlight and they all have stories to tell.

After growing up in San Diego we took our three children and moved to Clark, Colorado to live on a ranch. What a change and we learned so much. We went for one year and ended up staying eight years. We grew close as family, experienced things challenging, scary and fun. The people we met will always be a very special memory and the beauty of the mountains is a permanent vision. Our children look at life differently because of what they learned growing up in a small ranching town. Wealth was not a factor, you were judged on what kind of person you were and how you lived your life. Acceptance was there because in a small community you can't really exclude anyone. You learn to all get along and embrace your differences. If there is a need you find most are there to help out.

At 65 another opportunity showed itself… a motorcycle trip through the Alps. This required learning to ride after 40 years. It added excitement to our lives a real challenge and an amazing experience. We have done it twice now and each time we feel closer to God and marvel at the beauty in the country and the people. Yes, it is scary at times, and uncomfortable, but most of the time it is something I will never forget and count my blessings that I was able to have this adventure.

When we travel we do not stay in fancy places, but we do enjoy being comfortable and love eating food cooked lovingly. We don't buy a lot of things to bring back, on a motorcycle you don't have any room. We like to do what the people do that live there. Our home is small and we try not to accumulate a lot of stuff. I guess our goal has always been to live lightly. We aren't totally successful but it is a goal of ours. We put our money towards memories, given the choice. It is wonderful to have a home base to come back to but we try not to let it anchor us down. We often wait for opportunities to come our way and then we try to recognize them and follow where they may lead us. It has served us well so far.

I wish you well. Love and hugs, Susie

Pat and Bill Allen

Background: Bill and Pat Allen are a delightful retired couple living in San Diego, California. Bill is a former executive of high tech companies and Pat is a former teacher. We are fortunate to have them as good friends. When we get together we can exchange travel stories all night. They have had good luck in significantly reducing their travel costs by using home exchanges all around the world. Here are a few words from Pat regarding travel:

Home Exchanges

My husband and I, a retired couple living in San Diego, love to experience travel through home exchanges. Being able to set our own pace and schedule, prepare some of our own meals and enjoy the luxury of a larger living area, not to mention the obvious economic advantages, appeals to us. Combining the savings of using airline miles, not paying for lodgings and frequently trading vehicles makes traveling quite inexpensive.

In the beginning I was hesitant to let strangers into my home, but I have learned that communicating through e-mails, you can get to know a person and feel comfortable with them. The great majority of home exchangers are retired professionals much like us. A large part of the anxiety is relieved when one considers each has the same view of treating the other's home with the same respect as you would like your home to be treated.

In house trading it helps to have a flexible attitude and roll with the punches if things don't turn out exactly as you had hoped. You need to be able to separate the unimportant things from the big picture. Always keep in mind you are saving thousands of dollars by traveling this way. You can lock away anything of high value to you. We have always had positive experiences and numerous serendipitous lovely surprises when traveling by the home exchange program. Two of the websites we like are **www.homelink.com** *and* **www. intervac-homeexchange.com**.

Why I love to travel?

In short travel makes me feel incredibly happy and fully alive. The memories of places seen and shared with friends and relationships formed through travel are so much more lasting and rewarding than memories of material things, which quickly fade away. Travel experiences truly do broaden the mind and help us to see the world through different eyes and point of view of other cultures. I feel most fortunate to live in a country where its citizens are free to travel where they wish and speak their minds freely. Traveling, satisfying the wanderlust, is one of my life's greatest pleasures.

Cherie Sotsti & Greg Retkowski

Background: The word 'interesting' is pale in describing this vivacious young recently married couple that have much to teach all of us about living life to the fullest. Cherie has unhooked from life expectations and lives to travel. Greg works for six months and travels for six months. Read this from Cherie and Greg to see how they do it along with their love for travel and unique travel experiences and advice.

From Cherie:

I know exactly when I caught the travel bug. It was October 15, 1998. I got the Amelia Earhart Complex. Simply defined, the Amelia Earhart Complex is the sudden urge to get on an airplane and just disappear.

At the time I was 27-years-old and working 70 hours a week as the branch manager of a used-car dealership. Those were the days before unlimited "minutes", and my cellular phone bill was more than my mortgage. Back then, I knew a lot about racy cars, quick men, fast food, and short vacations. I had a life everyone wanted, but me!

What eluded me were the very things that define a rich life: love, integrity, patience, and generosity. The only book I could have written five years ago would have been titled: "How to Be an Immature Defensive Control Freak and Still Make Lots of Money."

That's when I met her. She was a 78-year-old woman who had traveled through 78 countries. Her experiences were her treasures; her memories were her children. Each year she and her husband chose a new country and explored it together. Their ages were always the same as the number of countries they had explored. That's when I got the idea of "30 in 30." I gave myself 3 years (until I was 30-years-old) to visit 30 countries.

Real change is never slow. A few weeks later I left my job, I left my house, and I left my life. I traded my briefcase for a backpack. I traded my savings for an airplane ticket. My friends thought I had lost my mind. But, I am not crazy. My story, however, is.

Traveling through 30 countries in three years, I spent more time with mosquitoes than movie stars. I've climbed up volcanoes, fallen down glaciers, laid on beaches, stood on mountaintops, and jumped out of planes and into rivers.

In 1998, I left a boatload of work in East LA and thirty months later I landed on a yacht in the South of France. I turned 40-years old in 2011 and the adventure continues. Now I've traveled through over 65 countries, which means I haven't been to over half the countries in the world.

At first I thought I would go back to work after "getting traveling out of my system." But traveling changed me. Instead of cramming myself back into a cubical, I've sold everything I own (both houses) and I'm still traveling the world. I don't own much, but I have a lot of great memories.

My friends sometimes ask me: "When are you going to buy a nice car?" My answer is this: "Why would I want to work 50 weeks out of the year to afford a car I don't want? On a recent trip, I wrote these words in my travel journal. It sums up why I continue to travel and how traveling has come to define who I am: "It is in these wide open spaces that I am healed and my broken places are filled. In this wild place there is room to be alive. Enough room to laugh and cry and love and be whole. Here I can be loud and quiet and finally at peace."

So many people live their lives in fear. We are afraid to loose our jobs, afraid to travel, afraid to try new things, afraid of what people will think, and afraid to hear opinions that are different from our own. In short, as humans, we are afraid of change.

When you travel, you have the opportunity to let new ideas in and let life affect you. I want to change and grow, which is why I embrace traveling and enjoy meeting people from different cultures. I hope I'm not the same person in ten years.

I believe that trust is given, not earned. I trust people and it is extremely rare that I am disappointed. People amaze me, and I try to live each day with wonder and gratitude.

There are many ways to travel and many opportunities to save money on a journey. Be flexible. Not having a time constraint is the best money-saver. When you are in a hurry, you have to buy things (like airplane tickets) on certain days. When you travel you don't need to plan every day and every moment. Leave open spaces in your schedule. Leave open spaces in your mind.

I travel with a backpack that has wheels. That way I can pull it easily through airports, and then put it on my shoulders when I have to walk up six flights of stairs. I always leave 25% of my space available in my pack. The best way to "blend in" in a foreign country is to buy your clothes on your trip. The only time this advice bit me in the butt was when I went to Thailand. There are no size 12 clothes for women in Thailand.

I've exchanged "things" for "experiences" in life. I rarely buy "stuff." When you have "stuff", you have to worry about it and protect it. I rarely spend money on a nice hotel—I'd much rather have a nice dinner.

Sharing the journey of travel with someone you love can be both amazing and frustrating. I am married and my husband and I currently travel together at least six months a year. I see it like this: you can have your way all the time, and then you get to watch the sunset alone. Or you can compromise sometimes and share the incredible adventure of life with someone special. I choose to share the adventure.

Listening to what is really going on for your travel partner is incredibly important. When you really "let the world in" it can cause great emotional upheavals. Once I had an idea that I would give out small candies to children in Zimbabwe. I was on a bus, traveling through remote villages, and children would run after the bus waving. I asked the bus driver to stop, and I stepped out to give the village kids a treat.

Then, over a dozen grown men from the village ran towards me with the most desperate eyes I have ever seen. I was terrified and the bus driver yelled at me to get on the bus. As I was stepping on the bus, the men grabbed the bag and it rained candy all over the place. As the bus drove away, the men scrambled on the floor for those little pieces of candy. All I could do for the rest of the day was cry. It broke my heart. Traveling is not always a vacation. Traveling is not just lying on a beach with a cocktail and a good book. There are days that will break you, and there are days that will mend you. My advice is this: let yourself break, and let yourself heal.

Finally—the big question is this: How do you start? The answer is simple. You buy a ticket. Buy the ticket first. (A plane ticket, boat ticket, or however you plan to travel.) The rest of your trip will fall in line once you buy your ticket and commit to go. Take the first step.

Also, I have helped many friends write their resignation letters. Here is a template that you may use:

Dear boss:

I quit.

Now—go enjoy this wild wonderful life. You have a limited number of years on earth. Some people are blessed with 80 or more years of health, while some only have a few years. What are you going to do with your limited time? There is a big world out there—go explore it!

Living a life defined by travel: "It is in these wide open spaces that I am healed and my broken places are filled. In this wild place there is room to be alive. There is enough room to laugh and cry and love and be whole. Here I can be loud and quiet and finally at peace."

- Cherie Sogsti

From Greg:

Hello Wayne,

A bit about me is mixed in with my anecdotes below, and there's a little more about me in my journals etc. on: **http://www.rage.net/~greg/**. Cherie writes colorfully about me when typing up our travel stories at: **http://www.wherescherie.com/**.

I guess I was born to travel, my parents both worked for airlines and met on an international trip. The biggest perk for airline employees is free travel for the family and discounts on hotels (it certainly isn't the pay). So I spent a lot of time on airliners from a very young age. I took a break from traveling throughout my 20's, and then brought it back into my live through a love of sailing. When I moved to San Francisco bay for high-tech work I looked at what sport the area was most well known for. Turns out to be sailing - so I bought a 22-foot sailboat and sailed all over the bay. I liked it so much that I bought a 41-foot sailboat with intentions to sail it on an extended trip. When the tech market tanked in

2001 I decided I rather just sail off into the sunset then scrounge for work while paying expensive bay-area rents.

Panama was one of our favorites. Cherie is much more eloquent about writing about our experiences there: http://www.wherescherie.com/dir/panama.php.

One of our trips was to Cuba. That's the poignant example of why I travel. I could read all I want in history books about the U.S. relationship to Cuba, I can take political theory courses to try and understand communism, I could read all the articles from newspapers and clips from CNN about Cuba to know the U.S. take on events there. But I couldn't really *know* and *experience* what it is like in Cuba without visiting there. I could be 'told' that communism is a bad deal, but I had to see it first-hand. I had to go there, see the place, talk to the people and have my own experiences. (and, yeah, turns out communism is a bad deal btw).

For the last 10 years I've been working for six months a year and traveling for the other six months. When I work I pick up a contract doing what I do (system administration and software development) for six months. Finding a job is like any skill in that if you practice it you get better at it and are less afraid of having to use it. Having to basically get a new job every year for the last 10 has made it anxiety-free for me when I'm traveling because experience has taught me that if you are willing to show up and put in an honest-day's work there's always work available when I'm ready to go back. My field is well suited for this as most of my work is project-based and at rapidly growing Internet startups.

I love doing the six/six because when I go back to work I am excited to go back to it, and when I'm heading off to travel I am excited to do that too. I am never doing either activity long enough that I get burnt out on it. And you can get burnt out on travel, there's only so many days sitting on a beach sipping pina coladas a person can take.

There's a good tax-incentive to doing it this way. Because of our progressive tax system it is much better to show, say, 40K a year for two years, then 80K one year and 0K the next. If you can work it where you work less than six months a year and that work is away from your 'home of record' you may even be able to deduct a per-diem rate from your taxes (consult your tax adviser, etc.).

The world is not a scary place. Although like anything, if you go into the world unprepared you can get into a lot of trouble. Using common sense, getting up to speed on the customs of a country, learning through guidebooks or other travelers which areas to avoid, and remaining aware of your surroundings, are important for having a trouble-free trip. We've also learned to just budget out that one bad thing will happen to you per year... Same as home. You may have your passport stolen, you may get food poisoning (I average once a year while I am traveling), you may miss some important mail which causes penalties on an overdue bill, but if you were home you'd just as likely have your car broken into or your bike stolen.

One important lesson is that anytime you say 'yes' to something you are saying 'no' to something else. For example, every day on our Alaska trip we spend seeing things in British Columbia is a day we won't be able to spend in Alaska.

This concept extends to all parts of life - if you say 'yes' to a big-screen TV or a new car you are saying 'no' to using that money to travel. If you buy a house you may be saying 'no' to traveling at all if you can't cover the mortgage cost without having a permanent job. Saying 'yes' to travel means saying 'no' to seeing your friends and family for the months you are gone.

I grew up having cats, and I love cats, but in the vein of every 'yes' means a 'no' I can't have one if I'm to travel six months a year. I try and make due visiting with other folk's pets. As for home, for the first eight years of my six-months-a-year of travel I'd rent an apartment month-to-month, which was never a great place because any great place required a year lease. It'd take me a month to get the utilities all turned on and the furniture moved in. I'd enjoy the place for four months, and then spend the last month closing down the apartment, moving out furniture, and turning off utilities. The last year we've been trying out living in an RV instead. When we go traveling we travel in the RV, or if we're going to do backpacking we'll just put the RV into a storage place. Much less hassle going between the 'working' state to the 'travel' state and back.

Before traveling it's good to really scrub through your bank statements and identify all the places your money is going, rent, phone bills, car payments, etc. Try and whittle those recurring costs down to the bone. We try and not have an empty residence when we are traveling for months at a time - we get out of our apartment and put our stuff in storage.

While traveling we try and bike / walk / public transit when outside the U.S. Most of the rest of the world either doesn't have majority populations with their own cars or have dense-enough urban centers that public transit is pretty darn good. And it takes away the worries about not knowing the local laws and customs when driving somewhere overseas. Our one overseas car accident was in Mexico. In the US the left turn signal means I am turning left - in Mexico it means you are clear to pass me on the left. You can imagine what happened.

We usually find airfare or hotels through one of those airline aggregators like Travelocity. Always better to book in advance if you can. However we usually have pretty good success doing things like hotels and campsites at the last minute, which allows us to keep our itineraries open-ended.

Traveling by RV we eat most of our meals 'at home', we'll go out to eat if there is some local dishes that a place is famous for. However going far away and trying to eat American food out at a restaurant is just going to be expensive and disappointing. Non-local items are cheaper in big cities, so stock up on food/fuel/ etc. while you are in one. Haggling isn't a skill Americans have but it is good to learn it and not be afraid to use it as most of the world does business this way.

We stay in touch via e-mail, Skype, and Facebook. We (on and off) maintain a blog of our travels to keep friends up-to-date on where we are and what we are up-to.

We usually get a Lonely Planet guide for the region we are going to. We also do a lot of Internet searches to find out about places before visiting. If traveling by vehicle we use Google Maps to plan routes.

When traveling in the U.S. we use Yelp a lot to find out which places are good (usually restaurants). It's like having a local friend who knows all the best places to eat. Before Yelp picking a restaurant would be done either by asking a local or two (and you never know what their ideas about cuisine are) or just picking one based on which place had the most colorful sign out front. Now, if a place has a few reviews on Yelp and they are positive we are almost guaranteed that it is going to be a good experience. Some bullet points:

- Be aware of your surroundings. Just every-so-often look around and notice if you are walking towards a worse part of town; if there are sketchy people around. Be aware of where your wallet is and that your backpack is zipped up.

- If you are in an area known for pickpocketing use a luggage lock to lock together all the zipper-pulls on your backpack. The same if the area is known for theft in hotel rooms, lock up your duffels with a luggage lock.

- Look like a local. Or at least dress and accessorize like you have about the same net-worth as the locals. If you can't really pull that off, like you are traveling in Haiti or something, just dress very plainly and don't have anything flashy (jewelry, etc.).

- If you find yourself in the wrong part of town, behave as if you know where you are going, act with a purpose, do not look aimless. Predators can sniff out people who are disoriented and fearful. Back track your steps.

- Have copies of your important documents, stored in a different place than the originals. This will help if you do have the misfortune of having your wallet or passport stolen.

- Try and not travel with anything that you'd be devastated to lose.

Noelia Da Mata

Background: It took me some time to think how to best describe this unique lovely young woman. As she describes below, travel has broadened her perspective of life giving her wisdom beyond her years. Growing up in Jersey in the Channel Islands off of France, she started traveling young and then established a successful career. After turning 30, she was looking for more in life and recently gave it all up to travel the world again. With her good friend, Annelise, they took a round-the-world adventure for a year starting and ending in Rio during Carnival. We met Noelia and Annelise in Iguazu Falls, Argentina, and as travel can afford you, became good friends later hosting them in our hometown of San Diego and most recently they hosted us in their hometown in the Channel Islands. Treat yourself to read about Noelia's life changing experience gained from travel:

What inspired me to travel was the curiosity of wanting to know what was out there in the big wide so called "scary world". I remember whenever I use to go on vacation for my 2-week break, I'd be sitting on the plane usually lucky enough to be on a window seat, and I'd be sitting there flying high above a certain country or two and I would wonder "what sort of place is that down there?" "Wow I wonder what that city is like, or are there are any village people living in these crazy mountains, and wow look at where that tiny village is positioned, I wonder what sort of people live there and what sort of life do they live, is it anything like mine, what foods do they eat, what morals and beliefs do they have and how do they survive? Are they happy?" etc. etc." These were only a few of the questions that baffled my mind as I flew within the short or long hours that I did.

I think it was always something to do with being so high above the clouds, where the sun was always shining that made me realize "there's a big wide world out there and I'd love to go explore it." The sense of freedom that I knew travelling would bring me, sent such a huge rush over my body and the excitement of accomplishing such a crazy idea was so exhilarating that I just had to look into how I would I ever possibly do such a thing. It was then that travelling the world became my ambition.

I started to save every single British pound I could. I'd make my own packed lunch for work, would cut out any luxuries like even buying myself a magazine and cut down completely on going out so often with friends. I would use the time to explore the world map and decide where I wanted to go. At first I looked at all the 7 wonders and thought I'd try and fit them in. Then I started looking at travel companies and seeking their advise on round-the-world tickets and it became quite easy to establish a route I was happy with. This just fed my ego with more excitement and once my ticket was booked that was it, the final piece of confirmation to myself that I was in fact deadly serious in putting my fantasy into a reality. This was in the year 2001 and at the time I was only 21-years young, all my friends had decided to go to university to get a degree yet here I was deciding to embark on a journey around the world after quitting my tourism job and finally building up the courage to tell my parents and boyfriend at the time.

I must say that I did prepare and organize myself extremely well. I did a lot of reading over the Internet, caught up with a mature friend who had been, and noted down the dos and don'ts. I had my list of essentials to take, clothing tips, health advice, what jabs to take etc. etc. It did in fact take me a good 10 months to prepare for such an adventure. Some parts I thought were going to be a bit tricky I would pre-organize with accommodation (i.e. hotels, transfer's and tours etc.) but for the majority of the time in places that were geared for travellers/backpackers I would generally just go with the flow and wouldn't necessarily know where I would be laying my head that particular night or how on earth would I ever get from A to B... but it seemed that one way or another everything would always resolve itself and I'd be shown a way or a place to stay or a friend to travel with.

I guess the beauty of this that should be brought into everyday life is that we as humans can never see the future yet we worry about it. So much what travelling taught me in this instance is not to worry because no matter what deep and scary experience you are in or you may think you are in there's always a way of solving it, or something will always form itself, show up to help you. What this in turn did for me was allow me to "Trust". This is a huge part in travelling... to Trust absolutely everything, most importantly your instincts because as you travel you really have no control over the certain situations or events that happen in and around you. You can't control the weather, the people you meet, the foods you eat that may make you as sick as a dog, the delays with planes, trains and buses that will leave you stranded for hours on end, the accommodation you booked which looks and is nothing to what it said on the website, etc. etc. ... you get the drift.

What you can control is how you react to them when they do or sometimes more than often don't seem to work out for you and it's from this reaction of yours that really defines who you are as a person in the sense that this is where you truly start finding out about yourself. You will learn many skills and acquire certain abilities along with a few other prominent things such as an abundance of patience, knowledge, gratitude, awareness, emotions, wisdom, etc... and it's with all this mixture that develops you beyond belief that no other job or life experience could ever possibly do for you. Travelling really enhances you as a person and offers you such great life experiences that to try and explain this in such words is virtually impossible but yet every traveller out there knows exactly what I mean and am talking about when I briefly mention this.

The interaction with different types of people who you meet both from travellers and local cultures give you such joy as each and every single one of us have our own story and uniqueness and we may feel like we are totally different worlds apart but when you look deeper we all learn that in actual fact we are very much the same... pure human beings experiencing life as we know it. It's fascinating to be amongst their cultures, to find out their beliefs, their fears as well as their love and zest for life. What foods do they enjoy, what smells, colours, and music am I constantly surrounded by. How do they survive and make the most of each of their living days? I could carry on with a huge list of other things that are open to you as you travel and once you start on the journey of discovery the more your five senses become alert and the stronger the desire to feed yourself with more and more knowledge. Its like being a child again and soaking up all that surrounds you that you don't feel like you need to work on learning it just becomes part of you and soon enough everything becomes almost automatic.

A lot of my travel experiences for me are stored within my memory and will be treasured forever, however I did take a few hundred if not thousand photographs and also wrote a small travel journal with various stories or certain emotions I felt when I embarked upon something extra special. Keeping in touch with home is so simple and it is easy to exchange e-mail or nowadays Facebook friendship with those who you meet along the way.

Occasionally I would buy a new piece of clothing and leave some of my old stuff with the hostel or give it to the families I would stay with. Travelling alone was also such a joy. You are never alone unless you choose to be and that was the wonderfully thing about it all. I had the best of both worlds and even if you are travelling with a best friend or a partner be sure to have a big talk before you go and express your own individual needs to each other so that there won't be any confusion, anything taken personally or bickering. I would say the most important key of all things is to keep communicating as you go along, keep checking in with one another and accept that you are all unique and will feel differently towards things occasionally.

Of course you are on a budget so when deciding on moving onto the next place it is worth spending some time looking at all possible transport options. Sometimes flying may be a little bit more expensive but if it's a place you need more time to explore then occasionally spend that little bit extra when you can afford to. If you are really on a budget I would always recommend taking a bus journey during the night as this saves you on a nights accommodation and you also tend to arrive during the day at your new destination which is safer too.

When deciding where to stay, a wonderful website to use is Hostelworld and it gives you ratings and comments from previous travellers. Look at location and depending on the type of person you are or what sort of mood takes you, you may decide to stay in a party-type hostel or a quieter family run one. Don't be afraid though to go on other travellers' recommendations that you meet along the way or others from a guidebook. Be careful when arriving at bus stations and going with a tout that is waiting or promoting their business, if you are in desperation and haven't pre-organized your place to stay then be sure to ask to see pictures, or a card, ask all the information needed possible and go on your gut instincts. You can usually pick up a real bargain this way but know that you take the risk of your own safety so best to go in groups and that the place itself and people running it may be a bit dodgy.

I would say that one of my most used and needed travel items was my money belt. In fact I had two. One tiny tiny one that was very thin which I could wear under my knickers and another which was a bigger and thicker which I wore when I needed to take my passport or travel documents with me and usually I'd only wear that under jeans or heavier clothing etc. I had a bank debit card with me and a credit card stored in a hidden place in my backpack that was also always padlocked. I always carried with me a first-aid packet and a photocopy of my documents to include insurance, passport and health jab card

I also made sure I had printed out my itinerary and had all the same documents left behind with a family member or friend; nowadays everything can be accessed through Internet and e-mail so it is so much easier.

On that note everywhere you go there is always someone doing business with regards to an Internet cafe of some sort and it's always fairly cheap to use. Some will offer great connection and computers with Skype set up and where you can place your USB key to download your photos from your camera onto Facebook or some other website like Picasa or flipper or you can simply just store them on your USB, perhaps make two copies just in case you loose one or get robbed. The most important tip is to always be street wise, use your common sense, remain balanced and trust your instincts on everything.

For me the greatest gift that travelling gives me is pure appreciation for the simplest of things. It brings me back and close to interacting with earth itself... nature at its best... natural landscapes and manmade buildings that before I wouldn't necessarily taken much notice of. This could be from a beautiful sunset to an amazing architectural building to a innocent smile from a local passerby to a ray of exploding flavours in a mouthful from a typical local dish to stepping foot on lands far beyond that give you the most breathtaking views ever.

Another priceless gift that travelling gives me is meeting all sorts of weird and wonderful people who become instantly your best friend ever because you find yourself sharing your life story with a complete stranger but yet it seems natural to and then you become the closest friends possible and the friendship just continues no matter the distance or time.

You do come back a very different person when you have been travel and it's not because your personality has changed but a simple fact that you have gone through and experienced so much in any one day, month and then year that you have developed beyond belief and it's with this fact alone that for me I am so grateful for all the learning's that travelling has given me for it has truly shown me a huge deal about the reality of life, what is meaningful, important to me, what I am actually capable of doing, how I am actually able to conquer what seems the hardest of all things, the strength in me as a person, and much much more than I can just not describe.

To sum up its not what some people seem to perceive as a "scary world out there" but a truly magical one that is waiting to be explored by many more of us as year by year it seems to grow to be more and more popular and doable. It's not just for gap year students but many people of all ages and walks of life, even families. Local communities in these third world countries are just waiting with baited breath for more travellers to pass through as they are so dependent on us in order to help them earn a living by offering their goods and services just so that they can survive. So it's really not as daunting as you imagine but rather an amazing life experience that will transform you and your life in an incredible way that you never thought possible. It will impact you for the rest of your life, that's certain!!!

Andy Achterkirchen

Background: We have been fortunate to have Andy as a wonderful neighbor for 23 years. This interesting man was a top scientist for a large aerospace firm in San Diego. Now retired, he donates much of his time to teaching math to less privileged high school students. Not willing to rest on his accomplishments, read his inspiring words how he has changed his life through travel.

Wayne,

For me, one of the most enjoyable things about traveling is meeting people, both local people and people from other countries throughout the world who are also traveling. Many times, though, differences in language makes meeting people challenging, which leads to my story.

Twelve years ago I was in Paris with relatives. We had a great time in Paris. We often ate in small restaurants near our rented apartment where no one spoke English. Although four of the five of us had studied French in school, none of us could remember enough to decipher some of the items on the menu.

When I returned home, I asked myself "Millions of people in the world speak more than one language. Why not I?" I decided to learn Spanish. I was 57 years old then. I started by taking some courses at a local community college in San Diego where I live. Then I went to Mexico where I attended Spanish language schools and lived with Mexican families, typically middle class families. I went for two to three weeks at a time and did this for eight times over a four-year period. I visited some of the oldest most beautiful colonial cities in Mexico and never had any problems.

More rewarding, I was able to meet some wonderful people whom I never could have met any other way. Meeting these people reinforced the feeling I had that people can live in different cultures and different environments but yet they are basically just like the people we know and associate with in our daily life. They are thoughtful, considerate, and want the best for their families. I still remember when I was in Oaxaca, Mexico and mentioned to the father of the family with whom I was staying that I was interested in buying a traditional Mexican woven rug. I told him I was planning on checking them out in the shops in town. He said to me that the place with the best selection and best prices was a small village about an hours drive from Oaxaca and that he would take me there. We drove for an hour, the last half on a dirt road and seemed to be in the middle of an isolated area with absolutely nothing around. Then as we reached the top of a little hill could see a small village. Each house had traditional Mexican woven rugs hanging in front with a weaving room in the front of the house. We must have visited at least ten of these houses before I found the rug I was looking for. I could never have done this by myself.

So I particularly enjoy traveling in Spanish speaking countries. However, when I am traveling in non-Spanish speaking countries I often hear people speaking Spanish. I introduce myself and meet them. It is a great way to meet people. And whenever I travel, I always learn at least a few words in the local language. A few words go a long way, particularly with children.

Kristy-Lee May

Background: Kristy is 27 years old from Melbourne, Australia. She lives to travel and has visited about 34 countries already. We met this outgoing young woman on our gulet boat excursion of southern Turkey. She has definitely been bite by the "travel bug." Learn more about her love for travel:

Hello Wayne,

I'm so happy for you guys. You're doing a fantastic job. I love that you are writing a book. Can't wait to see it.

My name is Kristy and I'm from Melbourne (Australia). The first time I went on a plane I was 21 and I jumped out of it. The second time I went up to Queensland (Australia) for a Christmas holiday. I loved the whole feeling of being in a plane and going somewhere new. I think this is when I caught the virus, better known as "the travel bug". I come from a large family (nine) so travel was far from the top of things we would do or learn about but I wanted more. I wanted to see and be in the places that I grew up watching on the idiot box. I wanted more for myself and what better way than to travel. Definitely something you can't be taught in any school.

My first overseas trip was to New Zealand when I was 22. I went for month and it was the most amazing thing I had experienced in my whole life (at the time). My next trip was 9 months later... I ended up in Asia, Europe, North Africa, Scandinavia, North and South America. That trip was for 10 months. Nine months later I spent two weeks in Nepal and another nine months after that I headed to Turkey, more Scandinavia, the Caribbean, Central America, again U.S.A and Vanuatu...for four months.

So far, I'm 27 and been to about 34-ish countries. Too many to keep track. My life has now become about travel and wanting to see more countries. I even just got a job with a local airline company. Don't get me wrong, there are many countries I would love to return too but I always wonder what I would be missing out on discovering in another country.

For all those people out there who are contemplating extended travel... Stop thinking about it and just do it. It's scary at first but you will not regret it. I can guarantee you that. It is worth every penny, sacrifice and second you have. Every country has something that you will like and dislike about it but that's how the world rolls. My personal favorites are Turkey, Cuba, Morocco, Switzerland, Jamaica and Portugal. It all comes down to the people you meet and encounter, food, weather and experiences. But I have loved all the countries I have been to.

So, you're worried about your budget? There so many things to factor in... time, season, and style of travel. I have always backpacked since it's the cheapest option which means my money goes toward the crazy things I want to do and I can do them for longer because I compromise by sleeping in hostels instead of hotels, travel by bus/train instead of flying and eat street food rather than in restaurants. I can't tell you how to travel. This is completely up to you and no one knows you better than yourself.

This also helps with planning your trip. When I first went to Thailand, I hadn't looked up any information. When I got there I felt completely lost and hated it for about the first week. So, I strongly suggest knowing why you want to go to a particular place. What do you want to see and do whilst you are there? What you take is also important and that again depends on how you travel. Are you backpacking or are you staying in luxurious resorts?! Backpacking essential is jeans whilst resort people probably should take some heels. You get where I'm going with this!

I use the web to look up EVERYTHING! Here are just a few sites I use:

*Country information - **lonelyplanet.com***

*Hostels - **hostelworld.com** and **hostelbookers.com***

*Hotels - **bookings.com**, **wotif.com**, and **lastminute.com***

*Cheap flights - **bestflights.com** and **skyscanner.net***

I don't travel with my partner. We did once - few years ago for about 5 weeks. It was great but we have different ideas on how to travel. I'm more backpacker style and he is more luxurious. Hopefully we get to the stage that Pat and Wayne are at one day... Until then we travel separately which isn't my ideal situation but like I said... One day! I also do not own any pets for the fact that I love to travel.

Methods of keeping in contact: Facebook, e-mail, and Skype!

Travelling can be scary (I'm sure I mentioned that earlier) but more in the case of safety, health, and security for you and your belongings. It's all common sense. Many countries are known for pickpockets, hijackings, health risks etc. So, you don't leave your things unattended and don't immediately trust ANYONE. I say, "if you can't afford to lose it then don't take it with you". I've never used a money belt and in saying that, I have only ever been successfully robbed...once! It's all about being aware of your surroundings and remembering what country you are in and what you've already heard/read about it in terms of safety.

I've chosen to try live a more sustainable life since travelling. I see all these families being completely self sufficient and I know it's hard to do that in a developed country but I do what I can. I've started a veggie garden, walk or use public transport when I can, try buy organic or direct from the farmers and energy saving light bulbs just to name a few things...

Why do I love to travel? The people, food, weather, cultural differences, geographical differences, festivals... There's so many reasons. I've never gone on a holiday to relax/do nothing. There's always something to see, do and discover and every country is worth discovering.

Good luck and let me know when the final print is. I'm already interested to see the finished product.

Love and miss you guys. Take care, Kristy

Joe & Dolores Mos

Background: Joe & Dolores live in Vancouver, Canada. We met this very personable couple on a repositioning trans-Pacific cruise from

Vancouver, Canada, to Japan on the Holland American Volendam cruise
ship. Dolores writes first, then Joe:

Hello Wayne

*Joe and I are considered seniors now (he is 81 and still vital and curious
about the world, especially financial and historic decisions and keeps alert with
daily readings). We just celebrated our 52nd wedding anniversary yesterday.*

*In our younger days were mainly active with the children skiing Sun
Valley, Parksville, and other regions but never in Europe as were preferred the
amenities in America. We were active in a Racquet club for years traveling most
of the National Parks in a Motor home with the children.*

*Winters: Half our life is spent in Sun City in Palm Desert, California,
a retirement community with all the amenities and two golf courses, which we
frequent. We belong to the golf association and play in tournaments and other
social engagements of every sort (over 50 clubs and organizations to amuse us).
Look up the Sun City Palm Desert website. Never a dull moment. I also volunteer
as an usher at the local McCallum theatre about twice a week Snowbirds visit
often in the winter. Summers it is too hot so we leave for Canada.*

*Summers: We recently built a home on the waterfront on Vancouver
Island away from the maddening crowd and have the two fold up bikes that
we can put in our car for touring the islands and a small sailboat for puttering
around the shallow bay. There we have a social network, tennis court,
community pool and several lovely golf courses too.*

*Now as we are older we prefer to cruise knowing we have the creature
comforts not having to look for hotels, lodging, meals etc. which previously was
certainly part of the adventure in travel experiencing different cultures. The
Internet now certainly makes all that searching easier.*

*We prefer to take longer cruises than shorter luxurious ones. The
benefit being we get to know the passengers better and gain lifelong
relationships with people like you and Pat who are now living your dreams. We
have the time now, and see more territory. We enjoy meeting people and thus
a longer cruise give us that benefit. We generally cruise in September, October,
and November, as the crowds are less and fewer school groups.*

*France is the country of our choice because Joe speaks fluently and I
speak a bastardized sort that makes the French squirm in agony. However they*

appreciate the miserable effort on my part. We enjoy the camaraderie, food, and idiosyncrasies of the French (speaking the lingo makes for more compatibility indeed).

We use the Internet frequently now to scout out bargains, use Lonely Planet and friends recommendations. Many of our friends are experienced travelers too. Read about places.

We take hand sanitizers always, as planes and washrooms are not germ free and always a blow up pillow, wristwatch with two faces for time zone but now use the iPhone.

Always, I carry a light rain wind jacket and a cashmere black cardigan underneath for warmth or over the shoulders in the eve, as ships can be chilly. Joe carries 2 pair of shoes, comfortable sandals, and black evening shoes. I carry 3 pair, one for evening, one for walking/jogging and sandals and always a cashmere sweater, extra Kleenex, a small flashlight for nights where you may be unfamiliar with the place. We load up Kindles with interesting books, periodicals and daily newspapers for long boring times which are rare. We seldom find life boring. It is always a task to take as few items of clothing as necessary. Luggage is a drag and hampers travel. Be very discerning about your packed items. Roll sweaters and other clothing items to avoid wrinkles. Wear the item at least five times.

I carry nuts and dried fruits for snacks and bottled water in a shoulder carrier or light fold up bag. Staying in touch with friends and family via the Internet in towns rather than the ship as it can be expensive and putting info on the thumb drive later sent. I carry a small computer.

We often ask ourselves what we would choose to do differently if we had to do it all over again and presently we are happy with our choices so far except Joe is ready for new fancier svelte gourmand cook, and a tiger in the bedroom).

Cheers, Dolores and best wishes.

And now a word from Joe:

We often talk of you two especially since we have booked another Holland America next October. Now that we qualify as ancient mariners, we have travelled everywhere and go only for the free laundry.

We feel very fortunate to have discovered the unconnected and independent life so many years ago. We have now been "Retired" that is not indentured to the system for 41 years. My frequent golf partners who are on their 401K's and Medicare have no comprehension of that time factor and think I can only have done that by being married to a rich woman, probably many times over. However, I must explain that if retirement in the vernacular refers to living a non-work committed life and still having some kind of income, I belong to the first generation that was able to do that. Previous generations either worked until they died, or had their income cease when they became unemployed. Learn a few languages and make a lot of friends.

Best wishes to both of you, Joe

Bruce Sherman

Background: Bruce and I have been friends since I graduated from college – for the number of years, let's not go there. He is married and is a talented investment advisor, and describes himself as semi-retired. I am glad he does because he directs of some of my investments. Bruce loves to travel and here a few comments from him:

Travel helps me make connections worldwide which helps me make investment decisions. The adventures, and seeing places I've heard about my whole life is enriching.

Just discovered Priceline for within the USA. Got a great deal. When I was younger I used to plan everything on my own, staying at cheaper hotels, being my own guide using a book etc. Now, for many destinations, we are choosing tours, with more expensive hotels, and guides, as my time and comfort and seeing all the sights easily is more important than the cash savings. Also meet interesting people on the tours, and have even picked up some clients for my investment management business from other travelers on the tours.

We bring Tylenol PM to get sleep and adjust when travelling across many time zones. I always carry prescription back drugs and ear infection drugs with me as I am predisposed to having problems in these areas when I travel.

I stop the mail and papers from being delivered. Have the neighbors watch the house for anything unusual or package deliveries. No pets.

I stay in touch with E-mail!

Aki & Kay Sasaji

Background: Aki and Kay live in Vancouver, Canada. We met this delightful Japanese couple on a repositioning trans-Pacific Ocean cruise from Vancouver, Canada, to Japan on the Holland American Volendam cruise ship. Aki retired from the travel industry and because English is his second language, he is concerned about his writing. We think he did a very good job of expressing his joy of travel. He tells us:

Dear Wayne

Kay & Aki are glad to hear from you. You and Pat had good two year-long trip, looking forward to read the book. We made a Panama cruise last year in end of April to May. It was a reposition cruise and very good price, came right back to Vancouver. We booked only one-way air. Now we booked a Mexican cruise from San Diego, departing April 10th. This one is also a reposition cruise coming back to Vancouver. We avoid peak season. Now I like to cruise. I can relax. I have lots of time since I retired from work. I visit Japan a lot and I make lots of side trips in Japan. We revisited Hakodate one month after we returned from the Volendum trip. Now days I use "Vacations to go" website and also keep an eye on newspaper travel sections for info. Also thanks to the Internet system we can keep in touch with my friends and relatives too from anywhere in the world. I would rather be staying one place and relax than traveling for sightseeing. During the summer time we like to stay in Vancouver. We don't want to miss such a comfortable weather so we spend most of our time for sports - play golf and lawn bowling. Thank you, Aki.

 *Appendix B*

Sample Travel Card

Appendix C

Measurement Conversions

In this appendix...

Some Easy Ways to Convert from Metric

Temperature Conversion Table – Celsius vs. Fahrenheit

Most countries in the world use the metric system. Here are a few basic rules that are easy to remember and calculate to help you convert from metric to the English system for some common measurements.

Some Easy Ways to Convert from Metric

Distance - Kilometers to Miles

Distances are often expressed in kilometers. Ten kilometers is 6.2 miles. An easy way to get a rough conversion of kilometers to miles is to divide the number of kilometers by half and then add back 10%. So, converting 10 kilometers goes like this: 10 / 2 = 5. Add 10% of 10 yield 6 miles (actual = 6.2 miles). For 80 kilometers, 80 / 2 = 40. Add 10% of 80 yield 48 miles (actual = 49.6 miles). The actual add back is 12% so for larger numbers you need to add a little more.

Distance - Meters to Yards

A very basic rule to remember is a meter is about one yard. So, if you see something saying 100 meters it is about a football field long. Actually, one meter is about 10% longer than a yard (1 meter = 1.09 yards).

Liquids - Liters to US Gallons

Again, a very basic rule is 1 liter is about a quart so 4 liters is about a gallon. Actually, 4 liters = 1.05 gallons.

Weight - Kilograms to Pounds

Here is another basic rule to remember. One kilogram is 2.2 pounds. To convert kilograms to pounds, multiple the number of kilograms by 2 and then add 20%. So, converting 1 kilogram goes like this: 1 X 2 = 2. Add 20% of 1 yield 2.2 pounds.

Temperature Conversion Table – Celsius vs. Fahrenheit

°C	°F	°C	°F	°C	°F	°C	°F
-25	-13	-5	23	14	57.2	33	91.4
-24	-11.2	-4	24.8	15	59	34	93.2
-23	-9.4	-3	26.6	16	60.8	35	95
-22	-7.6	-2	28.4	17	62.6	36	96.8
-21	-5.8	-1	30.2	18	64.4	37	98.6
-20	-4	0	32	19	66.2	38	100.4
-19	-2.2	1	33.8	20	68	39	102.2
-18	-0.4	2	35.6	21	69.8	40	104
-17	1.4	3	37.4	22	71.6	41	105.8
-16	3.2	4	41	23	73.4	42	107.6
-15	5	5	41	24	75.2	43	109.4
-14	6.8	6	42.8	25	77	44	111.2
-12	10.4	7	44.6	26	78.8	45	113
-11	12.2	8	46.4	27	80.6	46	114.8
-10	14	9	48.2	28	82.4	47	116.6
-9	15.8	10	50	29	84.2	48	118.4
-8	17.6	11	51.8	30	86	49	120.2
-7	19.4	12	53.6	31	87.8	50	122
-6	21.2	13	55.4	32	89.6	51	123.8

Note: a quick Fahrenheit estimate can be had by doubling the Celsius temperature and adding 30. For example 25°C = 80°F (actual is 77).

Appendix D

Recommended Reading

How to Escape Your Job and Career

If you are currently working and are concerned about interruptions of your career, the following two books may give you the insight of how to do it and why it may be good for you. In my judgment, **Timothy Ferris' "The 4-Hour Workweek"** is a masterpiece and is a must read even if you plan to remain at your job or create a new one.

- **The 4-Hour Workweek: Escape 9-5, Live Anywhere, and Join the New Rich**, Timothy Ferris, Crown Publishers, 2007.
- **Escape 101, Sabbaticals Made Simple**, Dan Clements and Tara Gignac, Brainranch, 2007.

Taking a RV Road Trip Around America

- **Live Your Road Trip Dream**, Phil & Carol White, RLI Press, 2008.

Appendix E

Contacts and Resources – Helpful Travel Websites and Apps

This appendix organizes the Internet resources referred to in this book.

The Internet is an amazing resource for today's traveler making finding information and bargains much easier if you know where to look. In this appendix, we provide a handy directory of some of the more popular and useful travel websites and smartphone apps to facilitate your research and learning. The best use of most of these travel websites and apps has been described previously in this book.

New travel websites and apps are always becoming available and may offer you even better features, information, and bargains. There are many other travel websites specializing in specific regions and travel options that can also be great resources for you. Be on the lookout for new travel websites and apps.

Other than finding bargains and information available to everyone, when this book was published the author has not benefited financially or from special arrangements from any of the resources listed in this book.

Comprehensive Travel Information Resources

Johnny Jet (www.johnnyjet.com)

Preparations

Passports, Visa Requirements, Travel Advisories, U.S. Embassies, and Proof of Onward Travel Needs
U.S. Department of State (www.travel.state.gov)
Travisa (www.travisa.com)
EmbassyWorld (www.embassyworld.com)

Vaccination Requirements and Travel Precautions
CDC (Centers for Disease Control and Preventions)
(wwwnc.cdc.gov/travel)

Latest Rules on Flights
U.S. Transportation Security Administration (TSA) (www.tsa.gov)

Trip Planning Assistance
Gecko Go (www.geckogo.com)
Trip Base (www.tripbase.com)
iExplore (www.iexplore.com)
mTrip – app for the Android and iPhone

Researching Events
Frommer's Whatsonwhen (www.whatsonwhen.com)
World Reviewer (www.worldreviewer.com)
Festivals Media (www.festivals.com)

Research City and Country Destinations
Wikitravel (www.wikitravel.org)
U.S. Department of State (www.travel.state.gov)
CIA (www.cia.gov/library/publications/the-world-factbook/index.html)

General Travel Research
Lonely Planet (www.lonelyplanet.com)
Rough Guides (www.roughguides.com)
Rick Steves (for Europe) (www.ricksteves.com)
VirtualTourist (www.virtualtourist.com)
Gadling (www.gadling.com)
World Hum (www.worldhum.com)
Trip Wolf (www.tripwolf.com)

UNESCO World Heritage Sites (http://whc.unesco.org)
Travel and Leisure (upscale) (www.travelandleisure.com)

Young Travelers and Students
STA Travel (www.statravel.com)
IIEPassport (www.iiepassport.org)
International Students Travel Confederation (www.istc.org)

Senior Travelers
AARP Destinations (www.aarp.org/travel)
Elderhostel Road Scholar (www.roadscholar.org)

Volunteering
International Volunteer Programs Association
(www.volunteerinternational.org)
Global Volunteers (www.globalvolunteers.org)
Volunteers For Peace (www.vfp.org)
Idealist (www.idealist.org)

Spa Vacations
Spa Finder (www.spafinder.com)

Educational Travel (i.e. cooking, language, cultural, art, photography, writing, golf, tennis)
Shawguides (www.shawguides.com)

Online Forum to Answer Travel Questions
Lonely Planet's 'Thorn Tree' Forum (www.lonelyplanet.com)
Frommer's Travel Talk (www.frommers.com/travel_talk)

Travel Bargains with Weekly Internet Newsletter
Travelzoo (www.travelzoo.com)
Frommer's Budget Travel (www.budgettravel.com)

Newspaper Travel Sections
Los Angeles Times (www.latimes.com/travel)
Boston Globe (www.boston.com/travel)
Chicago Tribune (www.chicagotribune.com/travel)

New York Times (www.nytimes.com/travel)
USA Today (www.usatoday.com/travel)
The Globe and Mail (www.theglobeandmail.com/travel)

Online Travel Clothing and Gear Stores
Magellan's (www.magellans.com)
TravelSmith (www.travelsmith.com)
REI (www.rei.com)
Rick Steves (www.ricksteves.com)

Travel Insurance
Travel Guard (www.travelguard.com)
USI Affinity Travel Insurance Services (www.travelinsure.com)
InsureMyTrip (www.insuremytrip.com)
TravelInsuranceCenter (www.worldtravelcenter.com)

Research and Track Frequent Flyer Programs
CreditCards (www.creditcards.com)
MileBlaster - smartphone app available for the Android, Nokia, iPhone, and iPad

World Weather
The Weather Channel (www.weather.com)

Currency Conversion
Oanda (www.oanda.com/currency/converter)
XE (www.xe.com)

International Electrical Plugs
Kropla (www.kropla.com/electric2.htm)

ATM Locators
MasterCard/Cirrus/Maestro (www.mastercard.com/atmlocator)
Visa/PLUS (www.visa.com/atms)

Inexpensive Phone Calls (VoIP)
Skype (www.skype.com) - also available as apps on the Android, BlackBerry, iPhone, iPad, and Windows Phone 7

Google Voice (www.google.com/googlevoice/about.html)

Country Calling Codes and Calling Cards
How to Call Abroad (www.howtocallabroad.com)
CallingCards (www.callingcards.com)

Language Translator
Babelfish (http://babelfish.yahoo.com)
Google Translate (http://translate.google.com) - also available as apps
on the Android, iPhone, and iPad

Tourist Offices
Tourist Office Worldwide Directory (www.towd.com)

Locating Availability and Pricing

Travel Search and Booking (i.e. Flights, Hotels, Car Rentals)
Kayak (www.kayak.com) - also available as apps for the Android,
BlackBerry, iPhone, IPad, and Windows Phone 7
Travelocity (www.travelocity.com) - also available as apps for the
Android and iPhone (more on the way)
Expedia (www.expedia.com) - also available as an iPhone app
Orbitz (www.orbitz.com) - also available as apps for the Android,
iPhone, and iPad
Yapta (www.yapta.com)
SideStep (www.sidestep.com)

Online Auctions
Priceline (www.priceline.com) - also available as apps on the Android,
iPhone, and iPad
Hotwire (www.hotwire.com)
BiddingforTravel.com (www.biddingfortravel.com) - also available as
apps on the Android, iPhone, and iPad

Last Minute Deals
LastMinuteTravel (www.lastminutetravel.com)
LastMinute (www.lastminute.com)
CheapCaribbean (www.cheapcaribbean.com)

Organized Tour Companies

smarTours (www.smartours.com)
Gate 1 (www.gate1.com)
Overseas Adventure Travel (www.oattravel.com) featuring smaller groups
Trek America (www.trekamerica.com) for U.S. tours

Adventure Tour Companies

Wildland Adventures (www.wildlandadventures.com)
Gap Adventures (www.gapadventures.com)
Tauck (www.tauch.com)

International Flights and Trip Planning

AirTreks (www.airtreks.com)

Low-cost airlines and where they fly in Europe

Flycheapo (www.flycheapo.com)

Choosing Seats on a Plane

Seatguru (www.seatguru.com)

Airline Fare Tracking

Yapta (www.yapta.com)

Hotel User Reviews and Things to Do

TripAdvisor (www.tripadvisor.com) - also available as apps on the
Android, iPhone, iPad, and Windows Phone 7

User Reviews on Businesses and Restaurants

Yelp (www.yelp.com) - also available as apps on the Android,
BlackBerry, iPhone, iPad, and Windows Phone 7

Specific for Hotels

HotelsCombined (www.hotelscombined.com)
Hotels.com (www.hotels.com)
Venere (www.venere.com)

Hostels and Budget Hotels

Hostelworld (www.hostelworld.com)
HostelBookers (www.hostelbookers.com)
Hostelling International (www.hihostel.com)

Last Minute Hotel Bargains
LateRooms (www.laterooms.com)

Spare Rooms and Private Studio Apartments
AirBnB (www.airbnb.com) - also available as an app on the iPhone
Crashpadder (www.crashpadder.com)

Homestays and Couch Surfing
Servas International (www.servas.org)
CouchSurfing (www.couchsurfing.com)

Inns and B&B's
BedandBreakfast.com (www.bedandbreakfast.com)

Home Rentals
HomeAway (www.homeaway.com)
Villas International (www.villasintl.com)
VRBO (www.vrbo.com)

Home Exchanges
Intervac (www.intervac.com)
HomeExchange (www.homeexchange.com)
HomeLink International (www.homelink.com)
Craigslist (www.craigslist.org)

House Sitting
HouseCarers (www.housecarers.com)
MindMyHouse (www.mindmyhouse.com)
The Caretaker Gazette (www.caretaker.org)

Discounted Cruises and Cruise Information
VacationsToGo (www.vacationstogo.com)
Cruises-N-More (www.cruises-n-more.com)
CruiseDeals (www.cruisedeals.com)
Cayole (www.cayole.com)
Cruise Critic (www.cruisecritic.com)
CruiseMates (www.cruisemates.com)

Car Rentals

Hotwire (www.hotwire.com)
AutoEurope (www.autoeurope.com)

Rail Passes

Amtrak (www.amtrak.com)
RailEurope (www.raileurope.com)
Rick Steves (www.ricksteves.com/rail)
International Rail (www.internationalrail.com)

Downsizing

Sell Your Stuff

Craigslist (www.craigslist.com)
eBay (www.ebay.com)

Other

Rent Your Home

E-Renter (www.e-renter.com) for background check
Ezlandlordforms (www.exlandloadforms.com)
HomeAway (www.homeaway.com)
Villas International (www.villasintl.com)
VRBO (www.vrbo.com)

News

CNN (http://www.cnn.com)
Google News (http://news.google.com)

Maps and Directions

MapQuest (www.mapquest.com)
Google Maps (www.google.com/maps) - also available as apps on the
Android, BlackBerry, iPhone, and iPad

Free E-mail Accounts

Google Gmail (www.google.com/accounts)
Yahoo Mail (www.yahoo.com)

Hotmail (www.hotmail.com)

Free Blogging
Google's Blogger (www.blogger.com)

Locate Cybercafes
Cybercafes (www.cybercafes.com)
Cybercaptive (www.cybercaptive.com)

Reduce Your Unwanted Phone Calls and Mail
National 'Do Not Call Registry' (www.donotcall.gov)
Direct Marketing Association (DMA) (www.the-dma.org)

Money Transfer
MoneyGram (www.moneygram.com)

Business/Travel Cards
Vistaprint (www.vistaprint.com)

Photo Editing, Organizing, and Sharing
Yahoo's Flickr (www.flickr.com) - also available as apps on the iPhone
and Windows Phone 7
Smugmug (www.smugmug.com)
YouSendIt (www.yousendit.com)

About the Author

Wayne Dunlap has a burning passion for travel and is a member of the exclusive Travelers' Century Club, having visited 100 countries and island groups on 6 continents as well as 43 states in the U.S. Recently, he and his wife, Pat, sold their business, rented their home, and traveled the world for 2 years visiting 51 countries. Wayne and his wife have taken over 70 trips taking cars, trains, buses, and organized tours. They have also done home exchanges and taken 26 cruises on 12 different cruise lines on ships ranging from 10 to 3,000 passengers. They now enjoy most of their traveling independently on their own.

As a former college professor, Wayne has a sincere desire to help others improve and add more meaning to their lives by realizing their travel dreams. He has taught high school and was an economics professor after his PhD program at the University of California, San Diego (UCSD). He was a Vice President of Sales and Marketing for technology companies before he and his wife ran their own successful business for 17 years. They also raised a wonderful son, Alden. Wayne is listed in Who's Who Among American Professionals, Who's Who in Computer Management, and Who's Who Among Students in American Universities and Colleges.

Wayne has been actively involved in his community serving as Chair of his local planning board getting many large projects completed while preserving the local environment, on the City of San Diego Small Business Advisory Board winning the Small Business Administration (SBA) Vision 2000 Award and presented the City of San Diego Special Commendation three times, and as a Little League and soccer coach for many years. Wayne also ran for the U.S. Congress and received almost three times the number of votes in his district that anyone had ever received for his political party.

Pat Dunlap shares Wayne's passion for travel taking over 70 trips and 26 cruises together and recently traveled the world for 2 years with her husband Wayne. Pat has been successful in business being a winner of "Entrepreneur of the Year for San Diego" for her own business and was a member of a fortune 500 company's 100% club for Sales for excellent customer support and business sales goals achieved.

Pat believes having had it all, but choosing to run away with her husband and best friend, has been the most rewarding lifestyle change one can make. Pat says: *"Visiting 100 countries and island groups together has given me lots of stories and many new friends, brought me closer in my relationship with my husband, and changed my life for the better."* Pat is originally from New York, but after living 35 years in San Diego, she now considers herself a San Diegan.

When they are not traveling the world, Wayne and Pat live and enjoy their friends and family in San Diego, California.

You can follow their worldwide travels on their:

Travel blog (www.UnhookNow.com) and

Travel photo files (www.flickr.com/photos/unhooknow/sets).

Keep Yourself Updated with the
Latest Travel Developments and Cost Saving Tips

The travel industry is moving forward quickly offering the traveler even more wonderful opportunities and bargains. In order to keep you updated on new developments and ways to save money, please visit our website and sign up for our *FREE travel tips* at *www.PlanYourEscapeNow.com*.

Give the Gift that They Will Remember Forever

Practically everyone has a dream to travel. Tell your friends how to order a copy of *Plan Your Escape*. It is also the prefect gift for friends, family, and colleagues on Christmas, Hanukah, and other special holidays, birthdays, anniversaries, retirement, a graduation present for young people thinking of living abroad, or any occasion that celebrates a new beginning, to help people you care about learn how to plan and how to afford a travel adventure. You and your friends can order copies at our website: *www.PlanYourEscapeNow.com*.

Premium Sales for Companies, Non-Profits, Associations, & Trade Promotions

Premium sales and trade promotions are available for organizations for incentives for your members and employees and to assist you in obtaining new members, as well as for Non-profits and Associations to raise money or for membership support. Visit our website: *www.PlanYourEscapeNow.com* for details.

Please contact Wayne Dunlap at:

e-mail: wdunlap@UnhookNow.com
Travel blog: www.UnhookNow.com

Plan Your Escape Now
PO Box 642,
Del Mar, CA 92014 USA